THE BOOK OF ART

A Pictorial Encyclopedia of Painting, Drawing, and Sculpture

W9-ABL-441

VOLUME 2

ITALIAN ART TO 1850

THE BOOK OF ART

A Pictorial Encyclopedia of Painting, Drawing, and Sculpture

ITALIAN ART TO 1850

Edited by

Professor Mario Monteverdi

Professor of History of Art,
Liceo Classico Manzoni, Milan

Grolier
INCORPORATED

NEW YORK   MONTREAL   MEXICO CITY   SYDNEY

HOW TO USE THIS BOOK

To obtain the maximum information and interest from this series it is necessary to understand its basic plan. With the exception of the first volume and the last two volumes, which are more general in their scope, each of the other seven volumes is arranged as follows:

First, a historical Introduction sets out the main lines of development within the school or period, with special reference to the major artists and the major works of art.

This is followed by a biographical section outlining the life and work of every major artist and important minor artists. The Biographies run in alphabetical order according to the name by which each artist is most generally known, whether it be surname, or Christian name (as for example LEONARDO da Vinci), or nickname (as TINTORETTO). With each biography is given a cross-reference to the page or pages on which he is represented in the plates sections which follow; a monochrome reproduction of one or more of his other works; and (where possible) a self-portrait or portrait of the artist and a specimen of his signature.

Next follow the sections of Color Plates, Drawings, and Sculpture. Each of these sections is arranged in chronological order according to the date of the artist's birth, though in a few cases minor adjustments to this order have been made for the sake of comparison or design. To illustrate painting techniques, particularly of frescoes and large easel paintings, some color plates show a detail rather than the whole work; but the use of such a detail is indicated in the caption, and a monochrome illustration of the whole work is normally given with the artist's biography; in such cases the size given in the caption refers to the whole painting. The location of every work of art is included in its caption. Every effort has been made to include also the size, medium, and date of each work represented in the plates, though this has not always been possible since not every museum has such information available for all the items in its collection. The reader will also appreciate that the precise dating of many works of art is the subject of scholarly controversy; however, no dates have been included here unless they have the authority of qualified experts and art historians.

A final section, entitled Influences and Developments, rounds off the volume by drawing together the main ideas and characteristics of schools and styles, and by exploring the internal and external influences that have made their impact on the development of the arts during the period concerned.

A list of basic reference books for further reading appears on page 16. Books containing material of special interest concerning an individual artist are listed at the end of the relevant biography.

To avoid repetitive explanation of basic technical terms such as *genre*, *chiaroscuro*, *baroque*, etc., an illustrated Glossary is provided in the volume entitled *How to Look at Art*. Also in that volume is an Index listing every artist mentioned throughout the series.

Taken as a whole, the series thus provides a comprehensive, carefully integrated, and highly informative survey of the achievement and significance of Western Art from its origins to the present day.

NOTE.—The terminal dates in the titles of some of the volumes are inevitably approximate. One volume will sometimes overlap with another. Some artists mentioned under French Art, for example, are also represented under the Impressionists, and the Post-Impressionists merge imperceptibly with the Moderns. In the ever-continuous process of Art it is difficult to contain schools or periods within precise boundaries.

Copyright © 1965 by Grolier Incorporated
First published 1965.
Second Impression 1966. Third Impression 1967. Fourth Impression 1967. Fifth Impression 1969.
Library of Congress Catalog Card Number: 65-10350

Designed and produced by George Rainbird Ltd., London
PRINTED IN ITALY by Amilcare Pizzi S.p.A., Milan

Contents

LIST OF COLOR PLATES

ABBREVIATIONS

attrib.	attributed, attribution
et al.	and elsewhere
in.	inches
S.	San (Santo), Santa (Italian and Spanish)
SS.	Santissimo, Santissima (Italian)
St.	Saint (English and German)
St. or Ste.	Saint (French)
Accad.	Accademia
B-A.	Beaux-Arts
Bibl.	Biblioteca, Bibliothèque
B.M.	British Museum, London
Cath.	Cathedral
Chap.	Chapel
Coll.	Collection
Fitzwm.	Fitzwilliam Museum, Cambridge, England
Gall.	Gallery, Galleria
Gemäldegal.	Gemäldegalerie

Inst.	Institute
Kunsthist.	Kunsthistorisches
Kunstmus.	Kunstmuseum
Met. Mus.	Metropolitan Museum of Art, New York
Mus.	Musée, Museen, Museo, Museum
Nat.	Nationale
Naz.	Nazionale
N.G.	National Gallery, London
	National Gallery of Art, Washington, D.C.
Pal.	Palace, Palazzo
Pin.	Pinacoteca, Pinacothèque, Pinakothek
R.A.	Royal Academy, London
Staatl.	Staatliche
Univ.	University
V. and A.	Victoria and Albert Museum, London

ACKNOWLEDGMENTS

The publishers and producers wish to express their gratitude to all the museums, art galleries, collectors, photographers and agencies who have courteously assisted them in obtaining the material for the illustrations reproduced in this volume. They would especially like to thank the following:

Accademia di Belle Arti, Florence
Accademia di Belle Arti, Venice
Accademia Carrara, Bergamo
Accademia di San Luca, Rome
The Albertina, Vienna
The Aldo Crespi Collection, Milan
Ampliaciones y Reproducciones Mas., Barcelona
Anderson Photos, Rome
Archives Photographiques, Paris
The Ashmolean Museum, Oxford, England
Bibliothèque Nationale, Paris
Biblioteca Reale, Turin
The Borghese Gallery, Rome
Museum Boymans-van Beuningen, Rotterdam
The Brera Gallery, Milan
The Trustees of the British Museum, London
Mr. F. Bruckmann, Munich
The Capitoline Museum, Rome
Casa Buonarroti, Florence
The City Museum and Art Gallery, Birmingham, England
Collection Conte Salvadego Molin, Brescia
The Contini-Bonacossi Collection, Florence
A. C. Cooper Ltd., London
Country Life Ltd., London
The Courtauld Institute Galleries, University of London
Deutsche Fotothek, Dresden
The Devonshire Collection, Trustees of the Chatsworth
    Collection, Chatsworth, England
The Doria Gallery, Rome
École des Beaux-Arts, Paris
Lord Fairhaven, Anglesey Abbey, Cambridge, England
Federico Aborio Mella, Milan
The Syndics of the Fitzwilliam Museum, Cambridge, England
Fratelli Alinari, S.A. (I.D.E.A.), Florence
John R. Freeman & Co., London
Gabinetto Fotografico Nazionale, Rome
Galleria Antica e Moderna, Florence
Galleria dell' Accademia, Venice
Galleria Nazionale, Palermo
Galleria Palatina, Florence
Galleria Nazionale dell' Umbria, Perugia
Galleria del Palazzo Mancini, Città di Castello
Galleria Sabauda, Turin
Gallery of the Marches, Palazzo Ducale, Urbino
Gemäldegalerie, Brunswick, Germany
Gemäldegalerie, Dresden
Photographie Giraudon, Paris
Photo Gundermann, Würzburg
Sir Giles Isham, Northampton, England
Kunsthistorisches Museum, Vienna
Kunstverlag Wolfrum, Vienna
Mr. Edward Leigh, F.I.B.P., F.R.P.S., Cambridge, England
The Liechtenstein Gallery, Vaduz, Switzerland
The Louvre, Paris

The Mansell Collection, London
The Metropolitan Museum of Art, New York
Monumenti Musei e Gallerie Pontificie, Rome
Musée Condé, Chantilly
Musée Royal des Beaux-Arts, Antwerp
Muséees Royeaux des Beaux-Arts, Brussels
Museo di Andrea del Castagno, Florence
Museo del Castello Sforzesco, Milan
Museo Civico, Bassano
Museo Civico, Padua
Museo Civico, Pesaro
Museo Correr, Venice
Museo Estense, Modena
Museo Nazionale del Bargello, Florence
Museo Nazionale, Florence
Museo Nazionale, Naples
Museo dell' Opera del Duomo, Florence
Museo dell' Opera del Duomo, Siena
Museo Poldi Pezzoli, Milan
Museo di Santa Croce, Florence
The Museum of Fine Arts, Boston, Mass.
The National Buildings Record, London
The Trustees of the National Gallery, London
The National Gallery of Art, Washington, D.C.
The National Gallery of Canada, Ottawa
Niedersächsisches Landesverwaltungsamt, Hanover
The Palatina, Florence
Palazzo Comunale, Siena
Palazzo Reale, Naples
The Earl of Pembroke, Wilton House, Salisbury, England
Pinacoteca, Bologna
Pinacoteca Nazionale, Siena
Pinacoteca, Parma
Pinacoteca, Prato
Pinacoteca Ambrosiana, Milan
Pinacoteca Civica, Borgo San Sepolcro
Pinacoteca Politico dei Minori Osservanti, Milan
Pinacoteca Tosio Martinengo, Brescia
The Pitti Palace, Florence
The Prado, Madrid
The Radio Times Hulton Picture Library, London
The Residenz, Würzburg
Rheinisches Bildarchiv, Cologne
The Royal Academy of Arts, London
The Royal Collection, London, by gracious permission of Her
    Majesty the Queen
Service Commercial Monuments Historiques, Paris
Staatliche Kunstsammlungen, Dresden
Staatliche Museen, Berlin
Staedel Institute, Frankfurt-am-Main
The Thyssen Collection, Lugano
The Uffizi Gallery, Florence
The Vatican Gallery, Rome
The Victoria and Albert Museum (Crown Copyright),
    London
Foto A. Villani, Bologna
Photo Vizzavona, Paris
The Walker Art Gallery, Liverpool, England
The Trustees of the Wallace Collection, London
The Wallraf-Richartz-Museum, Cologne

Italian Art to 1850

The story of art in Italy goes back long before the Christian era, but this book is concerned with modern art—that is to say, with Italian art beginning about the middle of the 13th century. Etruscan and Roman art of the pre-Christian period, and Christian art from 313 (when Christianity became a tolerated religion in the Roman Empire) can never be far out of mind, for they form the background of all Italian painting and sculpture. Nevertheless, there is a break in the 13th century, clearly discerned by the 16th-century biographer and art critic Vasari and by his contemporaries when they wrote of Cimabue and Giotto as the founders of modern art.

The beginnings of modern Italian art

This break with the past came in fact a little earlier than the career of Giotto. The history of modern Italian art begins in Pisa in 1259/60 with the sculptor Nicola Pisano. This was to a large extent because classical sculpture survived in comparative profusion, whereas painting was very largely lost. Most of what is known today was rediscovered in Pompeii and Herculaneum in the middle of the 18th century. More interesting than the relative precedence of sculpture over painting is the problem of why at this moment there was a desire for a different kind of art at all. It is true that Byzantine art, in such masterpieces as the mosaics at Ravenna, was a direct descendant of the humane and realistic art of Greece and Rome. Nevertheless, religious art in the Middle Ages tended to become more hieratic and symbolical, and the art of the Middle Ages is almost exclusively religious. Many secular works were made but comparatively few have survived, and in any case there can be no doubt at all that the important commissions were religious.

Nicola Pisano

Nicola Pisano was commissioned to make a pulpit for the Baptistery at Pisa with five panels in high relief of scenes from the life of Christ. Because he wanted to represent these scenes as dramatically as possible, Nicola turned to Roman sarcophagi, and in particular to one that still exists at Pisa. His extremely solid and realistic art was continued by his pupil Arnolfo di Cambio, and his son Giovanni Pisano, who introduced a greater intensity of emotional effect, due probably to his experience of Gothic art. Giovanni Pisano was the exact contemporary of Giotto, and the two men, in their different media, simultaneously evolved a style capable of expressing qualities of pathos and drama.

Cimabue and Pietro Cavallini, both painters, were working at about the same time as Nicola Pisano; both men were the direct forerunners, probably the teachers, of Giotto. Cimabue traditionally shares with Giotto the honor of breaking away from the Byzantine tradition and it is probably true to say that he was the last of the great Byzantines, just as Cavallini expressed the Roman monumental tradition that he had inherited from distant antiquity.

Giotto

Giotto, who lived until 1337, excelled both Cimabue and Cavallini and became the father of modern painting because he had the story-teller's gift for making the essential point of a narrative by gesticulation and facial expression and by small but telling details. The *Annunciation to St. Anne* (p. 171) is an example of this. The main scene takes place in a large box-like space, but the servant seated in a smaller box is essential to the composition, and by concentrating on her everyday task she provides a note of contrast to the apparition of the angel. Giotto's figures are simple in the extreme, but by comparison with contemporary paintings are almost startlingly illusionistic. Their this-world quality is comparable to Dante's use of the vernacular instead of Latin, in which serious books were then usually written. Giotto's art, like Dante's, was fundamentally religious even when he was painting portraits in parts of his great frescoes. The frescoes traditionally attributed to him at Assisi show his unprecedented power to create visual equivalents for a literary narrative.

The Giottesque tradition

Certainly most 14th-century art was influenced by Giotto. His works were all regarded as models for imitation by his successors, so that 14th-century Florentine painting tended to be a repetition of Giotto's ideas without his narrative and illusionistic gifts. Perhaps only Maso di Banco really understood Giotto's art. His own direct pupils like Taddeo Gaddi and perhaps Bernardo Daddi used his motives but combined them with the beauty of craftsmanship and the delicacy of color that distinguished the other great school of the 14th century —that of Siena—which started from Duccio di Buoninsegna.

Duccio and the Sienese school

Duccio's treatment of narrative was entirely different from that of Giotto, but in some ways as revolutionary. His masterpiece is the *Maestà* (pp. 67, 68, 167), painted between 1308 and 1311 for the altar of Siena Cathedral. Because of its position at the end of the nave, the front of the altarpiece consists of a very large image of the Virgin and Child enthroned in glory and surrounded by hosts of angels and saints. At first sight, this seems a more Byzantine picture than the *Madonna* by Giotto (p. 173). Duccio's altarpiece, however, which contains a great deal of gold, was really an elaborate icon and was meant to make its effect from a distance. The back of the altarpiece is entirely different. It consists of 26 narrative scenes from the life of Christ, which are more realistic since they are meant to be viewed from close up, and form a deliberate narrative sequence.

The wonderful craftsmanship of these paintings is characteristic of the Sienese tradition. Stylistically Duccio was almost certainly influenced by French Gothic, and the panels reveal a complete contrast with the bold and forceful painting of Giotto, not least in Duccio's use of line as compared to Giotto's three-dimensional forms.

Duccio's pupils aptly summarize these two 14th-century tendencies. Simone Martini in his *Annunciation* of 1333 (p. 175) continues the elaboration of Duccio's craftsmanship and is even more strongly influenced by French ideas. The brothers Pietro and Ambrogio Lorenzetti were influenced at first by Duccio, but had strong Florentine connections and were much more aware of the dramatic possibilities of fresco painting as practiced by Giotto. Pietro's *Deposition* (p. 180) and Ambrogio's *Effects of Good Government* (p. 177) show the influence of Florentine realistic ideas. The art of fresco painting in Siena was never carried as far as it was in Florence, perhaps because of the Sienese tradition of miniature and small-scale panel painting.

The International Gothic style

Partly because of the Black Death of 1348, which affected Siena and Florence very badly indeed, there was less outstanding work in the second half of the century. Most of the later painters combined elements of Giotto's narrative style with an attempt to retain the delicacy and craftsmanship of the Sienese tradition. The result, like most compromises, lost something of both. Giotto's work became in North Italy the foundation of several local schools, notably at Padua. In Verona the Giotto tradition grew almost imperceptibly into a form of Gothic known as International Gothic. This style began in France, possibly under the influence of Simone Martini, but reached its greatest height in the early 15th century, in the manuscript illuminations made for the Duke of Berry by the Limbourg brothers. The greatest Italian exponents of this lavish style were Gentile da Fabriano and Pisanello, who carried it on into the middle of the 15th century.

In Florence, where Gentile da Fabriano painted *The Adoration of the Magi* (p. 184) in 1423, the International Gothic style was for a time profoundly influential. Lorenzo Monaco changed his style entirely in the last years of his life, and both Masolino and the sculptor Ghiberti worked basically in the new style. In Siena, where the tradition of Duccio was still strong, Sassetta adopted the realistic elements of the International Gothic style.

The return to classical forms in Florence

The International Gothic style in Florence coincided almost exactly with the rise of Masaccio and Donatello, who in painting and sculpture returned to the strong dramatic and classical style of Giotto. They conscientiously avoided the elegance of the International Gothic in their search for the harsh and ruthless realism found in antique Roman portrait busts. At almost exactly the same moment Filippo Brunelleschi was returning to Roman forms in architecture, and the three men together created the new heroic style of the 1420's, which is the foundation of later Florentine art and the background to Michelangelo. Masaccio's frescoes in the Brancacci Chapel (pp. 196 and 197) form the strongest possible contrast to Lorenzo Monaco's *Coronation* (p. 185) or Gentile da Fabriano's *Adoration* (p. 184), which are only a few years earlier. In Masolino it is possible to see the effect of Masaccio's style on an artist who was fundamentally in sympathy with International Gothic ideas. In fact Masaccio's severe style was less influential than might be imagined, for almost all his successors, notably Masolino, Uccello, and Fra Filippo Lippi, reacted against his ideals and developed a style that moved consistently away from his.

Donatello and his influence

Masaccio died at the age of 27, and Donatello, who lived to be 80, imposed his more linear style not only on sculpture but on contemporary painting. Nevertheless, Masaccio's influence, in creating a three-dimensional space in which the figures are subordinated to the laws of perspective, remained the foundation of Florentine 15th-century painting, and even Fra Angelico modified his style in the direction of greater naturalism. Uccello was so fascinated by geometry and perspective that he carried it to an extreme. His images pass beyond a naturalistic representation and take on a formal abstract beauty of their own. The generation active in the middle of the century—Domenico Veneziano, Andrea del Castagno, and Fra Filippo Lippi—were all influenced by Masaccio at some point in their career, but it is in the

work of Castagno with its severity of outline and ruthlessness of presentation that the overwhelming influence of the sculpture of Donatello is most clearly visible. Donatello's statues for Florence cathedral have the gravity of the best Roman art, while his reliefs exploit the possibilities of perspective that had been worked out methodically by his friend Brunelleschi. Donatello's contemporary, Luca della Robbia, was more placid in temperament, though in his early marble works his feeling for solid form is as great as Donatello's. When he discovered the means of making colored terracotta he founded a form of craftsmanship that sustained a family business for more than a century and a half, and which, because of the prettiness sometimes associated with it, has obscured his reputation. Most of the other Florentine sculptors of the 15th century were influenced by Donatello, either in the use of very low relief, or by Donatello's interest in anatomy as a means of expressing violent action and therefore violent emotion. His closest follower in this latter respect was Antonio Pollaiuolo, and to a lesser extent the sculptor and painter Andrea del Verrocchio.

The later 15th century in Florence provides a marked contrast with the period around 1425. It was the period of consolidation in the works of the large studios run by Pollaiuolo and Verrocchio. It saw also the fresco cycles painted by Domenico Ghirlandaio, who was one of the most competent practitioners in the difficult art of fresco without ever having very much to say. His realism was prosaic rather than inspired, but posterity is indebted to him for having instructed the young Michelangelo in the rudiments of fresco technique.

Botticelli and his followers

The style of Botticelli is an altogether different matter, and both he and the much older Filippo Lippi were clearly concerned with line as a means of aesthetic expression and also as a means of introducing a lyrical quality into the fresco art they saw around them. Botticelli's most famous works, the *Allegory of Spring* and the *Birth of Venus* (p. 220), reject almost entirely the spatial construction of earlier generations in favor of a linear rhythm that to some extent recalls International Gothic. Both these allegories are intended as extremely elaborate representations of difficult themes—the re-creation of certain aspects of classical antiquity in terms of Christian philosophy. In his later works, such as the *Mystic Nativity* (p. 221), Botticelli's rejection of the prosaic realism of his day is the essential element in the creation of a deeply religious atmosphere.

To some extent the same ideas animated Filippo Lippi, although many of his works suffer from a lack of restraint, and a similar type of fantasy can be found in the weird and romantic paintings of Piero di Cosimo.

The 15th century outside Florence

During the 15th century the ideas that germinated in Florence took root in the rest of Italy. The most important non-Florentine painter of the period was Piero della Francesca from Borgo San Sepolcro. He seems to have received at least part of his training in Florence, although he worked with the least Florentine of all the leaders of the new movement, Domenico Veneziano. Domenico was particularly interested in the rendering of light and color—both of which are traditionally secondary in Florentine painting—but there can be no doubt that Domenico's exact observation of color and tone coupled with a study of Sienese painting formed the brilliant pale and lucid color sense that is Piero's greatest possession. The fresco cycle of the *Legend of the True Cross* at Arezzo is Piero's greatest achievement, and it has a calmness and clarity that by contrast make the contemporary Florentine works of Fra Filippo Lippi or Andrea del Castagno appear violent.

Piero had two pupils, both of whom came under the influence of Florentine ideas and reacted very sharply against them. Luca Signorelli, in his great fresco cycle at Orvieto, and in the early *Flagellation* (p. 219), which is still comparatively close to Piero, shows that the Florentine passion for using contour to suggest movement meant far more to him than Piero's simple forms. In fact, Signorelli was profoundly influenced by Pollaiuolo and looked forward to Michelangelo. The Umbrian Pietro Perugino adopted Piero's simple and clear spatial relationships in his landscapes, but he too was influenced by Florentine ideas. In his later works Perugino's original simplicity becomes boring and repetitive. Nevertheless he introduced into his frescoes in the Sistine Chapel (p. 223) a simplicity and clarity of composition that were badly needed in Florence at that time. Peru-

gino, like Signorelli, anticipated the 16th century in that he was Raphael's first master.

The Paduan school

The strongest effect produced by Florentine art outside Tuscany was undoubtedly in the North and specifically in Padua. Donatello spent ten years (1443 to 1453) there working on the high altar of the Santo, and on the equestrian statue of Gattamelata. Padua was the university city for Venice and the Veneto, and it is not surprising therefore that its art is rigidly classical. Donatello's work was the indispensable foundation for the art of Mantegna, the first and greatest Paduan painter. Mantegna's frescoes (pp. 102 and 215) must have been influenced to some extent by the cycle painted there by Giotto in the first decade of the 14th century, but they are more evidently derived from Donatello's interest in the actual forms of classical antiquity. Mantegna was trained by a minor painter called Squarcione, who was himself a passionate admirer of classical sculpture. Mantegna's romantic absorption in the grandeur of the Roman past is the foundation of his style, and has made him perhaps the only classical archaeologist who has also been a major painter.

The Bellini family in Venice

The softer, more sensuous art associated with Venice was the creation of Mantegna's brother-in-law, Giovanni Bellini. Jacopo Bellini had been a pupil of Gentile da Fabriano and his training showed him to be an International Gothic artist with an interest in antiquity. His two sons, Gentile and Giovanni, worked with him in the family shop until about 1470. Gentile was particularly famous as a portrait painter, but he was largely occupied on enormous decorations in the Doge's Palace and elsewhere representing scenes from Venetian history. Most of these have been destroyed, but the few survivals show that he was the founder of the decorative trend in Venetian painting that was continued in the works of Cosimo Tura and flourished again in the 18th century.

Giovanni Bellini (pp. 209-211) was the greatest artist of the family, and had a long and productive career. He began under the influence of his precocious brother-in-law, Mantegna, but he very soon softened the harshness of Mantegna's forms and began to study the effects of a richer, more saturated color scheme. He developed a style that retains much of Mantegna's tautness but is far more immediately pleasing. He seems also to have been influenced by the mysterious Sicilian, Antonello da Messina, who appeared in Venice in 1475/6 and painted a large altarpiece of which only fragments survive. Antonello da Messina was the only major painter of the 15th century who worked in southern Italy. There he learned the use of oil paint and a meticulous technique practically indistinguishable from that of contemporary Flemish painting, as may be seen from his *Annunciation* (p. 207). His Venetian altarpiece was painted in oil, and both this fact and the extraordinary breadth of his composition profoundly influenced Giovanni Bellini, who subsequently adopted this type of large-scale altarpiece for a whole series. Giovanni Bellini had a large and active workshop producing many small half-length Madonna pictures which influenced Venetian painters for generations to come; and almost all of the painters of the 16th century, notably Giorgione and Titian, were his pupils.

The Ferrarese school

The small, independant school of Ferrara produced a handful of painters of the highest quality. It was partly an offshoot of that at Padua, which explains the stony quality in the work of Cosimo Tura, Francesco del Cossa, and Ercole Roberti (pp. 212, 218, and 224). Tura was the first of the Ferrarese. He began from a Paduan style but was also deeply influenced by Piero della Francesca, who painted some frescoes, now lost, at Ferrara. Both Cossa and Ercole Roberti were deeply influenced by Tura, and they carried the spiky forms typical of the Ferrarese school to Bologna, where Lorenzo Costa softened the asperities of the Ferrarese style into a gentle, though rather dull, formula.

Leonardo da Vinci

By the middle of the 16th century the biographer Vasari realized that Leonardo da Vinci had begun a new epoch in the history of painting. Leonardo, however, cannot be considered solely as a painter — he was the most universal of all the universal men of the Renaissance.

His youthful career was that of a normal apprentice in a Florentine workshop, and one of his earliest pictures is *The Annunciation* (p. 227), which is dated 1470-75. It already shows Leonardo's new approach. The figure of the Virgin is not particularly different from those by other Florentine painters of the period, but there is a drawing that was made as a preliminary study for the draperies. Up till then painters normally invented draperies without reference to any particular garment. Leonardo, however, made studies of pieces of cloth arranged to fall in folds and examined the actual structure and texture of these folds, an innovation typical of his inquiring mind.

His contemporaries, so far from being inspired to make similar studies from nature, simply borrowed Leonardo's drawings. The wings of Leonardo's angels are also different from the conventional angels' wings in 15th-century painting, and it is probable that Leonardo, who subsequently made profound researches into the flight of birds, actually based the angels' pinions on the structure of a bird's wing. This scientific and analytical approach is what distinguishes Leonardo from all his contemporaries and most of his successors. At the same time it probably accounts for the small number of paintings completed by him, and the comparatively very large number of drawings and notebooks that have come down to us. His beautiful drawings of dissections were made for a treatise on anatomy that exists in an almost complete state.

Characteristically Leonardo refused to use the traditional fresco technique in his great painting of *The Last Supper* because it demanded not only intense concentration but also decisiveness of hand. Leonardo preferred to experiment, to reject and to try again, and this he was able to do with the new oil medium that he himself had pioneered in Florence. Unfortunately oil paint on a dry plaster wall does not last, and the fresco was already half ruined in his own lifetime. The influence of this and his other works in Milan created the Milanese school of the 16th century. Most of its members were hardly more than pale reflections of Leonardo.

During Leonardo's second Florentine period (1500-1506) he began his studies of light and shade and of facial expression that culminated in *The Virgin and Child with St. Anne* (p. 230) and the *Mona Lisa* (p. 229).

The latter presented a new solution to the problem of representing a figure at less than half length in a relaxed pose with the hands providing a satisfactory base for the pyramidal composition. At the same time Leonardo achieved the effect of a transient expression that, according to Vasari, he sought to induce by having musicians play while painting the otherwise undistinguished wife of a Florentine merchant.

While Leonardo was in Florence, the City Council took advantage of the fact that the two greatest painters in the world were rivals, both Florentines, and resident in the city. They commissioned from them two very large wall paintings for the huge new council room in the Palazzo della Signoria. Leonardo was to have one wall and his subject was a Florentine victory over the Pisans. The other wall was to be painted by Michelangelo and was also to represent an incident in one of the Florentine wars. What happened is highly characteristic of both artists. Leonardo made a number of studies and began to paint on the wall in a new and experimental medium that failed at once, whereupon he abandoned the whole project. Michelangelo began to produce an enormous picture that consisted almost entirely of scores of nude male figures in violent action. The cartoon was completed, and some superb drawings for individual figures have survived, but the actual fresco was never even begun. The cartoon remained in the palace for a decade or so, when it fell to pieces. During that period it was the most important school of drawing for all the Florentines and many non-Florentines of the generation born at the end of the 15th century.

Michelangelo

Michelangelo's character was quite different from that of Leonardo, although he too began many projects that came to nothing. He was primarily a sculptor, and always considered himself diverted from his true task when he found himself working first as a painter and later as an architect. He was a prodigy as a boy, and was trained under Donatello's pupil Bertoldo. His heroic sculpture reflects the sublimity of Donatello's art. Fortunately, he also served a short apprenticeship under Ghirlandaio, the most accomplished fresco painter of the age, from whom he learned the technique that

enabled him to accomplish the gigantic task of painting the whole of the Sistine Chapel ceiling (pp. 236 and 237) virtually single-handed in four years. He went to Rome originally to make a tomb for Julius II, the most splendid of the Renaissance popes and a man whose force of character was matched only by Michelangelo's. The project occupied the artist almost 40 years, but in its final form was a mere ghost of the original grandiose idea. In 1508 Julius II decided to divert Michelangelo's energies from the tomb by commissioning him to paint the ceiling of his private chapel in the Vatican Palace. Grudgingly Michelangelo complied, and he began with a project that involved comparatively small figure scenes with a great deal of purely decorative work. He found the figure scenes growing under his hands, dismissed his assistants, and settled down to painting an enormous series of figures that to some extent were a substitute for the figures he was not allowed to carve in marble. The Sistine ceiling, finished in 1512, is perhaps the highest point of the pure Renaissance style. Michelangelo's other fresco in the Sistine Chapel, *The Last Judgment* on the altar wall, executed between 1536 and 1541, reveals a complete change of style. This gave rise to what is now known as Mannerism. *The Last Judgment* (p. 238) and the later frescoes in the Pauline Chapel were as influential in the development of Italian painting in the later 16th century as was his lost battle cartoon of 40 years before.

The same changes of style can be seen in his sculpture. The early *David*, of 1504, is a masterpiece of the pure Renaissance style; a gangling youth with big feet and hands, he nevertheless is descended from Greek and Roman gods and proudly conscious of his virile beauty. The statues of the Medici Chapel, 20 years later, are already burdened with thought; while the late *Pietàs* are almost abstract in their flight from mere beauty. The *Rondanini Pietà*, which Michelangelo was still working on a few days before his death, has an unbearable poignancy that is in direct contrast with the early *David*; by comparison it is ugly, and even, apparently, tentative. This is because Michelangelo is attempting to render the lamentation over the dead Christ in terms of a far deeper religious sentiment. This sentiment is that which animated the saints of the Counter-Reformation, and it had to be expressed in new ways.

Raphael

The third great name of this period is that of Raphael. His background is entirely different, for he was born in 1483 in the beautiful but rather remote city of Urbino, where his father was a local painter of little talent. Fortunately Raphael went to Florence in about 1503 and there saw not only the battle sketches of Leonardo and Michelangelo but also the whole development of Florentine art of the last half century. He realized at once that he would have to start all over again, and for about four years he studied diligently, producing pictures like the *Madonna of the Goldfinch* (p. 248), which are carefully meditated studies of the problem of grouping two, three, or four figures. He was already learning the lessons of Florentine draftsmanship. The *Marriage of the Virgin* (p. 247) is virtually an improved Perugino; the *Madonna of the Goldfinch* is a first-class Florentine painting of the first years of the 16th century, while the *School of Athens* (p. 249) of 1509-12 is quite simply a great work. As a man who made himself a great artist by sheer hard work, Raphael is a rare but comforting figure. He always needed some extraordinary spur to bring out his full powers. The frescoes in the Vatican, which Julius II commissioned from him at the same time as Michelangelo's Sistine ceiling, provided him with a difficult task both technically and in the representation of such abstract ideas as Philosophy and Theology. Julius II deserves credit for discerning that this 26-year-old provincial, who had not so far painted anything on the grand scale, was capable of producing frescoes that in their own way rank with those of Michelangelo, then already considered the greatest living artist.

Mannerism

Raphael died aged only 37, but he was already advancing in a new tradition. The *Transfiguration* (p. 251) is one of the earliest works that can reasonably be called Mannerist. The emotionalism, the deliberate rejection of classical serenity in this picture made it enormously influential, and Giulio Romano, one of Raphael's principal assistants, took these ideas and exploited them still further in Mantua. Mannerism as a style developed in Rome and in Florence, and there was a fascinating but limited offshoot of it in Siena in the work of Beccafumi. In Florence the High Renaissance was continued in the work of Andrea del Sarto and Fra Bartolommeo, but the next generation—that of Pontormo and Rosso—brought up on Michelangelo's draftsmanship found themselves desperately searching for an original style in which they could use what they had learned from Michelangelo. At its best, in works like Pontormo's *Deposition* (p. 260), Mannerism was capable of producing startling equivalents for the tragic aspects of the Christian religion. Surprisingly also the elegance and pomp of the style suited court portraiture, as may be seen in the work of Bronzino. Both Beccafumi and Parmigianino carried the elegance and refinement of the style almost as far as it would go. Even in these sensitive hands it sometimes gave way to affectation on the one side and aridity on the other. Parmigianino developed from the style of Correggio, almost his contemporary, who represented the High Renaissance in the north of Italy.

Giorgione and the Venetian school

The true north Italian style of the 16th century, however, was that which Giovanni Bellini's pupils produced in Venice, where the ideas that underlie Mannerism hardly penetrated. Giorgione was the first of the great 16th-century Venetians who took over from Giovanni Bellini; but he introduced a note of romantic, almost elegiac poetry into his compositions and used a soft, glowing oil technique in place of the brighter, crisper colors of Giovanni Bellini. Many of Giorgione's works were produced for individual connoisseurs and his subjects are not invariably the simple, straightforward ones of earlier generations. Three of his most famous pictures —nearly half his known output—are of subjects that cannot be defined precisely: *The Tempest* (p. 239), the *Fête Champêtre* (p. 241), and the *Three Philosophers* (p. 240), which is an elaborated version of the traditional subject of the journey of the Magi.

Titian and Tintoretto

Giorgione died very young in 1510, and the leadership of Venetian painting fell upon Titian, who held it almost undisputed until his death in 1576. Titian lacked the sensibility of Giorgione, but there is a warm lyrical sensuality about his work, coupled with dazzling skill and inexhaustible imagination, so that his impact on Venetian painting lasted from Veronese to Tiepolo, who died in 1770. The one exception to this was in the work of Tintoretto, who in his turn was to influence El Greco. Titian was affected by Mannerism, and was not really impressed by Michelangelo. Tintoretto on the other hand saw the imaginative splendor of Michelangelo's greatest works and realized also that their impact was due at least partly to Michelangelo's complete mastery of the human figure and his use of contour as a means of expression. Tintoretto therefore sought to produce works that should have the grandeur of Michelangelo's ideas and the richness of Titian's color and texture. In his later works he developed a use of brightly contrasting lights and darks with looming figures silhouetted against a bright sky.

The sculptor Jacopo Sansovino, who was a friend of Titian, dominated 16th-century sculpture and architecture in Venice. His early sculpture is almost an imitation of Michelangelo, but unlike Tintoretto and like Titian, his ideal was the calm and order of true classicism. Veronese and Tintoretto died in 1588 and 1594 respectively. They were the last great painters of the 16th century and they tower above a host of minor Mannerists almost all of whom are tiresome in their attempts to rival Michelangelo. The new style, the Baroque, came into being at the beginning of the 17th century.

The Baroque and landscape painting

Both in painting and in architecture Baroque art made a sharp break with the past, but it is probably true that the new style is even more clearly to be seen in sculpture. Among painters the Carracci family on the one hand and Caravaggio on the other show the extremely broad limits of the new style and its main characteristics. These characteristics, which at first sight seem to be contradictory, are a new interest in naturalism coupled with a return to the classical standards of the antique and of Raphael.

The most important representatives of the classical style were Ludovico Carracci and his cousins Annibale and Agostino. Of the three, Annibale was by far the most considerable artist. His masterpiece is the ceiling of the gallery in the Palazzo Farnese in Rome, which can reasonably be compared with Michelangelo's Sistine ceiling in the Vatican.

It was, however, in Bologna that the Carracci first worked, and here that they founded an academy in which almost all the best painters of the next generation were trained. The somewhat sentimental religiosity of Guido Reni, as well as the work of Guercino and Domenichino, all owe much to the example of the Carracci; and it is possible too that the rise of landscape painting in the 17th century can be traced back to Annibale and to Domenichino, as well as to another Bolognese, Francesco Albani. The principal center for landscape painting, however, was Rome, where the two greatest artists in the middle of the century were both French—Poussin and Claude.

Annibale's ceiling in Rome, similar in its general layout to Michelangelo's, is much more decorative in feeling and the subjects themselves are less important, as befits purely secular decoration. The combination of figures painted in natural colors, figures painted in imitation of sculpture, and decorative details simulating bronze, was to be of the greatest importance in the development of the illusionist ceilings that are one of the principal glories of Baroque art, as, for example, the ceiling of the Palazzo Barberini by Pietro da Cortona, or the elaborately illusionistic ceiling of the Gesù by Baciccia. The work of the Fleming Rubens, one of the greatest of all Baroque artists, is particularly closely linked with this aspect of the style.

Caravaggio

The opposite tendency is represented by Caravaggio. He was a Lombard trained in a naturalistic technique who began by producing some strikingly realistic still-life paintings, and he developed a style in which extreme naturalism, sharp contrasts of light and shade, and a deliberately literal interpretation of religious subjects caused violent disagreement over the merits of his work. He was reacting sharply against the superficial generalization and vacuous idealization of late Mannerist art, but his businesslike treatment of such subjects as the Holy Family tended to shock many people. In spite of this, the honesty of vision and the dramatic power of his religious pictures ensured him a great following, both among patrons and also among his fellow artists. His influence, however, was strongest outside the main stream of Italian painting, and was particularly important in Naples, which was ruled by the Spanish. Through Naples, Caravaggio's influence penetrated to Spain itself, and in the work of Zurbarán and Velázquez it was responsible for some of the greatest masterpieces of the 17th century. Caravaggio's direct influence was also very strong in the north, and a whole group of painters known as the Utrecht school depended upon his example and upon that of his imitator Bartolommeo Manfredi. Many Dutch and Flemish painters, including Rubens himself, flocked to Rome in the 17th century and almost all of them were affected by Caravaggio's dramatic art. Even Rembrandt, who never visited Italy, was influenced by him.

Bernini

The most famous sculptor of the 17th century was Gian Lorenzo Bernini. His organizing ability and great versatility made him an ideal exponent of the grandiose style necessary for the decoration of the High Altar of St. Peter's, and the building of the huge colonnade outside. Bernini's portraiture was very penetrating, but at the same time conferred a superhuman dignity on the sitter. Not surprisingly, this appealed to the absolutist tendency of the age, and Bernini actually visited France to work for Louis XIV, though the trip produced little but a very fine bust of the king.

Among the other major artists of the period in Rome was the sculptor Algardi, Bernini's life-long rival who, as a Bolognese, represented the quieter, more classical aspect of Baroque sculpture. Pietro da Cortona, who was also one of the greatest architects of the age, was the other master of the somewhat inflated style necessary for such an immense ceiling as that of the Palazzo Barberini, crowded with scores of figures and filled with virtuoso feats of perspective. The last representative of the style, the Venetian Tiepolo, in accordance with the Rococo reaction of the early 18th century, lightened his ceilings by reducing the scale of the figures, but their effervescent quality and the brilliance of his color make him, in this respect at least, the last of the great Baroque decorators.

Landscape painting and the 18th century

Landscape painting of a highly romantic type was practiced by Salvator Rosa and later in Lombardy by Alessandro Magnasco. These landscapes, with their storm-tossed trees and wildly gesticulating figures, underlie the whole picturesque movement of the 18th century, and were also transmuted into the arcadian landscape practiced by a number of Venetian artists in the 18th century. Venetian 18th-century landscape was, however, dominated by the *veduta*; that is, a view of an actual place, most frequently Venice itself. Canaletto was not the first to paint views of Venice, but he was the greatest in the first half of the 18th century. The second half of the century saw a much lighter and more brilliant handling of the Venetian theme, full of atmosphere and dazzlingly painted small figures, in the paintings of Francesco Guardi. Venice in the 18th century was by far the most important of the Italian centers: it saw not only Tiepolo and the *veduta* painters, but a survivor of the straightforward Baroque tradition in Piazzetta, and a new kind of rather superficial genre painting in the work of Pietro Longhi. Two other Venetians brought the art of the 18th century to a close, though both formed their style in Rome; they were the etcher Piranesi and the sculptor Canova. Piranesi began as an architect but his imagination was haunted by the ruins of Rome and he spent his life in making large and extremely accurate etchings that, at the same time, are full of romantic grandeur. They were one of the principal influences on the Romantic movement of the end of the century, just as the sculpture of Canova was an important element in the Neoclassic style which, though invented and largely practiced by foreigners, was based on Rome. It was Rome itself that was the inspiration of much of the best art of the 18th century in Europe, just as it had been the art of classical Rome that inspired Nicola Pisano some five hundred years earlier.

Biographies

SOME BOOKS FOR FURTHER READING

The most important source for our knowledge about Italian art is Giorgio Vasari's *Lives of the Painters, Sculptors and Architects*, first published in Florence in 1550 and in a revised and enlarged edition in 1568: there are several editions in English, some available in paperback, but the largest and most complete is that by G. de Vere, in 10 volumes, London, 1912-15. The ideas that motivated many Italian artists are examined in A. F. Blunt's *Artistic Theory in Italy*, 1450-1600, Oxford, 1940. The most recent complete history of all the arts in Italy is A. Chastel's *Italian Art*, London, 1963. Some books on different periods or styles are:

H. Wölfflin, *Classic Art*, London, 1952.

C. Gould, *Introduction to Italian Renaissance Painting*, London, 1957.

R. Wittkower, *Art and Architecture in Italy*, 1600-1750, (Pelican History of Art) London, 1958.

E. Sandberg-Vavala, *Uffizi Studies*, Florence, 1948; *Sienese Studies*, Florence, 1953; *Studies in the Florentine Churches*, Florence, 1959.

M. Levey, *Painting in 18th-Century Venice*, London, 1959.

S. Freedberg, *Painting of the High Renaissance in Rome and Florence*, 1475-1521, 2 vols., Harvard, 1961.

E. Waterhouse, *Italian Baroque Painting*, London, 1962.

B. Berenson, *Italian Painters of the Renaissance*, London, 1953; *Italian Pictures of the Renaissance, Venetian School*, 2 vols., London, 1957, and *Florentine School*, 2 vols., London, 1963.

P. & L. Murray, *The Art of the Renaissance*, London, 1963.

J. Pope-Hennessy, *Italian Gothic Sculpture*, London, 1955; *Italian Renaissance Sculpture*, London, 1958; *Italian High Renaissance and Baroque Sculpture*, 3 vols., London, 1963.

P. Murray, *The Architecture of the Italian Renaissance*, London, 1963.

SEE ALSO UNDER THE INDIVIDUAL BIOGRAPHIES

ALESSANDRO ALGARDI

1595-1654

A classical Bolognese sculptor

Alessandro Algardi was a 17th-century sculptor who worked in a classical vein, as opposed to the Baroque master Bernini. Like the painters Domenichino, Guido Reni, and the Carracci, Algardi came from Bologna. The quiet classicism of all their works is characteristic of the Bolognese school.

Algardi was born in 1595 and was first trained in Bologna before going to Rome in about 1625. From that time on he was a rival of Bernini. He reached the peak of his career under Pope Innocent X, who was antagonistic to Bernini. Nevertheless, most of Algardi's major works, including the statue of *Innocent X* and the *Tomb of Leo XI*, are fundamentally "Bernini" works with some of the fire taken out of them. His most famous work is probably the huge relief of *The Meeting of Pope Leo I and Attila* in St. Peter's. His portrait busts show an extremely keen eye for character and are perhaps his finest works. He died in 1654.

R. Wittkower   Art and Architecture in Italy 1600-1750   London, 1958

Roberto Frangipane, after 1644
Rome, S. Marcello

HIS WORKS INCLUDE

S. Filippo Neri and the Angel, 1640
Rome, S. Maria in Vallicella

The Decapitation of St. Paul, 1641-47
Bologna, S. Paolo

The Meeting of Leo I and Attila,
1646-53   *Rome, St. Peter's*

Pope Innocent X, 1645
Rome, Pal. dei Conservatori

Portrait of Donna Olimpia
Maidalchini,
about 1650
Rome, Gall. Doria

See also page 393

The Meeting of Pope Leo I and Attila,
1646-53
Rome, St. Peter's

Pope Innocent X, 1645
Rome, Pal. dei Conservatori

Cardinal Bracciolini, after 1630
London, V. and A.

Frescoes, after 1377
Padua, Oratorio di S. Giorgio

The Crucifixion, about 1379
Padua, S. Antonio, Chapel of S. Felice

See also page 182

The Crucifixion, after 1377
Padua, Oratorio di S. Giorgio

Madonna, Saints, and Warriors of the
Cavalli Family, about 1365-70
Verona, S. Anastasia, Cavalli Chapel

ALTICHIERO   about 1320- about 1384

His style was derived from Giotto's Paduan frescoes

Altichiero was the most important painter working in a style based on Giotto's in North Italy during the second half of the 14th century. He was probably born at Verona in about 1320, and died about 1384. He painted a cycle of frescoes in the chapel of S. Giacomo in the Santo at Padua in 1379. A document still exists recording his payment for this work.

The whole basis of Altichiero's style was the fresco cycle painted by Giotto in the Arena Chapel in Padua, but to this he added an interest in naturalistic detail which anticipated the International Gothic style.

GIOVANNI ANTONIO AMADEO   1447-1522

The greatest of the 15th-century Lombard architect-sculptors

Giovanni Antonio Amadeo was born at Pavia. The stucco *Dance of the Angels* in the Portinari Chapel of S. Eustorgio in Milan is said to be an early work by him, and he was certainly working in the Certosa at Pavia by 1466. The very elaborate Colleoni Chapel at Bergamo was built by him between 1471 and 1477. From then on he was a successful and active architect, becoming the superintendent architect of Milan Cathedral. Like most Lombards of this time, his style is a mixture of half-understood Florentine influences and the local, highly decorative traditional style.

J. Pope-Hennessy Italian Renaissance Sculpture London, 1958

HIS WORKS INCLUDE

The Tombs of Bartolommeo and
Medea Colleoni, about 1475
Bergamo, Colleoni Chapel

St. Mary and St. Martha
Milan, Mus. del Castello Sforzesco

See also page 387

FRA ANGELICO

about 1387 or 1400-1455

A painter esteemed for his pure and devout works

Fra Angelico, the popular nickname given to the Dominican friar Fra Giovanni da Fiesole, aptly expresses the devotional charm of his work. It used to be thought that he was born in 1387, but the register of his entry into the Convent of Fiesole is not dated 1407, as had always been believed, and he may, therefore, have been born about 1400. Certainly his earliest works seem to have been painted in the 1420's. The earliest dated work is the famous *Madonna* painted for the Linen Guild in 1433. It shows that by 1433 Fra Angelico had been influenced by Masaccio, and was working in a style similar to that of Masolino. The modernism of Fra Angelico's style was much reinforced by the influence of the architect and sculptor Michelozzo, who was employed to reconstruct the convent of S. Marco, Florence, which housed Fra Angelico's community.

Angelico himself painted many frescoes in the rebuilt monastery during the 1430's and 1440's. Among these are a few relatively large frescoes, including the famous *Annunciation* of 1437-45; these frescoes are in the public rooms or on staircases and in corridors. There are many smaller frescoes in the individual cells, each

Portrait of Fra Angelico
by Luca Signorelli, about 1500
Orvieto, Cath.

HIS WORKS INCLUDE

The Last Judgment, about 1430
Florence, Mus. di S. Marco

Linaiuoli Madonna, 1433
Florence, Mus. di S. Marco

The Deposition, about 1435
Florence, Mus. di S. Marco

The Martyrdom of St. Cosmas
and St. Damian, about 1438-45
Paris, Louvre

The Annunciation, about 1438
Cortona, Mus. Diocesiano

The Madonna and Child with Saints
1437
Perugia, Mus. Naz. dell' Umbria

Frescoes, 1438-45
Florence, Convent of S. Marco

Frescoes, about 1449
Orvieto, Cath.

Frescoes, 1445-50
Rome, Vatican, Chapel of Nicholas V

See also pages 187, 188, 189

The Deposition, about 1435
Florence, Mus. di S. Marco

Christ Glorified in the Court of Heaven
(detail of Saints) from a predella of an
altarpiece, about 1430 *London, N. G.*

19

Noli me Tangere, 1438-45
Florence, Convent of S. Marco

of which is intended to form a subject for contemplation by the occupant. They vary a good deal in quality, and it seems that Fra Angelico employed assistants to do them. He was summoned to Rome in 1447 to work in the Vatican. About this time he also began the fresco cycle in Orvieto Cathedral, which was subsequently taken over by Signorelli. The frescoes in the chapel of Nicholas V in the Vatican still exist and show the increasing influence of Masaccio. Another chapel Fra Angelico painted in the Vatican has disappeared without trace.

The fact that so much of Angelico's style depends on artists like Lorenzo Monaco, Ghiberti, and Masolino has often obscured the strongly humanist elements in his works. He was long regarded as a sentimental maker of devotional images, but a closer examination of his works shows that this derogatory view is unfounded.

Angelico became Prior of Fiesole and was on friendly terms with some of the leading figures of his day. At the time of his death in 1455, he was working in Rome for Pope Nicholas V.

J. Pope-Hennessy Fra Angelico London, 1952

The Annunciation, 1437-45
Florence, Convent of S. Marco

ANTONELLO DA MESSINA

about 1430-1479

The only important South Italian painter of the 15th century

Antonello was born in Messina in Sicily and died there in 1479. The curious fact that his work is far closer in spirit to Flemish than to Italian painting has been explained in a number of ways, most of them implausible. It is certain, however, that Naples was strongly influenced by Franco-Flemish ideas, for it was ruled by René of Anjou. It is known that there were in the city works by leading Flemish painters, such as Jan van Eyck and Roger van der Weyden. The mysterious Colantonio, however, seems to have been Antonello's master. The idea that Antonello was trained in Flanders is improbable, since his style is derived from Jan van Eyck and not from Roger van der Weyden, as it would have been had he been in Flanders in the middle of the 15th century.

The extraordinary closeness to the Eyckian style is very evident in Antonello's early works, such as the *St. Jerome* and the *Crucifixion*. The *Salvator Mundi*, dated 1465, and the *Madonna and Child* in Washington show elements of grandeur and monumentality that have no parallel in Flemish painting, and which are probably derived from Sicilian mosaics. In all his later works is found the complete

Self-portrait (?) about 1475
London, N. G.

Salvator Mundi, 1465
London, N. G.

HIS WORKS INCLUDE

The Crucifixion, before 1465
Rumania, Sibiu Mus.

Portrait of a Young Man, about 1470
New York, Met. Mus.

The Madonna and Child, after 1475
Washington D. C., N. G., Mellon Coll.

Pietà, about 1476
Venice, Mus. Correr

See also page 207

The San Cassiano Altarpiece (fragment) 1476
Vienna, Kunsthist. Mus.

The Madonna and Child, after 1475
Washington D. C., N. G., Mellon Coll.

fusion of the Northern and the Italian Schools in his own expressive style. In 1475 Antonello went to Venice, where he was given the commission for the altarpiece of the Church of S. Cassiano. This was largely destroyed in the 17th century. Fragments of it exist in Vienna, and it has been possible to reconstruct its original appearance. It was one of the most important works produced in North Italy, since it appears to have been contemporary with the altarpieces by Giovanni Bellini and Piero della Francesca that were among the first to treat the subject of the Madonna and Child with Saints as an event actually taking place in the space in which the picture was placed. This made the altarpiece into an apparent extension of the chapel in which it stood. The invention of this idea, which was later exploited by Giovanni Bellini, cannot be definitely associated with any one of the three painters, but obviously Antonello's reputation must have been very high for him to receive such a commission from a Venetian church. The *Crucifixion* now in Antwerp must have been painted at this time, since it is dated 1475, and another *Crucifixion* in London is also of 1475. Both these dated works and indeed all his other pictures are painted in an accomplished oil technique, equal to that of the Flemish painters and in advance of that current in Venice and other parts of Italy. For this reason, Antonello has often been given the credit for introducing oil technique into Italy. Although this is undoubtedly an exaggeration, he certainly caused Giovanni Bellini to begin experiments in oil painting, and thus profoundly influenced the whole course of Venetian art during the next three centuries.

S. Botari   Antonello da Messina   London, 1957

The Crucifixion, 1475
Antwerp, Mus. Royal des B-A.

St. Jerome in his Study, about 1464
London, N. G.

ARNOLFO DI CAMBIO

died about 1302

The designer of Florence Cathedral

Arnolfo di Cambio is assumed to have been born at Colle Val d'Elsa near Siena. The first records of him go back to 1265 and refer to his collaboration with Giovanni Pisano on the pulpit for Siena Cathedral, as assistant to Nicola Pisano. In 1277 he was at Rome in the service of King Charles of Anjou, and shortly afterwards he was at Perugia and Orvieto. Later he was at Rome again, and in about 1294 he was summoned to Florence to build the new cathedral there, S. Maria del Fiore. He died in Florence sometime between 1302 and 1310, probably in 1302.

Arnolfo di Cambio was one of the greatest architects and sculptors of the late 13th century. Apart from the fame he acquired as the original architect of Florence Cathedral, he also showed an unusually powerful plasticity in his sculpture, in which he achieved a synthesis that preserved a sense of classical harmony and at times showed the emergence of an underlying Etruscan element. Unfortunately, he did not live to see the completion of the cathedral, and much of his original design was altered; the dome was built by Filippo Brunelleschi over a century later.

Sketch for Florence Cathedral, before 1296
Florence, Mus. dell'Opera del Duomo

Ciborium, 1285
Rome, S. Paolo fuori le Mura

Charles of Anjou, after 1277
Rome, Pal. dei Conservatori

The Tomb of Cardinal de Braye, about 1282
Orvieto, S. Domenico

HIS WORKS INCLUDE

Charles of Anjou, after 1277
Rome, Pal. dei Conservatori

The Tomb of Cardinal de Braye
about 1282
Orvieto, S. Domenico

Ciborium, 1285
Rome, S. Paolo fuori le Mura

Ciborium, 1293
Rome, S. Cecilia

The Madonna and Child, 1294-1301
Florence, Mus. dell'Opera del Duomo

See also page 371

23

GIOVANNI BATTISTA GAULLI called IL BACICCIA 1639-1709

Painter of spectacular illusionist decorations

Giovanni Battista Gaulli was born in Genoa in 1639. The name by which he is best known, Baciccia, is a dialect corruption of his second Christian name. He was influenced in his formative years by the rich, decorative and colorful style of Rubens and van Dyck, who both worked in Genoa in the first years of the 17th century, and by Correggio, whose illusionistic dome paintings he studied in Parma.

In Rome Baciccia came under the influence of his great contemporary in the field of Baroque decoration, Pietro da Cortona, whom he exceeded in warmth and richness of color, and in the creation of daring effects of illusionism in ceiling decorations. The most celebrated of these is *The Adoration of the Name of Jesus*, 1668-83, in the Gesù, mother church of the Jesuit order in Rome. The perspective illusion creates overhead a world of infinite distance and space. The figures in the painting merge almost imperceptibly into colored stucco figures that surge downward from the vault on to the wall below. The figures move out of the picture space and into the plane of the spectator, who is thus involved more closely in the dynamic effect of the decoration.

Baciccia worked in many other Roman churches, and also painted portraits, though these were quieter in feeling and more intimate in character.

Self-portrait
Florence, Uffizi

HIS WORKS INCLUDE

Portrait of Pope Clement IX
about 1668
Rome, Accad. di San Luca

Virtue, about 1671
Rome, S. Agnese in Piazza Navona

The Adoration of the Name of Jesus
1668-83
Rome, The Gesù

The Glorification of the
Franciscan Order, 1707
Rome, SS. Apostoli

See also page 289

The Child Jesus
Genoa, Pal. Rosso

St. Ignatius in Glory, after 1679
Rome, The Gesù

FEDERICO BAROCCI

1535/38-1612/15

A late 16th-century painter strongly influenced by Correggio

Federico Barocci was born at Urbino. A journey he made to Parma between 1555 and 1557 left him with a profound and sincere admiration for Correggio. Around 1560 he was active in Rome (in the Vatican) with Federico Zuccari, but a serious illness affected his health for the rest of his life; nevertheless Barocci worked intensely hard, especially on religious painting and portraiture, and he produced a multitude of remarkable drawings. He died at Urbino in 1612 or 1615.

Self-portrait
Florence, Uffizi

ꟻVBꟻ.

HIS WORKS INCLUDE

The Martyrdom of St. Vitalis, 1583
Milan, Brera

The Rest on the Flight into Egypt
Rome, Vatican Library

The Madonna of the Rosary
Sinigaglia, S. Rocco

The Assumption, late work
Dresden, Gemäldegal.

Self-portrait
Florence, Uffizi

See also page 351

The Martyrdom of St. Vitalis, 1583
Milan, Brera

The Holy Family
London, N. G.

The Adoration of the Child
London, N. G.

The Mystical Marriage of
St. Catherine, 1512
Florence, Pal. Pitti

HIS WORKS INCLUDE

Frescoes, 1510-14
Florence, Mus. di S. Marco

The Mystical Marriage of
St. Catherine, 1511
Paris, Louvre

The Madonna in Glory, 1512
Besançon, Cath.

The Madonna of Mercy, 1515
Lucca, Mus.

See also pages 234, 340

FRA BARTOLOMMEO   about 1474-1517

A painter whose religious conversion decisively influenced his art

Fra Bartolommeo, born near Florence about 1474, began his career in 1484 as a pupil of the competent but pedestrian painter Cosimo Rosselli. No works before 1499 are known. This is the date of the fresco of *The Last Judgment*, the battered fragments of which show clearly the influence he had on the young Raphael. In 1498 he was present when a mob broke into the convent of S. Marco and dragged away the prior, Savonarola, to imprisonment and eventual death. He was so affected by the horror of this experience that he became a monk in the convent in 1500. He took over the direction of the monastic workshop in 1504, and during the next few years developed a style based on balanced simplicity of composition, rhythmic movement, and a deliberate search for weight and nobility, leading sometimes to a rather inflated grandeur.

In 1508 Bartolommeo was in Venice for a few months, and in 1514 or 1515 he visited Rome. These contacts with other major artistic centers strengthened his rejection of Florentine late Quattrocento picturesque naturalism, agitated movement, and contemporary costume, in favor of a conscious striving for an impressive but generalized presentation. He is thus one of the major artists in the change from 15th to 16th-century art.

In 1508 Fra Bartolommeo took into partnership in the convent workshop Mariotto Albertinelli but, after the latter's defection to become an inn-keeper some years later, his assistants were never of an ability equal to his own. After his death in 1517 the workshop dwindled and disappeared.

S. J. Freedberg Painting of the High Renaissance in Rome and Florence Cambridge, Mass., 1961

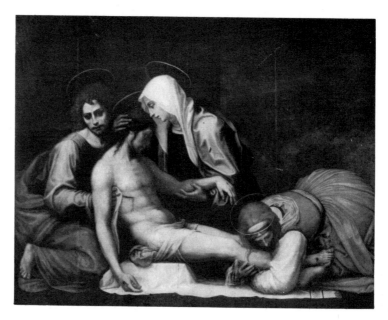

The Deposition
Florence, Pal. Pitti

EVARISTO BASCHENIS   1607/17-1677

An artist who painted musical instruments

Evaristo Baschenis, born in Bergamo, became a priest early in life. His still-life
paintings portray themes of great originality. Most of his pictures center on musical
instruments, generally superb lutes from the workshop of Amati, of full and rounded form, painted in minute detail. Each picture became virtually a portrait of a
collection of still-life objects, portrayed with an astonishing intensity. He also
extracted the maximum poetry—and even emotion—from the play of light and
the strong contrasts of detail and deep shadow, so that the relationships between
volume and light have something of the obsessive quality found in the work of
Caravaggio.

HIS WORKS INCLUDE
Musical Instruments
Brussels, Mus. Royaux des B-A.
Musical Instruments
Milan, Brera
Musical Instruments
Bergamo, Accad. Carrara

See also page 286

JACOPO DA PONTE, called BASSANO   about 1510/18-1592

A great painter from a famous Venetian family of artists

Jacopo da Ponte was born early in the 16th century in Bassano (hence the name he
is generally known by) and was the son of a painter and the father of four painter
sons, all of whom eventually worked in the family workshop. In the 1530's he was
in Venice as a pupil of Bonifazio de' Pitati, a minor but popular Venetian painter.
After he returned to his native Bassano, where he worked for most of his life, he
developed a robust and vigorous style, using strong effects of light and shadow. His
color is somewhat dark and gray, heavily impasted, but shot through with brilliant
effects of light. He was a pioneer in the creation of genre scenes with peasants and
herds of cattle set in mountainous landscapes and under dark and stormy skies.
His religious subjects often contained vivid groups of naturalistic figures and
animals, as well as still-lifes of game, vegetables, and fruit.

Although he worked almost all his life in a provincial center, Bassano's work
reflects with insight and feeling the grand art of Titian and Tintoretto, of whom he
is a worthy contemporary. He died in 1592.

HIS WORKS INCLUDE
The Good Samaritan, 1540-50
Hampton Court, Royal Coll.
Dives and Lazarus, about 1560
Cleveland, Ohio, Mus. of Art
The Crucifixion, 1562
Treviso, Mus. Civico
Descent of the Holy Spirit,
about 1562 or 1570
Bassano, Mus. Civico
The Mocking of Christ
Paris, Louvre

See also pages 264, 350

St. Roch Blessing
the Plague-stricken, about 1575
Milan, Brera

The Purification of
the Temple
London, N. G.

DOMENICO BECCAFUMI about 1486-1551

An important 16th-century Sienese painter

Domenico Beccafumi, the greatest Sienese artist of the 16th century, was born near Siena in about 1486. Here he came under the influence of Sodoma and Leonardo. When Beccafumi went to Rome, he was immediately affected by the work of Michelangelo and Raphael. After returning to Siena in 1512 he formed a highly personal and lyrical style, from an assimilation of the styles of Sodoma, Michelangelo, and Raphael. His work is characterized by shot color and elongated figures. Each figure, particularly in his religious paintings, is charged with a deeply emotional content. Beccafumi was also active as a sculptor, and produced a number of wood-engravings and etchings. He died in Siena in 1551. Most of his major works are still there.

An Angel, about 1515
Siena, Cath.

HIS WORKS INCLUDE

Descent of Jesus into Limbo
about 1528
Siena, Pin.

St. Michael, about 1542
Siena, S. Maria del Carmine

The Birth of the Virgin, about 1543
Siena, Pin.

See also page 338

Esther before Ahasuerus, late work
London, N. G.

GENTILE BELLINI about 1430-1507

A fine Venetian painter, overshadowed by his brother

GENTILIS BELLINI.

Gentile Bellini, the elder son of Jacopo Bellini and brother of Giovanni, was born probably in Venice. In his day he was famous both as a portrait painter and as a painter of huge ceremonial pictures containing scores of portraits. He painted most of these for the Doge's Palace in Venice and for various Venetian charitable foundations. Comparatively few of them have survived.

Gentile and his brother began their careers in their father's studio, and both were influenced by the prodigy Mantegna, who married their sister in 1454. In 1469 Gentile was ennobled by Emperor Frederick III. The principal event of his life, however, was his journey to Constantinople in 1479. The Turkish Sultan Mohammed II had sent a request to the Venetian Government for a good painter, and they recommended Gentile. He spent eighteen months in Constantinople, where he painted the Sultan's portrait. He created many huge decorations after his return to Venice, in 1481; these were later burnt in a series of fires.

Attrib. to Gentile Bellini
The Sultan Mohammed II, 1480
London, N. G.

The Adoration of the Magi
London, N. G.

HIS WORKS INCLUDE

Portrait of Catarina Cornaro
Queen of Cyprus, about 1492
Budapest, Mus. of Fine Arts

The Procession of the Cross, 1496
Venice, Accad.

The Miracle of the True Cross, 1500
Venice, Accad.

See also page 206

The Miracle of the True Cross, 1500
Venice, Accad.

Portrait of Caterina Cornaro,
Queen of Cyprus, about 1492
Budapest, Mus. of Fine Arts

29

VITTORE BELLINIANO
Portrait of Giovanni Bellini
Chantilly, Mus. Condé

IOANNES·BELUNUS

HIS WORKS INCLUDE

See also pp. 206, 209, 210, 211, 322

GIOVANNI BELLINI   about 1430-1516

The first great Venetian painter

Giovanni Bellini, son of Jacopo and brother of Gentile, was born probably about 1430. The two brothers worked in the family workshop until the death of their father in 1470/71. Giovanni, like Gentile, was influenced by the style of painting of his brother-in-law, Mantegna, though Giovanni's work was always gentler in feeling and softer in color and in light. A famous comparison between Mantegna and Giovanni Bellini is to be found in their two versions of *The Agony in the Garden*. Mantegna introduced into Venetian art a Florentine discipline derived from Donatello, but Giovanni Bellini transformed the severe humanism of Donatello and Mantegna into a softer and more tender humanity.

The influence of Antonello da Messina had inspired the experiments in oil painting which Giovanni had been making at least since 1473. From 1470, Giovanni was responsible for many Madonnas, not all of which were painted by his

The Madonna Enthroned with Saints (detail) 1505
Venice, S. Zaccaria

own hand. A series of paintings in the National Gallery, London, reveals the basic Giovanni Bellini type as well as the styles of his various assistants. He also began a series of large altarpieces similar to Antonello da Messina's S. Cassiano altarpiece of about 1476. Many of Giovanni Bellini's works still exist, among them the S. Giobbe altarpiece of about 1485, and they show the development of his style and its continuing enrichment over a number of years. As late as 1514 and 1515, when he painted the *Feast of the Gods* and the *Lady at her Toilet*, he continued to make discoveries similar to those of his young pupil, Titian. Bellini's art is the foundation of Venetian painting, and most of the major painters of the early 16th century were his pupils. Giovanni died in Venice in 1516.

R. Fry *Giovanni Bellini* London, 1910
P. Hendy and L. Goldscheider *Giovanni Bellini* London, 1945

St. Dominic, about 1515
London, N. G.

The Virgin and Child with St. Catherine and Mary Magdalen
about 1490-1500
Venice, Accad.

The Agony in the Garden (detail)
about 1465
London, N. G.

The Pietà
Venice, Accad.

The Agony in the Garden, about 1465
London, N. G.

31

The Madonna and Child with
Lionello d'Este
Paris, Louvre

JACOPO BELLINI

about 1400-1470/1

An artist of influence whose sons became great painters

Jacopo Bellini was a Venetian painter who went to Florence as a pupil of Gentile da Fabriano, and thus helped to introduce the International Gothic style into Venice. Later he worked as a portrait painter, and in 1441 painted a portrait of Lionello d'Este of Ferrara that was held to be better than one by Pisanello. Only a few pictures certainly by him now survive, but there are two large sketch books, one in Paris and the other in London, which contain drawings for completed compositions, and studies from the antique, as well as many miscellaneous drawings showing the influences that formed his style. His manner passed through his children into the heritage of Venetian art in general.

B. Berenson   Venetian Paintings in America   London, 1916

HIS WORKS INCLUDE

The Madonna and Child
Bergamo, Accad. Carrara

St. Jerome
Brooklyn, Mus.

Drawings
London, B. M., and Paris, Louvre

The Madonna and Child, 1448
Milan, Brera

The Madonna and Child
Venice, Accad.

See also pages 195, 309

St. Hubert, about 1440-50
Paris, Louvre

---

*Bernard Bellotto dit Canaletto
Peintre Du Roi*

BERNARDO BELLOTTO

1720-1780

A relation, pupil, and imitator of Canaletto

Born in Venice, in 1720, Bellotto was a pupil of his uncle, Antonio Canal, and he too was known by the name of Canaletto. On first sight it would seem that Bellotto reproduced the themes of his more distinguished relative almost to the last detail, but in fact he put a maximum emphasis on presenting an accurately realistic *veduta*, with a Flemish attention to detail. His views are usually suffused with a cold, metallic, or vitreous light—which was particularly suitable for catching the atmosphere of the northern regions where he stayed for a long time. After completing various journeys in Italy—to Rome, Turin, and Vicenza, from 1740 to 1745—he went to Munich; in 1746 and 1747 he stayed in Dresden at the invitation of the Elector of Saxony, Augustus III, and, apart from one visit to

HIS WORKS INCLUDE

The Old Bridge over the Po at Turin
about 1743
Turin, Pin.

View of Dresden, 1747
Dresden, Gemäldegal.

View of the Miodowa Road
about 1775
Warsaw, Mus.

See also page 303

32

Vienna and Schönbrunn (1759/60), remained there until 1766, when he went to St. Petersburg. From the following year until his death 13 years later, he lived in Warsaw as court painter to King Stanislas Poniatowski.

M. Levey Painting in 18th-Century Venice London, 1959

BONIFACIO BEMBO

active 1446-1478

A painter of the courtly life of 15th-century Milan

Bonifacio Bembo, born at Brescia some time between 1410 and 1420, became one of the last practitioners in North Italy of the International Gothic style.

He was inspired probably by Gentile da Fabriano and Pisanello, painters of similar pictures idealizing courtly life. He executed many of his works for the Sforza family, Dukes of Milan, and Bembo was given the citizenship of the city. Like most other artists of the International Gothic school, he introduced a fairy-tale quality into his pictures.

HIS WORKS INCLUDE

Francesco Sforza, 1471
Cremona, S. Agostino

Bianca Maria Visconti, 1471
Cremona, S. Agostino

Frescoes
Cremona, S. Agostino

St. Julian
Milan, Brera

See also page 311

GIAN LORENZO BERNINI

1598-1680

The greatest exponent of Baroque sculpture

Gian Lorenzo Bernini was born in 1598 in Naples, where his father, Pietro, a Florentine sculptor, had settled temporarily. By 1605 the family was in Rome, and the young Bernini soon gave proof of his extraordinary precocity. By the age of 14 he was carving a statue of Bishop Santoni, and he seems to have done some work in collaboration with his father. By 1619 he was working on his own. A group of his statues is datable between 1619 and 1625; all, except one, are now in the Borghese Gallery in Rome.

The exception is the *Neptune and Triton* of 1620, now in London, one of the few major works by Bernini to be found outside Italy. Both it and the *David* in the Borghese Gallery are splendid examples of early Baroque art, since both are expressive of violent movement, yet are simpler and much more energetic than Mannerist works with their complicated and twisted poses. The vitality of the young Bernini's sculpture is shown in his exceptional technical mastery. This is seen best in another early work, the *Apollo and Daphne*, about 1624, which expresses, in marble, the muscularity of Apollo and the contrast between the soft flesh of Daphne and the wood of the tree into which she is being changed.

In the 1620's Bernini also began to work as an architect, his first major commission being the Barberini Palace in Rome. In later years, Bernini's architecture was an important counter-balance to the architecture of Borromini, being far more closely based on classical Roman examples. It was at this time also that Bernini began his association with the Papal Court which, with one short break, lasted for the rest of his life. (This break was the Pontificate of Innocent X between 1644 and 1655, but even during this period Bernini continued to produce notable works).

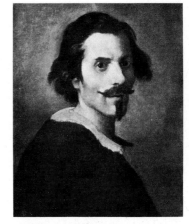

Self-portrait, about 1623
Rome, Gall. Borghese

HIS WORKS INCLUDE

Apollo and Daphne, about 1624
Rome, Gall. Borghese

Costanza Buonarelli, 1625
Florence, Mus. Naz. del Bargello

The Fountain of the Tritons, 1640
Rome, Piazza Barberini

Equestrian Statue of Louis XIV
1669-77
Versailles, and Rome, Gall. Borghese

The Blessed Ludovica Albertoni, 1675
Rome, S. Francesco a Ripa

See also pages 394, 395

A Male Figure
Florence, Uffizi

During this time he started the *Ecstasy of St. Theresa* (1645-52) in the Church of S. Maria della Vittoria in Rome. This is one of the most characteristically Baroque works of art, since the statue itself not only expresses a psychological state —which was something new in the history of art —but also employs technical means representative of the Baroque. Thus, the attempt to render ecstasy led him to combine

The Blessed Ludovica Albertoni, 1675
Rome, S. Francesco a Ripa

Equestrian Statue of Louis XIV, 1669-77
Rome, Gall. Borghese

Figure for a Fountain
Venice, Ca d'Oro

The Rape of Proserpina (detail) about 1622
Rome, Gall. Borghese

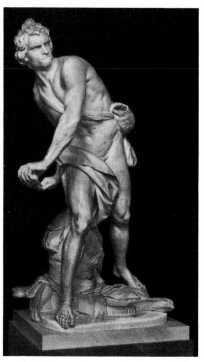

David, 1623
Rome, Gall. Borghese

the architectural setting with the statue in such a way that the use of colored and white marble and the introduction of a shaft of yellow light combine to produce an overwhelming effect.

Bernini's sense of grandeur is perhaps best seen in the enormous colonnades of St. Peter's, which contain the whole oval piazza in front of the church within their branching arms. The colonnades carry statues of hundreds of saints made under Bernini's supervision by his numerous assistants, and the quality and quantity of the work produced in this way is a testimony to the enormous influence exerted by Bernini throughout his very long life.

In 1665 Bernini was invited to Paris to draw up a plan for the Louvre, and also to make a bust and equestrian statue of Louis XIV. On his arrival in France he was given a princely reception; but the French artists managed to sabotage his plans for the Louvre, while Louis XIV himself disliked the equestrian statue. The bust, now in Versailles, is, however, the most perfect example of the way in which the Baroque style could be made an instrument of absolutism, expressing as it does the Roi Soleil's own conception of himself. Bernini's insight into character was very deep and can be seen in many of the busts still in Rome, while his religious works were invariably animated by the drama of the Counter-Reformation.

Scipione Borghese, 1632
Rome, Gall. Borghese

J. Pope-Hennessy   Italian High Renaissance and Baroque Sculpture   London, 1963
R. Wittkower   Gian Lorenzo Bernini—the Sculptor of the Roman Baroque   London, 1955

The Baldachin, 1624-33
Rome, St. Peter's

The Tomb of Pope Urban VIII, 1628-47
Rome, St. Peter's

HIS WORKS INCLUDE

The Mystic Marriage of
St. Catherine, about 1420
Siena, Pin.

The Marriage of the Virgin, 1430-35
New York, Met. Mus.

See also page 308

MICHELINO DA BESOZZO active about 1388-1442

A painter brilliantly successful in his own day, but now little known

The first record of the Lombard painter and miniaturist Michelino da Besozzo is in 1388, when he was working on a fresco cycle in the cloister of St. Peter's in Ciel d'Oro at Pavia. He was in Venice in 1410, and this brought him into contact, not only with the local art, but more important, with Gentile da Fabriano; in the following years he is often mentioned in the records of Milan Cathedral, the latest date being 1442. The dates of his birth and death are still unknown.

Mercury, 1564
Florence, Mus. Naz. del Bargello

HIS WORKS INCLUDE

Fountain of Neptune, about 1567
Bologna

Mercury, 1564
Florence, Mus. Naz. del Bargello

The Rape of the Sabine Women
about 1583
Florence, Loggia dei Lanzi

Venus
Florence, Villa della Petraja

Venus Bathing
Florence, Mus. Naz. del Bargello

Samson Slaying the Philistine, 1567
London, V. and A.

See also page 392

GIOVANNI DA BOLOGNA 1529-1608

The most famous Florentine sculptor after Michelangelo

Although he was born at Douai and started his career at Antwerp, Jean Boulogne, better known by the Italian name Giovanni da Bologna or Giambologna, arrived in Rome in 1545 and spent the rest of his life in Italy. He lived in Florence from 1553 until his death in 1608. Since Northern Europe was at this time much influenced by the Italian style imported into France by Francis I, Giambologna was already an Italian at second hand when he arrived in Rome, and was at once further influenced by Michelangelo. He became one of the greatest Mannerist sculptors. His style is unmistakable. Voluptuous curves, elongated limbs and very small heads make for simple shapes with clearly defined contours, delicate and sinuous. He is best known for his small scale works, although he carved a number of large statues, many of which were intended for the formal gardens of Florentine villas.

A River God, about 1570
Florence, Mus. Naz. del Bargello

36

GIOVANNI ANTONIO BOLTRAFFIO

1467-1516

A brilliant draftsman

Giovanni Antonio Boltraffio probably came from an aristocratic family and painted more for amusement than necessity. He was one of Leonardo da Vinci's select circle, meeting him on the different occasions when Leonardo stayed in Milan.

Boltraffio's palette was the richer in his later works for a touch of Venetian color inherited from Antonio da Solario. His aim in general was to convert Leonardo's *sfumato* technique into *chiaroscuro*, without losing sight of the Lombard traditions of the naturalistic treatment of light. His achievement of this is to be seen in the landscape backgrounds to those portraits and Madonnas that constitute the best of his paintings.

B. Berenson   The North Italian Painters   London, 1907

PAOLO VINCENZO BONOMINI called BORROMINI

1756-1839

An early Romantic

Paolo Vincenzo Bonomini, called Borromini, was a Bergamasque painter born in 1756. His modern reputation depends upon the macabre scenes of skeletons going about everyday activities. They are now regarded as early Romantic works, having affinities with the far greater art of Goya. He died in 1839.

Macabre Scene
Bergamo, S. Grata

Macabre Scene (detail)
Bergamo, S. Grata

Judith, about 1472
Florence, Uffizi

SB.

An artist who brought movement to painting, and broke with old tradition

Sandro Botticelli was born in Florence, and was active as a painter by 1470. The formation of his style is rather obscure. Since he is known to have been in close contact with Filippino Lippi about 1472, the traditional view that Botticelli was a pupil of Filippino's father, Fra Filippo Lippi, is probably correct. There is a group of pictures, for example, *The Adoration of the Magi*, which may be the work of Botticelli or Filippino, and the problem of attribution is not yet finally resolved.

In 1470 Botticelli received the commission for the allegorical figure of *Fortitude* now in the Uffizi, and this already shows unmistakable features of his style. In the next few years he seems to have been influenced by the anatomical researches of Antonio Pollaiuolo. The hard outlines and sharply defined forms of Pollaiuolo are in complete contrast to the soft and gentle style of Fra Filippo Lippi. About 1475 Botticelli began to develop his own style, in which movement is expressed by outline, and linear pattern is made more important than spatial depth.

It was probably in about 1478 that Botticelli painted *The Allegory of Spring* and in 1486 *The Birth of Venus*. Both these famous pictures have been connected with the Medici circle and its humanist interests. Both certainly have extremely

Fortitude, 1470
Florence, Uffizi

The Madonna Enthroned with Six Saints, 1483
Florence, Uffizi

complicated allegorical interpretations, with Christian implications in spite of their pagan subjects. This is in accordance with the ideas of Lorenzo the Magnificent and the Medici court, but there does not seem to have been an actual commission.

In 1481 or 1482 Botticelli was one of a number of Florentine artists commissioned to paint frescoes on the walls of the Sistine Chapel in the Vatican. These are among his least successful works, since he tried to crowd too much in the scenes and his gift for jewel-like color is not suited to large-scale frescoes. During the 1480's his style became more agitated and in the 1490's even neurotic. This is often said to be a result of Savonarola's revivalist teaching, but there is almost no documentary evidence to support this. The best example of his intense mental and anti-naturalistic style at this period is *The Mystic Nativity*, about 1500. During the last ten years of his life—he died in Florence in 1510—Botticelli was evidently old-fashioned and out of touch with the ideals of Leonardo, Michelangelo, Raphael, and their followers. It is probable that his intensely melancholy pictures, such as the *Pietà* in Munich, were painted during these years.

G. C. Argan *Botticelli* New York, 1957
H. P. Horne *Botticelli* London, 1908
L. Venturi *Botticelli* London, 1937
Y. Yashiro *Botticelli* London and Boston, 1925

La Derelitta, about 1495
Rome, coll. Pallavicini

HIS WORKS INCLUDE

Fortitude, 1470
Florence, Uffizi

The Adoration of the Magi, about 1477
Florence, Uffizi

Scenes from the Old Testament
about 1482
Rome, Vatican, Sistine Chapel

The Madonna of the Magnificat
about 1485
Florence, Uffizi

Mars and Venus, about 1485
London, N.G.

The Calumny of Appelles, about 1494
Florence, Uffizi

See also pages 220, 221, 222, 318, 319

The Murder of Holofernes, about 1472
Florence, Uffizi

The Allegory of Spring, about 1478
Florence, Uffizi

The Crucifixion, about 1533
Milan, Brera

HIS WORKS INCLUDE

The Nativity
Milan, Pin. Ambrosiana

Ecce Homo
Lugano, coll. Thyssen

The Madonna and Child
Boston, Mus. of Fine Arts

See also page 226, 323

BARTOLOMMEO SUARDI called BRAMANTINO

about 1450-1536

Painter and architect to the Duke of Milan

The date of Bartolommeo Suardi's birth is unknown, and widely differing theories have been put forward about it. The one most generally accepted is that he was born in Milan in about 1450, and got the nickname of Bramantino because he worked in Bramante's studio while the latter was in Milan. Suardi was influenced by Foppa, Butinone, and Ferrarese artists at first, until Bramante encouraged him in a more monumental style. Some scholars attribute the Milan *Crucifixion* to Bramante, and some to Bramantino, while others believe the two artists collaborated.

Bramantino is recorded in documents dated 1495 and 1504. In 1508 he was in Rome, possibly at Bramante's suggestion, working on the frescoes in the ceiling of the Stanza della Segnatura in the Vatican. Opinions vary as to his visiting Naples, though he definitely stayed in Florence, where he was somewhat influenced by Fra Bartolommeo, and, especially after his second stay in Milan, by Leonardo. His strange and rather sharp color shows the effect of his contacts with early Florentine Mannerism.

Bramantino died about 1536. His chief patron was Trivulzio, for whom he designed the tapestries now in the Castello Sforzesco in Milan. These were completed in 1509 by Maestro Benedetto, an artist in tapestry and embroidery.

HIS WORKS INCLUDE

Pietà, before 1530
Florence, Uffizi

Duke Guidobaldo II da Montefeltro about 1532
Florence, Pal. Pitti

Ugolino Martelli, about 1538
West Berlin, Staatl. Mus.

Lucretia and Bartolommeo Panciatichi, about 1540
Florence, Uffizi

Eleonora of Toledo and her Son Giovanni, about 1546
Florence, Uffizi

The Resurrection, 1548-53
Florence, SS. Annunziata

Martyrdom of S. Lorenzo
Florence, S. Lorenzo

See also page 262

AGNOLO BRONZINO

1503-1572

A painter of frescoes and court portraits

Agnolo Bronzino was a Florentine Mannerist painter, a pupil of Pontormo. He became court painter to the first Grand Duke of Tuscany, Cosimo I de' Medici,

Venus, Cupid, Folly, and Time, about 1545
London, N. G.

Maria de' Medici, 1553
Florence, Uffizi

and his principal works are court portraits of great elegance and restraint, cool in color and of a frigid impassiveness. He painted a few religious works, which are often entirely devoid of religious feeling, and even possess the coldly erotic quality of some of his mythological subjects. He completed the series of frescoes in the Church of S. Lorenzo that Pontormo had left unfinished, but these were of very poor quality and were destroyed in the 18th century.

S. J. Freedberg *Painting of the High Renaissance in Rome and Florence* Cambridge, Mass., 1961
A. McComb *Bronzino* Cambridge, Mass., 1928

FILIPPO BRUNELLESCHI   1377-1446

An architect famous for the feat of erecting the dome of Florence Cathedral

Filippo Brunelleschi is generally regarded as the pioneer of Renaissance architecture, preceding by a short time Leon Battista Alberti. In fact, the two men were very different; Alberti was above all a theorist, while Brunelleschi made his principal contribution by rediscovering the secrets of antique Roman construction.

Brunelleschi was born in Florence in 1377, and was trained as a goldsmith. He began his career by taking part in the competition held in 1401 for the commission for the second door of the baptistery in Florence. The competition was won by Ghiberti, but the reliefs submitted by both men still survive, and show that there was little to choose between them. A few other pieces of sculpture by Brunelleschi also exist, but soon after his defeat in the competition he turned to architecture.

Brunelleschi seems to have gone to Rome, where he studied classical buildings,

Portrait of Filippo Brunelleschi
Florence, Cath.

HIS WORKS INCLUDE

Two Prophets, 1390-1400
Pistoia, S. Jacopo
The Sacrifice of Isaac, 1401
Florence, Mus. Naz. del Bargello
Crucifix, about 1410-15
Florence, S. Maria Novella
Four Evangelists, about 1430
Florence, Pazzi Chapel

See also page 375

The Sacrifice of Isaac, 1401
Florence, Mus. Naz. del Bargello

The Cathedral Dome, 1420-36
Florence

The Pazzi Chapel, about 1429-43
Florence, S. Croce

41

S. Lorenzo, begun 1418
Florence

but this early part of his life is not clearly documented. It seems likely that he made several visits to Rome, possibly with Donatello. Certainly, the two were friendly and shared a passionate interest in classical antiquity.

In 1420 Brunelleschi was already working on the dome of Florence Cathedral. The opening was nearly 140 feet across and presented what appeared to be an insuperable problem, since it was not possible to make timber supports for the construction of so large a dome. Brunelleschi combined ancient Roman building methods with a form of ribbed dome evolved from Gothic examples; he finished the gigantic task after 16 years. The lantern above the dome was also built to his design, but not completed until after his death.

Among Brunelleschi's other major works were the two churches of S. Lorenzo and S. Spirito, both of which have a system of proportions based on simple mathematics and are among the earliest Renaissance churches of the Latin cross type. He also made experiments in the centrally planned type of church which was to be of great importance later in the 15th century. These include the Pazzi Chapel at S. Croce and the design for S. Maria degli Angeli, which was left unfinished. He died at Florence in 1446.

P. Murray   The Architecture of the Italian Renaissance Architecture   London, 1963

LUCA CAMBIASO   1527-1583

The Adoration of the Shepherds
Milan, Brera

An artist whose experimental drawings are of great interest

Luca Cambiaso was born the son of a painter, Giovanni, at Moneglia in Liguria. He greatly admired paintings executed by Perino del Vaga and Pordenone at Genoa, and these helped to set the Mannerist tone of his work. He was very active in Genoa, and traveled to Rome and Florence on many occasions. When Philip II, King of Spain, appointed him as Court Painter in 1583, he went to Madrid, where he met with an early death while engaged on some important works. Cambiaso was undoubtedly the greatest Genoese painter of the 16th century. In his work can be seen the outcome of Renaissance painting, and his highly decorative style reveals a certain eclecticism. He is interesting mainly for his drawings, which include some notable sketches in which the figures are built up from solid geometrical cubes.

HIS WORKS INCLUDE

The Nativity
Milan, Brera

The Madonna and Child with Saints
Houston, Mus. of Fine Arts

St. Benedict Enthroned with Saints
Genoa, S. Lorenzo

The Glory of the Blessed, about 1583
Madrid, The Escorial

See also page 352

The Madonna and Child with
Saints (detail) about 1559-67
Genoa, S. Lorenzo

ANTONIO CANAL called CANALETTO 1697-1768

A painter famous for his views of Venice

Antonio Canal, better known as Canaletto, was born in Venice into a family of scene painters. After a visit to Rome in about 1719 he was influenced by Panini, who was one of the finest of the painters specializing in views of Rome and its ancient ruins.

On his return to Venice in 1720, Canaletto began painting views of the city which portray the magical beauty of the architecture and its setting amid canals and the lagoon. The unique character of Venice had already been exploited by Gentile Bellini and Caravaggio, who used 15th-century Venice as a naturalistic setting for their narrative pictures. Glimpses across the lagoon also appear here and there in works by Giorgione and Titian. Only in the early part of the 18th century, when Carlevaris began his first series of views of ceremonial occasions in Venice, did this kind of picture emerge as a genre in its own right.

Self-portrait
Cambridge, England, coll. Lord Fairhaven

Canaletto's earliest views were painted on the spot, but he later abandoned this method and returned to the more traditional method of working from detailed drawings, which were often done with the help of a camera obscura. Occasionally he even worked from Carlevaris' etchings. The biggest market for his pictures was

Eton College, about 1754
London, N. G.

Venice: A Regatta on the Grand Canal
(detail) about 1735   *London, N. G.*

HIS WORKS INCLUDE

Ideal View
Parma, Pin.

The Feast of the Ascension, 1729
Milan, coll. Aldo Crespi

The Stone Mason's Yard, about 1730
London, N. G.

The Gate, 1767
Venice, Accad.

An important series of paintings and
most of Canaletto's drawings are in
the Royal Collection at Windsor.

See also pages 298, 299

among the foreign tourists who visited Venice in considerable numbers. He worked up a connection with the wealthy English doing the Grand Tour, through the British Consul in Venice, Joseph Smith. The latter formed a large personal collection of Canaletto's works, which was eventually owned by the English king, George III.

Smith also arranged for Canaletto to visit England, where, from 1746, with short intervals in Venice, he stayed for about ten years. During this time he painted many views of London and other places in England, and also did a number of *capricci*. These are imaginative compositions which include a variety of buildings and monuments arranged in ideal compositions, each part being a faithful representation, but in an unrealistic conjunction. Canaletto had a certain difficulty in establishing himself in England, partly due to the numerous imitations of his work which had been made by English artists, who resented his introduction into their closed market, and partly because during the latter part of his life his own style altered considerably. His huge production led to his abandoning the delicate touch characteristic of his earlier works, in favor of a hard, mechanical rendering of detail. Though popular with the less educated of his admirers, this technique destroyed all the beautiful freedom and lovely tonal qualities which had until then been characteristic of his work. He had a considerable influence upon the development of landscape painting in England, in that he helped to establish the painting of actual views—as against the creation of ideal landscapes—as a worthwhile and honorable genre in its own right.

W. G. Constable   Canaletto   Oxford, 1962

ANT·CANOVA·F·A.

HIS WORKS INCLUDE

The Monument of Pope Clement XIII
1787-92
Rome, St. Peter's

Cupid and Psyche, 1797
Paris, Louvre

Napoleon, 1803
London, Apsley House

Pauline Bonaparte Borghese,
about 1808
Rome, Gall. Borghese

The Monument of Pope Pius XI, 1818
Rome, St. Peter's

The Stuart Monument, 1819
Rome, St. Peter's

See also page 397

ANTONIO CANOVA   1757-1822

A sculptor whose work became synonymous with Italian Neoclassicism

Antonio Canova became the most famous of the Italian Neoclassic artists, but his early work was in a Venetian Rococo style. His abandonment of the Rococo and conversion to the stricter ideals of Neoclassicism took place in 1779, and was confirmed when he took up residence in Rome in 1781.

Canova was born in the village of Possagno, near Treviso. His early training gave him great technical virtuosity, and as soon as he had adopted the fashionable Neoclassic style with its ideal of Greek purity of form, he began to receive important commissions. The first of these, executed between 1782 and 1787, was the *Monument of Pope Clement XIV*, which was followed by that of *Pope Clement XIII*. In 1802 he was, for diplomatic reasons, urged by the Vatican to accept an invitation from Napoleon to visit Paris.

In Paris Canova fell under the spell of Napoleon, although he resented the French looting of Italian works of art. He made a number of figures which repre-

Napoleon (detail) 1808
Milan, Brera

Italian Venus, about 1812
Florence, Gall. Palatina

sent the Emperor as a Greek god. One of these was captured by Wellington and is now in the Wellington Museum in London.

After the fall of Napoleon, Canova was responsible, with English help, for obtaining the return to Italy of many of the works looted by the French. It was at this time that he visited London and saw the Elgin Marbles. These were probably the first Greek works of really high quality that he had ever seen, and they made a deep impression on him. Perhaps the best known of Canova's numerous statues is that of *Pauline Bonaparte Borghese*, which shows Napoleon's sister reclining at her ease as a well-fed, complacent Venus.

MICHELANGELO MERISI called CARAVAGGIO   1573-1610

A painter who had a profound influence on 17th-century European art

Detail, believed to be a self-portrait, from David and Goliath, about 1606
Rome, Gall. Borghese

Michelangelo Merisi is better known as Caravaggio, from the name of the village near Milan where he was born. From 1584 to 1588 he was apprenticed in Milan to a minor Bergamasque painter called Simone Peterzano, who was a distant and insignificant follower of Titian. After this brief training he went to Rome, though the exact date of his arrival is not known.

Caravaggio's early life in Rome was spent in great poverty, and he maintained himself by hack-work for academic painters like the Cavaliere d'Arpino, and by painting small, detailed naturalistic portraits and still-lifes of a northern and often slightly Venetian type, strong in their effects of light and shadow. His first major patron was Cardinal del Monte, who commissioned several pictures, mostly of genre subjects such as the *Lute Player* and the *Gypsy Fortune-teller*.

In 1597 the Cardinal obtained for him a commission to decorate a chapel in S. Luigi dei Francesi in Rome, with an altarpiece and two wall paintings of scenes from the life of St. Matthew. This was the first of his public works, and it set the pattern for most of those that followed. His originality of vision and the daring with which he presented sacred figures in the most humble settings and with vividly realistic detail offended the clergy and caused the rejection of his pictures. The two scenes on the wall of this chapel were repainted several times, because of his difficulties with the relative proportions of the figures; these difficulties occurred largely because he painted directly onto the final canvas. This was a method that he always used but it was unusual in his day. It accounts for the fact that no drawings by him are known.

His *Martyrdom of St. Peter* and *Conversion of St. Paul*, painted in 1600 and 1601 for a chapel in S. Maria del Popolo in Rome, were also rejected in their first versions and replaced by more orthodox representations of the themes. These, like the paintings for S. Luigi, exploit his characteristically powerful contrast of light and shadow, and his dramatic realism. The chief accusation against him was his lack of decorum—that his Virgins were peasant women, his pilgrims had dirty feet, and that his saints and apostles were common types. In *The Death of the Virgin*, painted for a convent chapel, and removed after a public scandal, the figure of the Virgin was said to have been painted from the decomposing body of a drowned prostitute. Yet despite these accusations of irreverence and impropriety, among his principal patrons were churchmen and noblemen of blameless reputation. His great gifts of simplicity and immediacy were admired by some of the most celebrated artists of his day, including Rubens, who twice copied his *Deposition* and later arranged for the purchase of one of his pictures by the Dominican church in Antwerp.

Caravaggio's private life matched his public reputation. A stormy troublemaker, given to violent brawling, he eventually became a murderer and fled from Rome in 1606 to escape justice. In 1607 he was in Naples and then in Malta, where he had the Grand Master of the Order of the Knights of Malta as his patron. He was received into the Order, but after a brawl in which he wounded one of the Knights Justiciary, he was imprisoned and expelled. He escaped to Sicily, where the stages of his flight are marked by the completion of large altarpieces. Harried by the vengeance of his Maltese victim, he fled eventually to Naples, where, during a

Eros Triumphant, about 1600
West Berlin, Staatl. Mus.

St. Matthew and the Angel
(accepted version) about 1599
Rome, S. Luigi dei Francesi

The Martyrdom of St. Matthew
Rome, S. Luigi dei Francesi

brawl of great savagery, he was so badly wounded that he was reported dead. He survived, however, and fled again to a small Tuscan port under Spanish control, while he waited for the pardon from Rome which his friends were endeavoring to obtain for him. On his arrival at Porto d'Ercole, however, he was mistaken for a wanted criminal and thrown into prison. Upon being released a few days later he found that the ship which had brought him had sailed, carrying with it, as he thought, all his goods. The rage into which he fell provoked an attack of malarial fever from which he died. After his death it was discovered that all his possessions were in fact in the local customs house.

Caravaggio's last pictures, painted in Malta and Sicily, exhibit even stronger effects of light and shadow, and they have greater directness of feeling and a poignant simplicity. Unfortunately, their rapidity of execution, the thinness of the color with which they are painted, and the increasing use of shadows has caused them to darken and to deteriorate. His influence upon northern painters—chiefly Dutch and Flemish artists working in Rome—was far greater than on Italians, though Neapolitan painters were quick to adapt his spectacular effects to their own more commonplace realism. He had a short-lived influence on Guido Reni and Guercino, but it is among the painters from Utrecht such as Baburen, Honthorst, and Terbrugghen that his greatest following is to be found. Ribera in Naples, Velázquez and Murillo in Spain, La Tour and the Le Nain brothers in France, Rubens, for a short while after his return to Flanders from his Italian journeys, and Rembrandt during the early years of his career, were among the great artists who were strongly influenced by him.

R. Hinks   Michelangelo Merisi da Caravaggio   London, 1953
W. Friedländer   Caravaggio Studies   Princeton, 1955

The Death of the Virgin
about 1606
Paris, Louvre

The Calling of St. Matthew, about 1599
Rome, S. Luigi dei Francesi

The Supper at Emmaus, about 1600
London, N. G.

47

POLIDORO CALDARA DA CARAVAGGIO · 1495/1500-1546

A 16th-century Mannerist

Polidoro Caldara was born at Caravaggio at some date between 1495 and 1500. At a very early age he went to Rome, where he became an assistant to a pupil of Raphael. He stayed in Rome until 1527, when, as a result of the sack of the city, he went to Naples and to Sicily, where he died. He practiced a form of Mannerism derived from Raphael, and his monochrome paintings show his style at its best.

St. Stephen Preaching
Milan, Brera

VITTORE CARPACCIO · active 1490-1523/6

A painter of poetic narrative skill

Vittore Carpaccio was born in Venice, probably about 1465. Most of his artistic education came from Gentile and Giovanni Bellini, and Antonello da Messina. He was also influenced by Mantegna and the Ferrarese Francesco del Cossa and Ercole Roberti. His taste for detail was stimulated by his interest in Flemish painting.

In the series of the *Legend of St. Ursula* and in the two series painted for the Church of S. Giorgio degli Schiavoni in Venice, his work began to reflect the new ideas introduced by Giorgione. This resulted in an uneasy conflict between the detailed and rather naïve naturalism of the 15th century and the broader tonal effects and more generalized presentation of the 16th century, with which he was much less successful. His great gift was for the poetic, seen in fantastic narratives such as the *St. Ursula* series. In these he was particularly adept in achieving delicate effects of lighting to create a fairy-tale atmosphere.

J. Lauts Carpaccio London, 1962

HIS WORKS INCLUDE

The Miracle of the Cross, 1495
Venice, Accad.

The Legend of St. Ursula
about 1490-1500
Venice, Accad.

The Legend of St. George, 1502-7
Venice, S. Giorgio degli Schiavoni

The Legend of St. Jerome, 1502-7
Venice, S. Giorgio degli Schiavoni

The Presentation in the Temple, 1510
Venice, Accad.

See also pages 232, 326

The Arrival of the Ambassadors,
about 1498
Venice, Accad.

AGOSTINO CARRACCI

A painter remembered chiefly for his engravings

Self-portrait
Florence, Uffizi

Agostino Carracci was principally an engraver who executed many plates after works by Venetian artists. He was born in 1557 at Bologna, into a family which probably originated in Lombardy. His first works show the influence of the late Mannerists, revealing a special interest in Tuscan and Roman painting and engraving. His journeys to Parma and Venice certainly soon contributed to his more intense and subtle treatment of light and color. After 1582, Agostino, his brother Annibale, and his slightly older cousin Ludovico, founded in Bologna an academy for the training of painters. This became the most famous school of its day and attracted many of the most promising of the younger artists. Agostino's best qualities are revealed in his engravings, which were one of the main factors in the widespread dissemination of Italian art across Europe. Between 1595 and 1600 he was in Rome, where he collaborated with his brother Annibale on the frescoes in the Farnese Palace. In 1600 he went to Parma again in the service of Duke Ranuccio Farnese: he died there in 1602.

HIS WORKS INCLUDE

The Last Communion of St. Jerome
about 1593
Bologna, Pin.

The Assumption, about 1593
Bologna, Pin.

Composition with Figures
and Animals, about 1596
Naples, Mus. Naz.

Christ and the Adulteress, about 1597
Milan, Brera

See also pages 273, 356

Cephalus and Aurora, about 1597   *London, N. G.*

ANNIBALE CARRACCI

The greatest of a famous family of Bolognese painters

Annibale Carracci was not only the greatest painter in his family, but also one of the truly great artists of his period. He seems to have been trained partly by his cousin, Ludovico, although he soon outshone his teacher in his fluent imagination, the firmness and crispness of his handling, and the breadth of his composition. He was in Parma in about 1585 with his brother Agostino, and probably also in Venice at about the same date. He shared with Ludovico and Agostino the founding of the academy which they ran in Bologna. This academy became the most celebrated training-ground for the major Bolognese painters of the next generation, which included Domenichino, Guido Reni, and Guercino.

Christ and the Woman of Samaria,
about 1593
Milan, Brera

Christ Appearing to St. Peter:
"Domine quo vadis?", about 1604
London, N. G.

The Triumph of Bacchus and Ariadne, 1597-1604
Rome, Pal. Farnese

HIS WORKS INCLUDE

The Butcher's Shop, about 1585
Oxford, Christ Church College

Allegory, about 1585
Hampton Court, Royal Coll.

Self-portrait, with his Father and his
Nephew Antonio, about 1590
Milan, Brera

The Resurrection of Christ, 1593
Paris, Louvre

The Alms of St. Roch, 1595
Dresden, Gemäldegal.

Frescoes, 1597-1604
Rome, Pal. Farnese

The Assumption, about 1607
Rome, S. Maria del Popolo

See also pages 275, 354

The ceiling of the gallery (detail)
1597-1604   *Rome, Pal. Farnese*

Annibale worked with the other members of his family on frescoes in the Fava and Magnani palaces in Bologna, and in 1595 he went to Rome to work for Cardinal Farnese on the decoration of his great palace there. The gallery in the Palazzo Farnese ranks as one of the great decorative schemes of all time. The room takes the form of a barrel-vaulted tunnel about 65 feet long and some 20 feet wide, without any architectural features except the windows along one wall and six niches and a door in the wall facing them. The artist constructed an elaborate illusionistic architectural framework which encloses panels containing large mythologies. Against colonnades, open to the sky, are seated large figures of nude youths, reminiscent of those in Michelangelo's Sistine ceiling. Playful figures of small children are silhouetted against the intense blue of the sky. The contrasts between the framed mythologies, the fictive bronze reliefs, the nude figures of the youths, and the illusion of the marble architecture and statuary are handled with consummate skill, and with a lightness of touch and a wit absent from the works of his great predecessors. This was Annibale's finest work and almost his last, since he fell ill in 1605 and painted very little thereafter.

The greatness of the Farnese decoration lies in its summing-up of the grander aspects of the High Renaissance. In it all the traditions that Annibale had absorbed from Raphael, Correggio, Titian, Veronese, del Sarto, and Michelangelo have been assimilated so that they nourish his talent. He had some assistance in the work, notably from Domenichino for the small, inset landscapes, from his brother Agostino, and from Albani. He also executed a number of altarpieces and similar devotional works.

A. McComb   *The Baroque Painters of Italy*   Cambridge, 1934
E. Waterhouse   *Italian Baroque Painting*   London, 1962
R. Wittkower   *Art and Architecture in Italy, 1600-1750*   London, 1958

LUDOVICO CARRACCI 1555-1619

The founder of a famous academy

Ludovico Carracci was the elder cousin of Agostino and Annibale. The three of them founded an academy, which Ludovico continued to run after his cousins had left Bologna. His own style was one of mild, rather sentimental piety, and after the departure of his cousins what little fire there had been in his art died out. He became a painter of typical Counter-Reformation altarpieces.

Ludovico hardly ever left Bologna, except for short journeys to Venice and Parma, and in 1602 to Rome. These brief contacts with more lively artistic centers had little effect on him. He survived both his more celebrated cousins, but was no more than a provincial painter of considerable technical skill and pedestrian imagination. His importance lies in his connection with the academy at Bologna.

St. Raymond, about 1612
Bologna, S. Domenico

HIS WORKS INCLUDE

The Annunciation, about 1585
Bologna, Pin.
The Madonna of the Bargellini, 1588
Bologna, Pin.
Frescoes, 1604-5
Bologna, S. Michele in Bosco
See also pages 272, 355

Christ and the Woman of Cana
Milan, Brera

ROSALBA CARRIERA 1675-1757

A fashionable woman portraitist

Rosalba Carriera was a painter of attractive portraits that were extremely popular in her own day. She traveled widely all over Europe, exploiting a new fashion for pastel portraits, so that her works are to be found in most of the greater European galleries. She was a Venetian and a pupil of her brother-in-law, Gianantonio Pellegrini. She seems to have known Watteau in Paris, and she worked for a long while in Vienna. She created a number of "ideal" subjects, which consist principally of rather affected semi-nude girls of a provocative kind. In this respect she precedes the French painter Greuze, who exploited the same subject.

Rosalba Carriera's art is one of the most typical representations of the more vacuous aspects of aristocratic society of the 18th century, but sometimes she brings to life the charm and elegance of Rococo ideals. Her long life ended dramatically: she became blind, and died in Venice in 1757 tormented by madness.

Self-portrait (detail)
Venice, Accad.

HER WORKS INCLUDE

Portrait of a Woman
Treviso, Mus. Civico
Catherine Sagredo Barbarigo
Dresden, Gemäldegal.
Boy of the Leblond Family
Venice, Accad.
See also page 292

51

ANDREA DEL CASTAGNO

Christat and St. Julian, about 1455
Florence, SS. Annunziata

HIS WORKS INCLUDE

Frescoes, 1445-50
Florence, S. Apollonia

The Trinity, about 1455
Florence, SS. Annunziata

Portrait of a Gentleman
Washington D. C., N. G., Mellon Coll.

Illustrious Florentines, about 1455
Florence, Mus. di Andrea del Castagno

See also page 204

An influential Florentine painter

Andrea del Castagno was born near Florence. He must have been very precocious, since he was given a commission as early as 1440. This, however, was a minor state commission similar to a modern poster. He was instructed to represent various rebels against the state as hanging by one foot from a gallows. As a result he became known as "Andreino of the Hanged Men." His earliest important commission was for frescoes in Venice in 1442. These, however, were undertaken in collaboration with an older man, whose manner is not known, so that it is difficult to guess what Castagno's own earliest style was like. It seems, however, that he was much influenced by Masaccio, Uccello, and Donatello.

From 1444 until his death from plague in 1457, Castagno worked in Florence. Most of the frescoes which he painted in this period are now in the Castagno Museum in Florence. They include the remains of the magnificent decoration from the Villa alla Legnaia, representing famous men and women. These figures were painted on the wall in an illusionist way, so that they appear to be emerging from stone niches. Their style, vigorous and sculptural, almost harsh in its energy, was much influenced by Donatello. Castagno's last major work is the fresco of *Niccolò da Tolentino*, painted in 1456 in Florence Cathedral.

The violence of Castagno's style has often been exaggerated, owing to a myth, propagated by Vasari, that Castagno had murdered Domenico Veneziano. In fact, Domenico survived Castagno by four years.

S. M. Richter Andrea del Castagno New York, 1943

The Last Supper, about 1445
Florence, S. Apollonia

Equestrian Portrait of Niccolò
da Tolentino, 1456
Florence, Cath.

PIETRO CAVALLINI

active about 1270-1325

The earliest great representative of the Roman school

Pietro Cavallini is the earliest Roman painter whose life is known to us in any detail. There is a series of mosaics in the Church of S. Maria in Trastevere in Rome, one of which was once signed and dated 1291. There is also a very damaged fresco of the *Last Judgment* in S. Cecilia which is probably of 1293. He was working in Naples in 1308 and some of the frescoes in S. Maria Donna Regina are probably his. These are the last works attributable to him, although there is a legend that he lived to be a hundred, and he may have died as late as 1325. His earliest works go back to about 1270 and it is probable that Cavallini, Arnolfo di Cambio, and Cimabue were working in Rome in the 1270's, at the beginning of the 13th-century Renaissance of the arts there. It is possible also that Cavallini worked at Assisi and that his simple classical style both in fresco and mosaic is an essential link between the tradition of Roman antiquity and the art of Giotto.

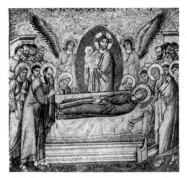

The Death of the Virgin, 1291
Rome, S. Maria in Trastevere

HIS WORKS INCLUDE

The Nativity, 1291
Rome, S. Maria in Trastevere
The Last Judgment, about 1293
Rome, S. Cecilia

See also page 166

The Last Judgment (detail)
about 1293
Rome, S. Cecilia

The Last Judgment (detail)
about 1293
Rome, S. Cecilia

BENVENUTO CELLINI

1500-1571

Florentine sculptor and goldsmith

Benvenuto Cellini is one of the most fascinating and best-known personalities of the 16th century. He was perhaps the finest craftsman of his day, rather than a truly great artist, but his fame rests chiefly on his autobiography. He emerges from this as an amorist of almost incredible accomplishment and an obvious liar, but the circumstances of his career are characteristic of the uprooted lives led by many Italian artists in the early 16th century. He was born in Florence in 1500 and grew up to worship Michelangelo. He was trained as a goldsmith, but his irrepressible pugnacity soon led to his being banished from Florence. He went to Rome in 1523 and was present at the Sack of 1527.

Before long, however, Cellini was in serious trouble on account of alleged murders and he went to France to work for Francis I. The French king was enthusiastically introducing Italian Mannerist art into France, mainly at Fontainebleau. The splendidly sophisticated *Nymph of Fontainebleau*, a statue now in the Louvre, is the most characteristic production of this epoch. Inevitably, Cellini fell out with the

HIS WORKS INCLUDE

Salt Cellar, about 1540
Vienna, Kunsthist. Mus.
Nymph of Fontainebleau, 1543-44
Paris, Louvre
Perseus, 1545-54
Florence, Loggia dei Lanzi
Narcissus
Florence, Mus. Naz. del Bargello

See also page 390

Medal, obverse: Cardinal Bembo
London, V. and A.

Medal, reverse: Pegasus
London, V. and A.

Perseus, 1545-54
Florence, Loggia dei Lanzi

other Italian artists in the service of the king as well as with the French themselves, and after narrowly escaping imprisonment he returned to Italy. In 1558 he appears to have reformed and taken steps toward entering a religious order. This, however, was purely temporary, and the attempt was abandoned in 1560.

It was during the years 1558 to 1562 that Cellini's autobiography was written. It contains interesting accounts of some of his major works, in particular his masterpiece, the *Perseus* group in Florence. On the whole, the small figures on the pedestal are more satisfactory than the statue itself, imitative of Michelangelo. The smaller figures are closer to the goldsmith's art, and Cellini was perhaps at his best in such small-scale work as his medals or the salt cellar now in Vienna, made for Francis I. He died in Florence in 1571.

Autobiography (new translation by George Bull)   London, 1956
J. Pope-Hennessy   Italian Renaissance Sculpture   London, 1958

M.D.C.
CC EDEBAT

HIS WORKS INCLUDE

St. Charles Borromeo Distributing Alms to the Poor, about 1628
Milan, Cath.

St. Charles Borromeo Blessing the Cross after the Plague, about 1628
Milan, Cath.

The Madonna of the Rosary
Milan, Brera

See also page 274

GIOVANNI BATTISTA CRESPI called IL CERANO

about 1557-1633

Painter, sculptor, and architect

Giovanni Battista Crespi took his nickname Cerano from the small town where he was born, near Novara. Having made the customary visit to Rome in about 1590, he established himself in Milan. Here he was one of the major representatives of the Counter-Reformation school of painting that was fostered by Cardinal Federico Borromeo and that culminated in the foundation of the Ambrosian Academy, of which Cerano himself was appointed head. He was a prolific artist, and introduced into the traditional themes of the late Mannerism of Lombardy a tendency to pathos and religious sentiment which was typical of the 17th-century Baroque manner.

Sometime about 1620 to 1625 Cerano, Morazzone, and Giulio Cesare Procaccini together painted one very unusual work for a kind of artistic competition, possibly unique in the history of painting. This curiosity, entitled *The Martyrdom of S. Rufina and S. Secunda*, became known as the "three-handed picture."

GIACOMO CERUTI

active about 1720-1740

Portrait of a Priest
London, N. G.

One of the strangest figures in 18th-century art

Three cities—Brescia, Bergamo, and Milan—claim to be Giacomo Ceruti's birth-place, but to judge from the district where most of his work was done, and from other evidence, he was probably born at Brescia, possibly in about 1690. The only records of him refer to paintings he completed between 1724 and 1738. His religious works are not very important, and fall far short of the portraits and groups of figures which reveal his exceptional personality.

Ceruti may be considered a true descendant of Caravaggio. He intensified Caravaggio's grimly realistic poses, his sense of drama, and his close observation of nature. Ceruti's favorite subjects were those which emphasized the distressing aspects of daily life, such as beggars (hence his nickname " Pitocchetto " which means " Little Beggar "), hired mercenaries, gypsies, cripples, and paupers. Instead of making them an excuse for genre pictures as the Caravaggesques had done, Ceruti exalted them as the melancholy heroes of society. He was thus the Italian painter who showed the most intuitive foresight of the social revolution which was to take place in Europe at the end of the century.

Two Boys Playing Cards
Brescia, Pin. Tosio Martinengo

HIS WORKS INCLUDE

Soldiers Playing at Cards
Milan, coll. Sciltian
Young Girl with a Fan
Bergamo, Accad. Carrara
The Beggar, 1737
Bergamo, coll. Bassi Rathgeb
The Laundress
Brescia, Pin. Tosio Martinengo
The Dwarf
Padernello, coll. Salvadego

See also page 304

CIMABUE

about 1240-1302

Traditionally the master of Giotto

Cimabue, whose real name seems to have been Cenni di Pepo, was a Florentine artist born probably in 1240. He is known to have been in Rome in 1272, but before that date he worked on the mosaics in the Baptistery at Florence, and he may also have painted the *Crucifix* in S. Domenico at Arezzo before 1272.

Very few works by him have survived, but there is a large altarpiece, the *Santa Trinità Madonna* in Florence which is traditionally his masterpiece, and which may date from about 1285. It seems certain that he worked as a fresco painter in the

HIS WORKS INCLUDE

Crucifix, about 1272
Arezzo, S. Domenico
The Santa Trinità Madonna,
about 1285
Florence, Uffizi
Frescoes, about 1290
Assisi, S. Francesco
St. John, 1302
Pisa, Cath.

See also page 165

Upper Church of St. Francis at Assisi, probably in the 1280's. Two large Crucifixions and other frescoes in the choir and transept are attributed to him, but they are now almost entirely ruined. The famous *Madonna and Child with St. Francis* in the Lower Church of St. Francis is one of his most famous works, but has probably been extensively repainted. His only documented work is the mosaic figure of St. John in the apse of the cathedral at Pisa, which is documented in 1301/02. The remainder of the mosaic has been remade. A document of 1302 is the last record of Cimabue.

Cimabue has long been famous because of the mention by Dante which associates him with Giotto, and all Florentine writers have stressed that Cimabue was the first Florentine artist to break away from the Byzantine style, and thus to prepare the revolution wrought by Giotto. To some extent this is a Florentine myth, since it takes no account of developments in Rome, nor is it quite fair to Florentines of a slightly earlier generation, such as Coppo di Marcovaldo. What is certainly true is that Cimabue's art has a dramatic quality and rhythm of line which takes it outside the rather narrow range of purely Byzantine image-making. His work is thus more realistic and more human, and these qualities were certainly passed on by him to Giotto.

E. B. Garrison   *Italian Romanesque Panel Painting*   Florence, 1949
A. Nicolson   *Cimabue*   Princeton, 1933

The Madonna and Child with St. Francis, about 1295
Assisi, S. Francesco

St. Francis (detail of left)
Assisi, S. Francesco

ANTONIO ALLEGRI called CORREGGIO   1489/94-1534

A painter distinguished by his subtly varied chiaroscuro

Correggio, whose real name was Antonio Allegri, was born at Correggio near Parma in either 1489 or 1494, though the later date is generally preferred. After some training from minor local artists he went to Mantua, where he was somewhat influenced by Mantegna, who was his teacher, according to one tradition. If he was, this would involve acceptance of the earlier birth date. Correggio was also strongly affected by Leonardo, whose influence on all North Italian artists was tremendous. From Leonardo he evolved his extremely sensitive use of light and shadow, his delicate modulations of color and a curious softness of form which presages the emotional qualities of the Baroque and even of 18th-century French painting. Both his altarpieces and his mythologies are characterized by this extreme softness of handling, and the emotional content of his large Madonnas has a voluptuousness which is paralleled by his often overtly erotic mythological subjects. Correggio was also one of the first to produce a very beautiful type of Nativity in which the Christ Child becomes the source of light for the whole composition, illuminating the setting and the worshippers. This type of Nativity was developed by Domenichino and later Baroque painters for whom the device became an indispensable feature of the theme.

It was in his great cupola decorations that Correggio developed the most daring aspects of illusionist perspective. The Camera di San Paolo in the convent of St. Paul in Parma is decorated with a painted trellis bearing garlands and framed medallions with large putti disporting themselves above a series of illusionistic

Self-portrait (?)
London, Courtauld Inst. Gall.

The Virgin and Child with St. Jerome,
about 1528   *Parma, Gall.*

The Madonna of the Basket
London, N. G.

HIS WORKS INCLUDE

The Madonna of St. Francis
about 1515
Dresden, Gemäldegal.

The Holy Family, 1516
Hampton Court, Royal Coll.

Frescoes of the Camera di San Paolo
about 1518
Parma, S. Paolo

The Vision of St. John on Patmos
1520-23
Parma, S. Giovanni Evangelista

The Madonna in Adoration
about 1522
Florence, Uffizi

Jove and Antiope, 1524/25
Paris, Louvre

The Assumption, 1526-30
Parma, Cath.

Night, about 1530
Dresden, Gemäldegal.

Mercury Instructing Cupid
before Venus
London, N. G.

See also pages 258, 259, 342, 343

57

Camera di San Paolo, about 1518
Parma, S. Paolo

The Adoration of the Magi, about 1514   *Milan, Brera*

Mercury Instructing Cupid before
Venus *London, N. G.*

lunettes containing mythological subjects. Both the idea of the trellis and the illusionistic medallions are debts which Correggio owed to Mantegna and Leonardo, but in the dome of S. Giovanni Evangelista, also in Parma, he used ideas derived from Michelangelo. The large nude figures of the saints seated round the base of the dome clearly show his knowledge of Michelangelo's Sistine ceiling, finished in the previous decade.

In 1522 Correggio negotiated with the authorities of Parma Cathedral for the huge decorations of the dome, which were probably executed between 1526 and 1530. Here the effects are even more illusionistic than those in S. Giovanni, and are a clear anticipation of the extreme illusionism of the High Baroque style of a century later. The effect of the cathedral dome is, however, extremely disturbing. The swirling mass of figures, seen from below, produces an impression of, as one of the priests so unkindly phrased it, "a hash of frog legs." The illusionism is given full rein also in the pendentives, for the central octagon appears to be supported upon shell niches in which figures are seated. This effect is contrived entirely through the artist's control of light and shadow.

Correggio's last works were a series of highly erotic mythologies of the loves of Jupiter painted for the Duke of Mantua. Here again, in the softness of handling and in the sensuous grace of the figures, he is clearly an ancestor of the 18th century.

A. E. Popham Correggio's Drawings London, 1957
C. Ricci Correggio London, 1930

FRANCESCO DEL COSSA

1436-1478

A fresco painter of the Ferrarese school

Francesco del Cossa was born at Ferrara in 1436. He was the son of Cristoforo, contractor and master-mason. Early in life he was admitted to the circle of artists at the Este court, thereby winning an excellent reputation but inadequate financial rewards. For this reason, on March 25, 1470, he brought a petition before Duke Borso. On the Duke's refusal he left Ferrara for Bologna, where he worked until his early death from plague in 1478.

Francesco was influenced at first by Cosimo Tura, and from him gained a surrealist view of nature. He echoed Piero della Francesca's feeling for space in the frescoes of the *Months*, charming and amorous, which he painted in the Schifanoia Palace at Ferrara, and in altarpieces at Bologna. In addition, his color always has a specially intense tone, and this makes him one of the most interesting representatives of the Ferrarese school of painting.

B. *Nicolson   The Painters of Ferrara   London, 1951*

St. Vincent Ferrer (?) (detail)
about 1473
London, N. G.

St. Vincent Ferrer (?) (detail) about 1473
London, N. G.

HIS WORKS INCLUDE

March, April, May, about 1470
Ferrara, Pal. Schifanoia

The Annunciation, before 1472
Dresden, Gemäldegal.

St. Vincent Ferrer(?), about 1473
London, N. G.

St. Lucy, 1470-75
Washington D. C., N. G.

See also page 218

LORENZO DI CREDI

1456/60-1537

A fellow pupil of Leonardo

Lorenzo di Credi was a worthy but not outstanding Florentine painter. He is best known as the chief assistant of Verrocchio and the temporary collaborator of Leonardo da Vinci. His religious works are somewhat static, but he was an ardent follower of Savonarola. His religious devotion is perceptible in his altarpieces.

HIS WORKS INCLUDE

The Annunciation
Florence, Uffizi

Self-portrait
Philadelphia, coll. Widener

Venus
Florence, Uffizi

Noli me tangere
Paris, Louvre

See also page 327

GIUSEPPE MARIA CRESPI

Painter of religious subjects, portraits, and genre

Giuseppe Maria Crespi was born at Bologna in 1665 and was called Lo Spagnolo, "the Spaniard," perhaps simply because he liked to dress in Spanish fashion. Rather than study the work of his fellow citizens, the then famous Academicians, he preferred to choose masters who were less well known but who were gifted with particularly spirited brushwork.

By 1690 Crespi had been to Venice, where he was impressed by Sebastiano Mazzoni's coloring, while at Parma he learned a valuable lesson from Correggio's frescoes. He evolved an entirely personal style, which was very successful from a decorative point of view, as is demonstrated by *Hercules and the Seasons* and *Olympus* in the Palazzo Pepoli at Bologna. These works show a rich imagination and wit as well was some fanciful whims skillfully expressed in new pictorial forms. In his brushwork—which was both fresh and thick—he rebelled against the classicist rules imposed by the official Bolognese school. This not only made him one of the most original artists of the first half of the 18th century, but it inspired Piazzetta to develop a new approach to light, and in so doing was instrumental in creating a new phase of painting in 18th-century Venice.

In Crespi's painting *chiaroscuro* is brought down to a "natural" level; his work hinges not so much on drama as on anecdote. His settings are sometimes reminiscent of Dutch painting. Crespi was a keen and close observer of reality, which he transformed with his light effects and thick, fluid application of paint. He favored genre subjects, even some of his religious pictures being represented as scenes taken from daily life. In 1709 he received commissions from the Grand Duke of Tuscany, and in 1743 one of his paintings was bought by the King of Sardinia. A man devoted to his family, he became blind in his last years, and died in Bologna in 1747.

Self-Portrait
Bologna, Pin.

The Fair at Poggio a Caiano, 1709
Florence, Uffizi

The Market
Milan, Brera

CARLO CRIVELLI

active 1451-1494

An artist whose work is characterized by elaborate decoration

Carlo Crivelli, son of Jacopo—also a painter—was born in Venice about 1430 or shortly afterwards. In his early years he followed the school of Squarcione, a merchant turned painter, who was more famous for his teaching than for his own works. Mantegna was the most outstanding of his pupils, and it was he who had the greatest influence on Crivelli.

In 1457 Crivelli faced legal proceedings for stealing a certain Tarsia from her husband. After serving a six months' sentence, he left Venice. In 1465 he was at Zara, and from 1468 onwards he was in the Marches, where he settled at Ascoli Piceno. He worked extremely hard in the district until his death, which, according to one rather unreliable tradition, occurred at Fermo in 1495. More probably it was at Ascoli in 1499 or 1500. Carlo Crivelli's style was whimsical and decorative, characterized by a real concern for technique and style, with a strong element of Late Gothic fantasy.

The Madonna and Child, about 1475
Bergamo, Accad. Carrara

St. Catherine of Alexandria and St. Jerome; predella panels from the Altarpiece of the Virgin and Child with St. Jerome and St. Sebastian, after 1490
London, N. G.

HIS WORKS INCLUDE

The Cook Madonna, about 1469
Washington D. C., N. G.

St. George, about 1469
Boston, Isabella Stewart Gardner Mus.

Pietà, begun 1473
London, N. G.

The Dead Christ, about 1494
Milan, Brera

See also page 208

BERNARDO DADDI

about 1290-1349/51

A painter of Giottesque frescoes

Though records of this painter are few and incomplete, it is almost certain that he was for a while a pupil of Giotto. Born in Florence toward the end of the 13th century, Bernardo Daddi first followed his master's methods in the treatment of form. Later his work reflected the Sienese influence of the Lorenzetti brothers in delicacy of line and color. His art is one of the most successful and coherent fusions of Giottesque and Sienese themes.

There are records of Daddi between 1312 and 1347, and it is therefore supposed that he died soon after the latter date, around 1350.

O. Siren Giotto and His Followers Cambridge, 1917

HIS WORKS INCLUDE

Frescoes in the Chapel of SS. Stefano and Lorenzo, 1333 and after
Florence, S. Croce

Triptych, 1328
Florence, Uffizi

The Madonna of the Magnificat, 1334
Florence, Mus. dell' Opera del Duomo

Polyptych, 1344
Florence, S. Maria Novella

The Maestà, 1346
Florence, Orsanmichele

See also page 176

The Last Communion of St. Jerome
1614
Rome, Vatican, Pin.

HIS WORKS INCLUDE

The Scourging of St. Andrew, 1608
Rome, Oratory of S. Gregorio Magno

The Last Communion of St. Jerome
1614
Rome, Vatican, Pin.

Scenes from the Life of St. Cecilia
1614
Rome, S. Luigi de' Francesi

The Hunt of Diana, about 1617
Rome, Gall. Borghese

Frescoes, about 1628
Rome, S. Andrea della Valle

See also page 282

A Girl with a Unicorn, about 1609
Rome, Pal. Farnese

DOMENICHINO   1581-1641

A classical painter who competed unsuccessfully with the fashionable Baroque style of his day

Domenichino, whose real name was Domenico Zampieri, was born in Bologna. He became a pupil of Ludovico in the academy that the Carracci had founded there. In 1602 he went to Rome to work for Annibale Carracci on the decorations in the Palazzo Farnese, where he is generally believed to have been responsible for many of the landscapes. His sensibility, subtle composition, and tender color made him the most classical of the Bolognese painters of his day, and account for his considerable influence on the French artists Poussin and Claude. He was a man of difficult and morose temperament, withdrawn and reserved, whose life was embittered by his inability to compete with the more florid aspects of Baroque illusionism. These increasingly popular qualities were entirely alien to his art and temperament.

Domenichino's greatest work was done in the Church of S. Andrea della Valle, in Rome, where he decorated the choir and the pendentives of the dome, between 1624 and 1628. These contrast strongly with the exuberant illusionism of Lanfranco, who, to Domenichino's great grief and mortification, received the commission for the dome itself. He again competed unsuccessfully with Lanfranco in Naples in 1631, where he was harassed by the local factions of artists. He fled several times before their threats of personal violence, returning on each occasion with fearful reluctance. Eventually he died there, to be succeeded by his detested rival, Lanfranco.

D. Mahon   Seicento Art and Theory   London, 1947
E. Waterhouse   Italian Baroque Painting   London, 1962

The Calling of St. Peter and St. Andrew, 1628
Rome, S. Andrea della Valle

Landscape with Tobias and the Angel
London, N. G.

DOMENICO VENEZIANO

An artist whose style changed from the lyrical to the realistic

Domenico Veneziano was a rather mysterious painter active in Florence in the mid-15th century. On account of his name, he is thought to have come from Venice, but nothing is known about him until 1438, when he wrote from Perugia to Piero de' Medici in Florence in hope of a commission. He died in Florence in great poverty in 1461, and Vasari says that he was then 56.

Only two works are signed by Domenico. One, *The Carnesecchi Tabernacle*, a fresco now in the National Gallery, London, is much damaged. The other, the *St. Lucy Altarpiece*, is in the Uffizi in Florence, but the panels have been dispersed, so that in effect there are six pictures certainly by him. *The St. Lucy Altarpiece* is one of the most important works painted in Florence in the 15th century, since it reveals an entirely new feeling for the beauty of light and for the changes in color wrought by the effects of light. Other works attributed to him include *The Adoration of the Magi* in Berlin and the fresco of *St. John the Baptist and St. Francis* in S. Croce in Florence. These two works are so different that it is probable that *The Adoration* is very early and the *St. John and St. Francis* very late, since the latter has much in common with the style of Castagno.

The Martyrdom of St. Lucy, predella panel from The St. Lucy Altarpiece, about 1444   *West Berlin, Staatl. Mus.*

HIS WORKS INCLUDE

The Carnesecchi Tabernacle
about 1430-38
London, N. G.

The Adoration of the Magi
about 1435 (attrib.)
West Berlin, Staatl. Mus.

St. Lucy Altarpiece, about 1444
Florence, Uffizi

Predella Panels, about 1444
West Berlin, Staatl. Mus.
Washington D. C., N. G.
Cambridge, Fitzwm.

St. John the Baptist and St. Francis
after 1454 (attrib.)
Florence, S. Croce

See also page 192

The Annunciation, predella panel from The St. Lucy Altarpiece
about 1444   *Cambridge, Fitzwm.*

The St. Lucy Altarpiece, about 1444
Florence, Uffizi

Jeremiah, about 1425
Florence, Mus. dell'Opera del Duomo

David, about 1435
Florence, Bargello

DONATELLO

A sculptor of great influence in 15th-century Florence

Donatello was born in Florence in 1386 and died there eighty years later. The fact that he lived to so great an age is of paramount importance in the development of Florentine art, since his style dominated the sculpture of the 15th century, and to a large extent the painting also. Masaccio's death in about 1428 at the age of 27 meant the removal of the only painter whose stature as an artist was comparable to his. During the middle decades of the 15th century Donatello's dramatic and linear style had a profound effect on painters such as Castagno.

Donatello was apprenticed to a goldsmith, but received his first real training under Ghiberti, working on the first of Ghiberti's Baptistery doors at Florence. This was in 1403, but by 1406 Donatello was working on his own and received commissions for sculpture for the cathedral. The early marble statue, *David*, shows that at this date he still retained much of the gracefulness of Gothic sculpture as well as reminiscences of Ghiberti. But by 1417, when he carved the over-life-size statue of *St. George* and a relief of *St. George Killing the Dragon*, he had found his own style. The figure is simple and classical, while the relief uses perspective in a thoroughly pictorial way; this shows that, with Brunelleschi, Donatello must have

Cantoria, 1433-39
Florence, Mus. dell'Opera del Duomo

been one of the first Florentines to use mathematical perspective as a means of creating the illusion of space.

During the next years Donatello extended his knowledge of ancient Roman art, particularly portraiture, which he used to give a new force of characterization to his figures. At the same time he began to work in very low relief, exploiting the possibilities of perspective. This can be seen in the highly dramatic *Herod's Feast* of 1427, made for Siena, which was undoubtedly one of the causes of the great stylistic change in Ghiberti's work between his first and second Baptistery doors. Donatello probably visited Rome on several occasions, and was certainly there in 1423, staying for more than a year. On his return he was commissioned to make the cantoria or musicians' gallery for the cathedral in Florence, the counterpart to

St. George Killing the Dragon, about 1417
Florence, Orsanmichele

the one by Luca della Robbia. The dancing figures are clearly derived from Roman sarcophagi and, along with Luca's smaller figures, were of great influence on Florentine artists of the period. The over-life-size figures carved for the campanile of the cathedral are more important, since many of them are made deliberately ugly, in order to explore the dramatic possiblities of uncompromising realism, similar to that found in ancient Roman portraits. The most famous example of this is that of the prophet Habbakuk, called *Lo Zuccone* or "Baldhead," which is traditionally supposed to have been one of Donatello's own favorite creations.

In 1443 Donatello went to Padua, where he stayed for ten years. During this time he created a large equestrian statue—the first since the ancient statues of

St. Louis of Toulouse, about 1430
Florence, Mus. di S. Croce

Pulpit, about 1460
Florence, S. Lorenzo

The Magdalen, about 1455
Florence, Baptistery

Judith and Holofernes, about 1455
Florence, Piazza della Signoria

Roman emperors—of a mercenary soldier called *Gattamelata*. He also made the high altar for the Basilica of S. Antonio, a complex work with three standing figures and reliefs in stone and in bronze. The reliefs, which record St. Anthony's miracles, show his use of ancient architecture as a means of creating a setting. The whole Paduan school of painting in the second half of the 15th century depended directly on these works.

During the last years of his life in Florence, Donatello continued to produce works of the greatest tragic content, such as the agonized wooden statue of the *Magdalen* in the Baptistery. He also experimented with distortions and extreme foreshortenings in his relief style, best seen in the bronze pulpits for the Church of S. Lorenzo, which were incomplete at his death. Donatello's austere and classical style is usually regarded as typical of humanist art.

H. W. Janson Donatello (2 vols.) Princeton, 1958
J. Pope-Hennessy Italian Renaissance Sculpture London, 1958

St. Sebastian (detail)
Milan, Brera

HIS WORKS INCLUDE

The Madonna and Saints
Glasgow, City Art Gall.

The Rest on the Flight into Egypt
Florence, Pal. Pitti

The Lamentation over the Dead Christ, early work
London, N. G.

Circe, about 1530
Rome, Gall. Borghese

See also page 242

DOSSO DOSSI   about 1479/90-1542

A court painter to the Este family

Dosso Dossi's real name was Giovanni Luteri. It has been said that he was given his nickname because he originated from Dosso, near Trento, but it is more likely that his father came from Trento and that Dossi was in fact born at Ferrara. The first reference to him places him at Mantua in 1512. After 1516 the records show that he was working in Ferrara, often with the collaboration of his brother Battista. In 1531 to 1532 he worked at Trento, and farther afield at Pesaro, Reggio Emilia, and Modena. He died probably at Ferrara in 1542.

Dosso Dossi was successful in blending Venetian tone and color with the splendid plastic strength of the 15th-century Ferrarese school, creating visions of fantasy inspired by the poetic atmosphere of the Este court—the atmosphere of Ariosto's famous poem *Orlando Furioso*. The outstanding example of this is his *Circe* in which an eerie light illumines gorgeously dressed figures. In the last phase of his art Dossi emulated Titian with a pungent Mannerism and a polemic, anti-classic feeling, though he also drew inspiration from Raphael's monumental manner.

B. Nicolson The Painters of Ferrara London, 1951

A Muse Inspiring a Court Poet (?)
(detail) *London, N. G.*

DUCCIO DI BUONINSEGNA   about 1255-1318/19

The first great painter of the Sienese School

Duccio is first recorded in 1278 when he was working for the city of Siena. His career was punctuated by a series of fines, mostly for unspecified offences, so that it is probable that he was politically minded. In 1285 he received a commission for a large altarpiece of the *Madonna* from the Church of S. Maria Novella in Florence. This is now usually identified with the *Rucellai Madonna*, which is undoubtedly of the right date, though somewhat different in style from Duccio's great masterpiece, the huge *Maestà* painted between 1308 and 1311, for the high altar of Siena Cathedral. Most of this altarpiece is now in the cathedral museum, but a few of the smaller panels from it have found their way to London, to the Frick Collection in New York, and to the National Gallery in Washington.

The *Maestà* originally consisted of a huge painting of the *Madonna and Child Enthroned with Saints* on the side facing the nave of the cathedral, while the back of the altarpiece, facing the choir, consisted of a series of small panels of scenes from the life of Christ. The narrative scenes show a dramatic power and a mastery of

The Madonna and Child, about 1305
Siena, Pin.

Maestà (back) 1308-11
Siena, Mus. dell'Opera del Duomo

perspective that make Duccio comparable to Giotto as an innovator, while the extremely subtle color and the linear patterns are the elements in the altarpiece that were taken up by successive generations of Sienese painters. The *Maestà* is, in fact, the foundation of the whole Sienese School. Other elements in Duccio's style are taken from French Gothic art and late Byzantine icons. Duccio died in Siena in about 1318 or 1319.

E. S. Vavala Uffizi Studies Florence, 1948

The Crucifixion, about 1311
Boston, Mus. of Fine Arts

HIS WORKS INCLUDE

The Rucellai Madonna, 1285 (attrib.)
Florence, Uffizi

The Madonna of the Franciscans
about 1285   *Siena, Pin.*

The Maestà 1308-11
Siena, Mus. dell'Opera del Duomo

See also pages 167, 168

Maestà (front) 1308-11
Siena, Mus. dell'Opera del Duomo

HIS WORKS INCLUDE

The Madonna, Crucifixion and the Life of Mary Magdalen, 1529-32
Vercelli, S. Cristoforo

Angel Musicians, about 1537
Saronno, Santuario

See also pages 233, 325

GAUDENZIO FERRARI   1471/81-1546

A painter of joyful and decorative frescoes

Gaudenzio Ferrari, a North Italian, first appeared as a painter at Varallo. His style was the result of several dissimilar influences, such as those of Leonardo, Perugino, and Correggio, and showed a taste for naturalistic detail and picturesque costume derived probably from German art. His principal works are fresco cycles in the Chapel of Sacro Monte at Varallo. At the expense of artistic unity he included painted terracotta figures in an attempt to increase the vivid realism of the scene. His paintings are distinguished by their narrative skill and the bright and luminous colors. The scenes are filled with movement.

Ferrari is well documented, not only at Varallo, but in many other towns in North Italy. He eventually settled in Milan, where he worked until his death.

E. Halsey Gaudenzio Ferrari London, 1904

VINCENZO FOPPA

1427/30-1515/16

An artist who initiated a new trend in Lombard painting

Vincenzo Foppa of Brescia was the artist who directed the development of 15th-century Lombard painting into the Renaissance and away from the International Gothic tradition. Foppa's very early training was within this tradition, but a journey he probably made to Padua about the middle of the 15th century would have brought him into contact with the humanist innovations, though he interpreted these as a rediscovery of the real nature of things. He gained access to the Duke of Milan's court, working in the Sforza capital, Pavia, and in Liguria, Bergamo, and Brescia.

The frescoes Foppa painted for Pigello Portinari in a chapel in the Church of S. Eustorgio in Milan were of fundamental importance for the new trend of Lombard painting. He fell under the spell of Bramante's monumental vision, but remained unaffected by the influence of Leonardo, managing throughout to maintain a style of his own. Typical of Foppa is a luminous effect that heralds the 16th-century Brescian school of painting, and in which, as well as in his faithful adherence to realism, may be detected intimations of Caravaggio far ahead. Foppa died between May, 1515 and October, 1516, at Brescia.

J. Ffoulkes and R. Maiocchi Vincenzo Foppa London, 1909

The Miracle of St. Peter Martyr
at Narni, about 1468
Milan, S. Eustorgio, Portinari Chapel

Madonna and Child with Saints,
before 1486
Pavia, Mus. Civici

HIS WORKS INCLUDE

The Madonna of the Hedge, 1445-50
Settignano, coll. Berenson

The Three Crosses, 1456
Bergamo, Accad. Carrara

The Madonna and Child, about 1460
West Berlin, Staatl. Mus.

Polyptych, about 1476
Milan, Brera

The Adoration of the Kings, about 1502
London, N. G.

See also pages 205, 321

A Boy Reading, about 1470
London, Wallace Coll.

St. Dorothy and the Infant Christ
before 1466
London, N. G.

FRANCESCO DI GIORGIO MARTINI

1439-1502

One of the most versatile artists of his generation

Francesco di Giorgio Martini was born in Siena in 1439 and died there in 1502. He was active as a painter and sculptor, and he was also an architect and the author of a treatise on architecture. His fame among contemporaries was as a military engineer, and he was probably the inventor of the land mine.

Martini's sculpture was influenced by Donatello's humanist art, but he was trained by Vecchietta, and his early paintings were done in collaboration with Neroccio, who was a more traditional Sienese artist. Not much is known of his activity as an architect, although he certainly worked on the palace at Urbino, where he may have carried out some of Laurana's designs. It is known that in 1490 he met Leonardo da Vinci in Milan, and the two shared an interest in architectural theory. Francesco's most important work as an architect is S. Maria del Calcinaio, near Cortona, built at the end of his life.

A. S. Weller   Francesco di Giorgio   Chicago, 1943

The Deposition (detail) about 1475   *Venice, S. Maria del Carmine*

HIS WORKS INCLUDE

The Coronation of the Virgin, 1471
Siena, Pin.

The Flagellation, 1480
Perugia, Gall. Naz. dell'Umbria

See also page 317

TADDEO GADDI

died 1366

One of the most important of Giotto's pupils

HIS WORKS INCLUDE

Scenes from the Life of the Virgin
1332-38
Florence, S. Croce

Triptych, 1334
West Berlin, Staatl. Mus.

The Madonna and Child, 1355
Florence, Uffizi

The Madonna and Child Enthroned
with Saints and Angels
Bern, Kunstmus.

See also pages 181, 305

Gaddi, a Florentine painter of the 14th century, came from a family of artists. His father Gaddo was a contemporary of Giotto, and his son Agnolo, a very well known painter with a rather superficial and prosaic style, was also active in S. Croce in the second half of the century. In 1313, when Gaddi was still a boy, he left his father's studio for Giotto's; he collaborated with Giotto for 24 years or more. Records of his work date from 1327 till his death in 1366. Giotto's influence is apparent in his early work, but it is soon replaced by a clearly stronger adherence to the Sienese style, particularly as regards color contrasts and line.

70

GENTILE DA FABRIANO   about 1370-1427

A courtly exponent of the International Gothic style

Very little is known of the early days of Gentile di Niccolò di Massio, better known as Gentile da Fabriano. He was born at Fabriano in the Marches in about 1370 or possibly before. He was probably encouraged in his early training and youthful ventures by local masters such as Allegretto Nuzi, who in a rather provincial way interpreted the Florentine and Sienese themes of the 14th century.

A hypothetical, but probable, first journey in North Italy would have been extremely important in enabling Gentile to establish closer contact with the International Gothic style. If he did make this journey, he must have seen works by the Sienese painter Taddeo di Bartolo, active in Padua between 1389 and 1393. After returning temporarily to his home town in about 1400, he painted a polyptych for the Franciscan church in Val di Sasso. From 1403 or 1404 until 1419 he was in Venice and Brescia, where he devoted himself to important works, such as the frescoes in the Greater Council Chamber and the so-called Broletto paintings. All these works are now lost.

During this period Gentile established a working partnership with Pisanello, who, still in his formative period, was much influenced by the older master. Gentile often visited Florence, Siena, and Orvieto. It was in Florence that he created the *Adoration of the Magi* in 1423 and the *Quaratesi Altarpiece* two years later. In these he achieved a perfect balance in his art, adding to the local tradition a delicate, Late Gothic sensitivity with an all-pervading lyrical atmosphere,

The Quaratesi Madonna, 1425
London, Royal Coll.

The Presentation in the Temple, about 1423
Paris, Louvre

The Coronation of the Virgin
Milan, Brera

HIS WORKS INCLUDE

The Adoration of the Magi, 1423
Florence, Uffizi

Four Saints from the Quaratesi
Altarpiece, 1425
Florence, Uffizi

The Madonna and Child
with Angel Musicians
New York, Met. Mus.

See also page 184

St. Valerian, St. Tiburzio,
and St. Cecilia, 1620
Milan, Brera

The Flight into Egypt, predella panel from the Adoration of the Magi, 1423
Florence, Uffizi

at the time when Masaccio's revolutionary style was beginning to reveal itself.

On January 28, 1427, Gentile was working in Rome on the *Legend of St. John the Baptist*, now destroyed, in St. John Lateran. He died in October of that year, while still at Rome. He had reached his full artistic maturity even when he was at Venice and Brescia, but constantly sought to perfect his art. Barely conscious of the Renaissance tendencies which were beginning to be apparent during his lifetime, he remained faithful to his own world of fantasy, richly colored, lavishly and exquisitely decorated, and inspired by a poetical naturalism of northern origin.

R. Offner Italian Primitives at Yale University New Haven, 1927

ORAZIO GENTILESCHI   about 1563- about 1640

A court painter who worked in Paris and London

A follower of Caravaggio, Orazio Lomi is better known by his nickname Gentileschi. He was born into a Florentine family living at Pisa, and was trained by his half-brother Aurelio in the style of the Tuscan late Mannerists. Gentileschi reached Rome in 1585, and a few years later he got to know the work of the young Caravaggio. This gave him the stimulus to develop an entirely personal luminous style, which was highly lyrical even when he tackled realistic and dramatic subjects. He was in the Marches soon after 1610 and from there went on to stay at Genoa from 1621 to 1623. He later spent two years in France; finally, he landed in England in 1626, where he became Court Painter to Charles I.

Gentileschi's style became even more refined with time. His palette became softer and the treatment of light increasingly transparent and delicate. His color schemes heralded the final development of Caravaggio's idea that is seen in the work of the Dutchman Vermeer.

Gentileschi had a daughter, Artemisia, born in Rome in 1597, who adhered to Caravaggio's more dramatic ideas. After a period in Florence, she settled in Naples in 1630. In 1638 and 1639 she made a journey to England to visit her father, returning later to Naples, where she pursued a daring, darkly dramatic style of painting. She died there in about 1651. Gentileschi himself died in London about 1640.

E. Waterhouse Italian Baroque Painting London, 1958

HIS WORKS INCLUDE

David and Goliath, after 1610
Dublin, N. G.

The Madonna and Child, 1610-15
Urbino, Ducal Pal., Gall. of the Marches

St. Valerian, St. Tiburzio, and St. Cecilia, 1620
Milan, Brera

The Annunciation, 1623
Turin, Pin.

See also page 276

LORENZO GHIBERTI

1378-1455

The sculptor of the "Doors of Paradise"

Lorenzo Ghiberti was born in Florence in 1378 and died there in 1455. He is famous for two of the three sets of bronze doors of the Baptistery in Florence, which occupied almost the whole of his life. He is also well known for the autobiography written in the last years of his life, a document unique in its period. It is the first autobiography of a practicing artist since classical times, and it tells much about the way in which Ghiberti regarded himself as a humanist artist intent on recording the forms of classical antiquity. Ghiberti owned a collection of antique sculpture, but in spite of this he was far less truly classical in feeling than his contemporaries Donatello, Brunelleschi, and Masaccio.

In his autobiography Ghiberti states that he was in Rimini in 1400, when he

The North Doors, 1403-24
Florence, Baptistery

The Expulsion from the Temple, from the North Doors, 1403-24
Florence, Baptistery

The Triumphal Entry into Jerusalem, from the North Doors, 1403-24
Florence, Baptistery

HIS WORKS INCLUDE

The Sacrifice of Isaac, 1401
Florence, Mus. Naz. del Bargello

The North Doors, 1403-24
Florence, Baptistery

St. Matthew, about 1428
Florence, Orsanmichele

St. Stephen, about 1428
Florence, Orsanmichele

The East Doors, 1425-52
Florence, Baptistery

See also pages 376, 377

The East Doors, 1425-52
Florence, Baptistery

St. John the Baptist, 1414
Florence, Orsanmichele

heard that a competition was being held for a design for a pair of bronze doors for the Baptistery in Florence, similar to those by Andrea Pisano already there. He gives a rather highly colored account of his victory in the competition, in which he defeated both Brunelleschi and Jacopo della Quercia, as well as several lesser men. He began the doors, for the north side of the Baptistery, in 1403 and worked on them until 1424, commissioning a large workshop with many assistants, several of whom subsequently became famous in their own right.

The North doors show scenes from the New Testament. They follow very closely the pattern established in the earlier doors by Andrea Pisano; that is, the style is still largely Gothic but reveals an occasional hint of classical antiquity in the individual forms. These doors were so successful that in 1425 Ghiberti was commissioned to make a third pair, for the east side. Decorated with Old Testament sce-

Jacob and Esau, from the East Doors, 1425-52
Florence, Baptistery

nes, they were completed in 1452 and showed a marked contrast to his earlier doors. This time Ghiberti was given a free hand, and used an entirely new relief style in which perspective plays the most important part. The individual reliefs are much larger and contain many more figures set in architecture or landscape to give the impression of real space. This stylistic change was due to Ghiberti's study of the work of Donatello and Brunelleschi. Although he was less original than they, the doors show Ghiberti's superb craftsmanship and his very real desire to work in the antique manner. The last pair of doors is often referred to as the "Doors of Paradise," and was so called by Michelangelo.

R. Krautheimer and T. Krautheimer-Hess Lorenzo Ghiberti New York, 1957

DOMENICO GHIRLANDAIO

1449-1494

A prosperous painter with an elegant style

The fresco painter Domenico Bigordi, born in Florence in 1449, was generally known as Ghirlandaio. This surname was derived from his father Tommaso, a goldsmith, who used to make the gold and silver circlets that girls wore as ornaments on their heads.

Domenico is supposed by tradition to have started on his artistic career under Baldovinetti, retaining, especially in his early works, the latter's well-regulated sense of harmony infused with a fresh ingenuous quality. He often painted in collaboration with his brother Davide, and he knew the works of Verrocchio. He sometimes studied Andrea del Castagno, though with more stupefied admiration than understanding. However, he was influenced by the analytical tendencies in Flemish painting which were known in Florence mainly through Hugo van der Goes' *Portinari Altarpiece*. His output of frescoes was enormous. In addition to his native city, he worked in San Gimignano and in Rome. His workshop was extremely prosperous, and many artists gathered there, among them the young Michelangelo.

Ghirlandaio, who died in Florence in 1494, was not a profound artist, but an

Self-portrait, 1482
Rome, Vatican, Sistine Chapel

HIS WORKS INCLUDE

The Life of S. Fina, 1475
San Gimignano, Collegiata

The Calling of the Apostles
about 1482
Rome, Vatican, Sistine Chapel

Mary and St. John the Baptist, 1485
Florence, S. Maria Novella

The Adoration of the Shepherds, 1485
Florence, S. Trinità

Giovanna Tornabuoni, 1488
Lugano, coll. Thyssen

See also pages 225, 320

The Visitation, 1491
Paris, Louvre

The Birth of St. John the Baptist,
about 1490
Florence, S. Maria Novella

75

agreeable one. He told the story of Florentine life, describing it in an elegant (and sometimes mannered) prosaic style, even when dealing with religious subjects. He showed a special flair for endowing his portraits with vivid characterization.

G. S. Davies   Domenico Ghirlandaio   London, 1908

A Legend of St. Justus and St. Clement
of Volterra, about 1484
London, N. G.

HIS WORKS INCLUDE

Marchese G. M. Rota and Capt. Brinzago
Seriate, coll. Piccinelli

G. B. Vailetti, about 1710
Venice, Accad.

Contessina Secco-Suardi in Male Attire about 1720
Rome, coll. Secco-Suardi

Filippo Marenzi, 1720-25
Bergamo, Accad. Carrara

See also page 290

VITTORE GHISLANDI called FRA GALGARIO   1655-1743

A monk who became a fashionable painter

Born at Bergamo on March 4, 1655, the portrait painter Ghislandi was christened Giuseppe. His father Domenico was also a painter. Giuseppe changed his name to Vittore, when at the age of 20 he entered the religious order of the Paolotti. He was known as Fra Galgario after the monastery where he later lived.

Ghislandi had a complex artistic development. He spent a long time in Venice studying the Venetian school of painting, and on returning to Bergamo he established closer contact with the local tradition. Finally, in Milan, he knew the German Salomon Adler.

Ghislandi was one of the most accomplished portrait painters of 18th-century Italy. He died at Bergamo in December, 1743, and his major works belong chronologically to the 18th century. Faithful to a realism derived from Caravaggio, he paid close attention to psychological factors, creating a concentrated, eloquent art, full of life and rich in color and light.

R. Wittkower   Art and Architecture in Italy, 1600-1750   London, 1958

LUCA GIORDANO

1632-1705

A decorative painter of the Neapolitan school

Luca Giordano was one of the Neapolitan painters belonging to the generation that succeeded the true followers of Caravaggio. The artists of this generation found their leading exponent in Mattia Preti. Giordano was born in Naples in 1632, and at first followed the example of his father, a modest imitator of Ribera; he later worked under Ribera himself. Preti, however, was the real source of his youthful inspiration, though when he went to Rome, shortly after 1650, he most of all admired Pietro da Cortona. From Pietro he drew the incentive for a nobly decorative style of painting, fluently and flamboyantly executed. It was on account of his phenomenal speed in working that he was nicknamed "Luca fa presto."

When, in 1667, Giordano went to Venice (which he had already visited in 1654) his work acquired more light and a brighter color. After he had painted the ceiling of the ballroom of the Palazzo Medici-Riccardi in Florence in 1682-83, his great reputation led Charles II, King of Spain, to entrust to him the ceilings of the Escorial, which are probably his masterpieces. He returned to Naples in 1702, and remained there until his death on January 12, 1705.

Self-portrait, from the Allegory of Peace
Madrid, Prado

HIS WORKS INCLUDE

Jesus Among the Doctors
Rome, Gall. Doria

The Deposition
Venice, Accad.

The Marriage at Cana, 1659
Naples, Mus. Naz.

See also page 288

The Unbeliever's Mule Adoring the Sacrament: Study for a Miracle of St. Anthony of Padua
London, B. M.

Cupid and Psyche
London, Royal Coll.

Attrib. to Giorgione
Portrait of a Man
Brunswick, Gemäldegal.

The Three Philosophers,
begun about 1501
Vienna, Kunsthist. Mus.

Portrait of Laura, 1506
Vienna, Kunsthist. Mus.

GIORGIONE

A genius of the Venetian School

Information about the lives of many artists is very limited, but the biography of Zorzi da Castelfranco, known to his contemporaries as Giorgione, is an almost complete mystery. The only certain fact is that he died in 1510, during a plague that broke out in Venice. The artist's birth may be calculated from the fact that when he died he was said to have been 34. If this is true, the date of his birth would be 1476 or 1477. His birth-place was Castelfranco in the Veneto. Some say that he came of very humble stock, while others claim that he belonged to the well-to-do Barbarelli family. The writers of his day spoke of him as a melancholy and romantic young man, good-looking, well-educated, and an amiable companion of intelligent conversation, who had a passionate fondness for music; but this could be an idealized picture drawn from the characteristics of his art.

There is a tradition that Giorgione studied under Giovanni Bellini, but this was customary in Venice during the last years of the 15th century. Critics have not unraveled the mystery of his development, but rather have added to it, at times ascribing numerous works to him—some of which were later transferred to other artists and documented as such—and at times reducing the catalogue to only six works. However, it is possible to assess his characteristics and to define the phenomenon of "Giorgionism" which had such tremendous repercussions in the first decades of the 16th century. His far-reaching influence explains the importance of his revolutionary development of the relationship between light and color.

It is supposed that Giorgione early in life left his native Castelfranco for Venice,

The Castelfranco Madonna
Castelfranco, S. Liberale

Attrib. to Giorgione
The Proving of Moses *Florence, Uffizi*

where he made contact with Giovanni Bellini. He also met Vittore Carpaccio, who passed on to him the latest researches of Antonello da Messina, particularly with regard to light. Although he probably did not lose contact with Bellini, Giorgione became an independent master and exerted a definite influence on the greatest artists in Venice at that time, including Titian, who was his pupil and is now believed to have been about ten years younger than his master.

Attrib. to Giorgione
The Golden Age (detail) *London, N. G.*

Attrib. to Giorgione
The Golden Age *London, N. G.*

Attrib. to Giorgione
A Man in Armour *London, N. G.*

Venus Asleep, about 1509
Dresden, Gemäldegal.

The accepted chronology of Giorgione's masterpieces is based on the probable course of his artistic development. In order, they are the *Castelfranco Altarpiece*, *The Tempest*, the portrait of *Laura*, the almost completely faded frescoes on the Palazzo Fondaco dei Tedeschi, *The Three Philosophers*, and *Venus Asleep*. His first experiences of Bellini and, through Carpaccio, of Antonello da Messina were enriched by a naturalism which gradually led him to make his figures, forms, and landscapes melt into the atmosphere. The clearly defined contours so dear to the 15th century were therefore gradually dissolved and finally disappeared altogether, leaving the light to create shapes as it falls on colored substance. Giorgione's images were inspired by his observation of nature, yet were turned into a fantastic and romantic vision filled with a sense of poetry.

By discarding drawing and painting by color alone, Giorgione made an extraordinarily far-reaching discovery that not only laid open a hitherto unexplored way for Venetian painting, but was also destined to be the cause of further research and future achievements as far ahead as the Impressionist revolution. Giorgione constantly displayed a love of landscape, so that the landscape itself becomes the true protagonist of many of his paintings. This makes his work a prelude to the freedom of choice in subject matter that has become one of the fundamental characteristics of modern painting.

G. M. Richter Giorgione Chicago, 1937

GIOTTO   1266/67 or 1276-1337

The father of Renaissance art

Giotto di Bondone revived the painting of his time by freeing it from the Byzantine tradition. He was probably born in Florence, though some people now think that it was at Vespignano in the Mugello. The date is determined from an entry made by the Florentine writer Antonio Pucci which records his death at the age of 70 on January 8, 1337. The birth date given by the biographer Vasari as 1276 might be a clerical error.

Giotto is traditionally believed to have been a pupil of Cimabue, and this is not impossible even though some characteristics of his style are reminiscent of Coppo di Marcovaldo, a vigorous Florentine painter who worked on the Baptistery in Florence. Although differences of opinion still exist concerning Giotto's early activities, many experts believe that he went to Assisi when very young and was perhaps one of Cimabue's apprentices there. According to this widely held theory he must have worked there until 1290 or 1295, alongside Roman artists from Pietro Cavallini's group, on frescoes of stories from the Old and New Testaments in the Upper Church of St. Francis. He could therefore have derived the monumental and solemn classical atmosphere of his painting from Cavallini. It seems that Giovanni di Muro, the Franciscan superior-general, entrusted him with his first masterpiece, *The Legend of St. Francis*, in about 1297. It must be admitted, however, that some scholars have denied that Giotto ever worked at Assisi.

Noli me tangere (detail) about 1306
Padua, Arena Chapel

Giotto's presence in Rome in about 1300 is proved by his much restored works there, for example, the mosaic *Christ Walking on the Waves* and the fresco *Pope Boniface VIII Proclaiming the Jubilee*. There is also a polyptych in the Vatican Museum which was probably done with the help of assistants.

Giotto next went to Padua, where, between 1303 and 1305, he painted scenes

Pope Boniface VIII Proclaiming the Jubilee, about 1300
Rome, S. Giovanni in Lateran

St. Francis Denouncing his Father, about 1297
Assisi, S. Francesco

St. Francis and the Birds, about 1297
Assisi, S. Francesco

The Massacre of the Innocents, about 1305
Padua, Arena Chapel

HIS WORKS INCLUDE

The Legend of St. Francis
about 1297-1300
Assisi, S. Francesco

Frescoes, about 1305
Padua, Arena Chapel

The Ognissanti Madonna, about 1310
Florence, Uffizi

The Life of St. Francis, about 1320-25
Florence, S. Croce, Bardi Chapel

The Assumption
Florence, S. Croce

The Lives of St. John the Baptist and St. John the Evangelist
Florence, S. Croce, Peruzzi Chapel

See also pages 169, 170, 171, 172, 173

Interior of Arena Chapel: to the East
Padua

Interior of Arena Chapel: to the West
Padua

The Death of St. Francis, about 1325
Florence, S. Croce, Bardi Chapel

from the lives of Christ and the Virgin in the chapel that Enrico Scrovegni, Lord of Padua, had built on the site of the old Roman arena. On his return to Florence, he painted the *Madonna* for the Ognissanti church. He went again to Rome, probably to Rimini in about 1311, to Venice in about 1314, and it is thought that he may have gone to Avignon in 1316. He may also have been summoned to Ferrara, Ravenna, and later, between 1330 and 1335, to Naples and Milan. In the meantime Giotto had undertaken the task of directing the construction of the cathedral at Florence after Arnolfo di Cambio had died. The bell-tower which is named after him was erected according to his plan. Presumably Giotto took advantage of the collaboration of Andrea Pisano in this work. The latter is remembered chiefly as a sculptor and the creator of the bronze reliefs on the first door of the Baptistery at Florence. In Florence Giotto married Guida di Lapo del Perlo who bore him eight children, one of whom, Francesco, became a painter. He bought property and land, was appointed Superintendent of the cathedral works, and supervised the city walls and fortifications. Meanwhile, about 1320-25, he painted the scenes from the life of St. Francis in the Bardi Chapel of S. Croce, and returned to the same church perhaps four years later to carry out the scenes from the lives of St. John the Baptist and St. John the Evangelist in the Peruzzi Chapel. He died in 1337.

The Test by Fire, about 1320
Florence, S. Croce, Bardi Chapel

On the strength of these and other less important works the young Giotto was celebrated by his contemporaries; Dante mentions him in "The Divine Comedy" in the stanza

Credette Cimabue nella pittura
tener lo campo, ed ora ha Giotto il grido,
sì che la fama di colui oscura.

Il Purgatorio XI, 1.94-96

(Cimabue believed he held the field in painting, but now Giotto
has the cry and the other's fame is obscured.)

Giotto's new conception of art, his powerful expression of the third dimension, his lofty poetical vision and the humanity in his narrative make him one of the world's greatest painters. He had a very widespread influence on contemporary artists and their successors. In Assisi, Florence, Padua, Rimini, and many other places, regular schools of painting were based on his works. The artists of the early Tuscan Renaissance, above all Masaccio, looked to him as the brilliant forerunner of a new conception of form and space. Even Michelangelo found Giotto an ideal predecessor in his solution of the problems of form as well as in the moral content of his art.

R. Fry Vision and Design London, 1920
Cesare Gnudi Giotto London, 1960

The Adoration of the Magi,
about 1305
Padua, Arena Chapel

The Resurrection of Lazarus,
about 1305
Padua, Arena Chapel

The Presentation in the Temple, about 1305
Padua, Arena Chapel

The Kiss of Judas, about 1305
Padua, Arena Chapel

Polyptych, 1360-65
Prato, Pin.

GIOVANNI DA MILANO

A painter of frescoes and altarpieces

The real name of Giovanni da Milano, a Lombard painter of the 14th century, was Giovanni di Giacomo di Guido da Como. The earliest references to him, already as a painter, show him to have been at Florence in 1346. His formative years must have been spent in Lombardy, under the influence of Giusto da Menabuoi among others. Later, at Florence, he frequented Taddeo Gaddi's studio. He worked in Tuscany until about 1369, and in that year was engaged in Rome on the decoration of two Vatican chapels. There are no later records and nothing is known of Giovanni's death. His work was a synthesis of typical Lombard realism, a Giottesque sense of space, and a luminosity of color which heralds the International Gothic style.

HIS WORKS INCLUDE

Polyptych, 1360-65
Prato, Pin.

Triptych, 1360-65
London, N. G.

The Story of St. Joachim and St. Anne
about 1365
Florence, S. Croce

The Madonna and Child
with two Donors, about 1365
New York, Met. Mus.

Pietà, 1365
Florence, Accad.

See also page 183

Polyptych (detail) 1360-65
Prato, Pin.

Madonna with Angels and Saints,
1461   *London, N. G.*

BENOZZO GOZZOLI

about 1421-1497

A fresco painter of great charm and narrative skill

Benozzo di Lese, surnamed Gozzoli, was born in Florence. Until he was over 30 his activities were centered on other artists, in particular Fra Angelico, whose assistant and collaborator he was from 1447. In 1459 he painted the *Procession of the Magi* in the chapel of the Medici-Riccardi palace, and in this work revealed his own talent as an imaginative story-teller. He then worked at San Gimignano from 1463 to 1465, and between 1467 and 1484 he devoted himself to painting frescoes for a large part of the cemetery at Pisa. Here he gave free rein to his humanist tendencies, which had previously been unrealized because of his taste for fanciful narrative. Benozzo died at Pistoia in 1497.

The Procession of the Magi (detail) 1459
Florence, Pal. Medici-Riccardi

The Dance of Salome and Beheading
of St. John the Baptist, about 1461
Washington D. C., N. G., Kress Coll.

B Gozzoli.

HIS WORKS INCLUDE

The Procession of the Magi, 1459
Florence, Pal. Medici-Riccardi
The Madonna with Angels and Saints
1461
London, N. G.
The Miracle of S. Domenico, 1462
Milan, Brera
Predella, about 1461
New York, Met. Mus.
Scenes from the Life of St. Augustine
about 1463
San Gimignano, S. Agostino and Collegiata

See also page 203

GIOVANNINO DE' GRASSI   active before 1389-1398

Painter, architect, and sculptor in the International Gothic style

Little is known about the early life of Giovannino de' Grassi. He may have been
born in Milan or Como in about the middle of the 14th century. In 1389, already
at a mature age, he was working on the construction of Milan Cathedral as painter,
architect, and sculptor, and continued to hold these offices intermittently until he
died in 1398 in the Lombard capital. Giovannino was one of the few representatives of the International Gothic style in Italy, having connections in style with the
Franco-Belgian and Bohemian miniaturists. He influenced Gentile da Fabriano
during the latter's first period in North Italy, and, more directly, Stefano da Verona, Pisanello, and Michelino da Besozzo.

HIS WORKS INCLUDE

'Offiziolo' of Gian Galeazzo Visconti
1370-80 (?)
Florence, Bibl. Naz.
Christ and the Samaritan Woman
(bas-relief), 1396
Milan, Cath.
A collection of drawings is kept in
Bergamo, Biblioteca Civica

See also page 306

Caprice with a Ruined Arch,
about 1775 *London, N. G.*

The greatest exponent of the veduta

Francesco Guardi is associated with Canaletto in his search for a new emotional content in the *veduta*, or view, although his was a different approach and he used different means of expression. He went beyond Canaletto in that he developed a more appropriate style, which affected the future of landscape painting in the 19th century. Francesco was born in Venice on October 5, 1712, into a family of painters who had come down from a valley of the Trentino. At a very early age he joined the family workshop which, after his father Domenico had died in 1716, was supervised by his elder brother, Giovanni Antonio. Throughout the 18th century Giovanni Antonio enjoyed a greater reputation than Francesco. His younger brother Niccolò was also a painter, while his sister Cecilia married Giovanni Battista Tiepolo and was the mother of Domenico and Lorenzo, who were also painters, draftsmen, and engravers.

Guardi did not achieve a fully developed personal artistic style until he was nearly 40, at the time when Canaletto was in England. He then devoted his attention entirely to the *veduta* and achieved exceptional results. His paintings, however, were much more appreciated by foreign tourists than by the recognized artistic circles in Venice. At first Guardi undertook some religious works, full of tension and drawn with quick, nervous brush strokes, nearer in style to Magnasco and Marco Ricci than to Crespi of Bologna. It is often difficult to distinguish

HIS WORKS INCLUDE

Tobias, about 1747
Venice, S. Raffaele

S. Maria della Salute
Milan, coll. Aldo Crespi

The Doge's Procession to S. Zaccaria
Paris, Louvre

The Mendicanti Canal
Bergamo, Accad. Carrara

View of Cannaregio, 1764
Washington D. C., N. G.

Ball in the Conti del Nord, 1783
Monaco, Pin.

Lagoon, about 1790
Milan, Mus. Poldi Pezzoli

See also pages 301, 302, 364

Venice, the Punta della Dogana with S. Maria della Salute
London, N. G.

Venice, Piazza San Marco, about 1765
London, N. G.

Francesco's hand from that of Giovanni Antonio, and more than one painting of this period could be the result of their collaboration. There are also certain floral compositions which have been associated with Francesco Guardi's name, but his real talent lay in the *vedute*, the vivid Venetian scenes, and the *capricci*, products of fantasy. These subjects, with old Roman ruins rising from backgrounds of lagoons, are typical of Canaletto, but they are treated in a fresh, vivacious manner.

Venice springs into life and movement in Guardi's *vedute* in a way that Canaletto could never have realized within the limits of his bright, polished, illuministic dream-world. It is through the portrayal of daily life in action that Guardi's romanticism is seen, in the lively spontaneity of each brush stroke, and the rich textures that the light throws into rough, crumbly relief. One new element which he brought into some of his interior scenes was the spirit of the reckless, hollow gaiety of Venetian festivities, telling of a society already fading and on the point of extinction, unaware of its impending tragedy. This softens into an elegaic, melancholy despair only in some of the lagoon paintings, where Guardi reaches the heights of poetry in exquisitely pure compositions. He received a certain amount of recognition only after 1760 and was admitted to the Venetian Academy of painting on September 12, 1784, nine years before his death in Venice.

M. Levey Painting in 18th-Century Venice London, 1959

The Mendicanti Canal
Bergamo, Accad. Carrara

87

Doubting Thomas
London, N. G.

GIOVANNI FRANCESCO BARBIERI called GUERCINO
1591-1666

One of the first Baroque painters

Giovanni Francesco Barbieri, nicknamed Guercino, "Squint-eye," because of a cast in his right eye, received his first training in his home town of Cento near Bologna. He was a pupil of Ludovico Carracci and strongly influenced by Caravaggio's dramatic use of light and shade. His early works combine many features derived from both masters. He visited Venice in 1618, and was in Rome from 1621 to 1623, when he painted his finest work, the fresco of *Aurora* on the ceiling of the Casino Ludovisi. This enchanting illusionistic work was the high point of his career for he later dwindled into a purveyor of large-scale religious and mythological subjects of formal dullness and emptiness, both of thought and handling. He returned to Cento in 1623, and on the death of Guido Reni in 1642 took over the latter's flourishing practice in Bologna, where he worked for the rest of his life.

D. Mahon *Studies in Seicento Art and Theory* London, 1947
R. Wittkower *Art and Architecture in Italy, 1600-1750* London, 1958

A Saint
London, B. M.

HIS WORKS INCLUDE

Susanna and the Elders, 1618
Madrid, Prado

St. William of Aquitaine and St. Felix
Bologna, Pin.

Aurora, 1621-23
Rome, Casino Ludovisi

St. Petronilla, 1621
Rome, Gall. Capitolina

The Dead Christ, 1630
London, N. G.

The Martyrdom of St. Peter
Bologna, Pin.

See also page 284, 357

Aurora, 1621-23
Rome, Casino Ludovisi

FRANCESCO LAURANA

about 1430-1502

An obscure sculptor, famed for his portrait busts of women

Almost nothing is known of the youth of Francesco Laurana, except that he was Dalmatian by birth, probably born at Zara, and that he is first recorded in 1458 at Rimini, where he may have been working with Agostino di Duccio. He is last mentioned in 1502. His career took him from Naples and Sicily to the south of France. He seems to have worked on the Triumphal Arch of Alfonso of Aragon in Naples, which was influenced by the humanist ideas of Alberti and his circle.

From 1461 to 1466 Laurana worked in the south of France, before returning to Sicily in 1467, where he brought French influences to the local school. He was at Urbino between 1474 and 1477 and it is during this period that he seems to have made the very geometrical, rather enigmatic, busts of women that are clearly translations into three dimensions of the monumental style of Piero della Francesca. These busts are his most typical works, although few of them are documented. He later returned to France and worked in the Old Cathedral of Marseilles, where he reverted to a more Gothic manner.

J. Pope-Hennessy   Italian Gothic Sculpture   London, 1955

Triumphal Arch, about 1470
Naples

HIS WORKS INCLUDE

Eleanor of Aragon, 1468
Palermo, Mus. Naz.
Battista Sforza, about 1476
Florence, Mus. Naz. del Bargello
Bust of a Woman
Washington D. C., N. G.

See also page 386

LEONARDO DA VINCI

1452-1519

The most versatile of all Renaissance artists

Leonardo da Vinci was born in 1452, the illegitimate son of a Florentine lawyer. He was brought up in Florence with his half-sisters and brothers, and was apprenticed to the painter and sculptor Verrocchio. As early as 1472 Leonardo was enrolled in the Guild of Painters in Florence, but for the next six years at least he continued to work for Verrocchio. There is a tradition, which goes back to the 16th century, that Leonardo painted the angel in profile in the unfinished *Baptism of Christ*, the rest of which is attributed to Verrocchio. According to this tradition Verrocchio felt himself so outstripped by Leonardo that he ceased to paint and devoted himself entirely to sculpture. Certainly there are very few pictures that can be attributed to Verrocchio, but it is probable that he preferred sculpture and felt that he could leave painting to his young collaborator. Several other pictures of the 1470's are almost certainly by Leonardo, including *The Annunciation* and the very beautiful *Portrait of a Young Woman*, probably Ginevra de' Benci, painted on the occasion of her marriage.

In 1481 Leonardo was occupied on a large *Adoration of the Magi* for the Monastery of S. Donato a Scopeto near Florence. This picture was never completed, although numerous drawings exist; it seems likely that Leonardo stopped work on

Self-portrait, about 1512
Turin, Bibl. Reale

The Virgin of the Rocks, after 1483
London, N. G.

it when he went to Milan. The composition is important in that it solves the problem of representing a crowded scene in such a way that the figures at the apex of the group dominate the whole. They are not submerged by the gesticulating figures at the side, each of which is given a different facial expression.

There is a copy of a letter which was perhaps sent by Leonardo to the Duke of Milan, in which Leonardo claims to be "as good as any man" and highly skilled in an extraordinary variety of things including military engineering, sculpture, architecture, and painting. Leonardo probably arrived in Milan about 1482, and in 1483 he received a commission for an altarpiece for a church in Milan: for many years controversy has raged over the identity of this picture, since there are two versions of *The Virgin of the Rocks*, one in Paris and the other in London. There seems no doubt that the documents refer to the London picture, but the version in Paris is stylistically earlier and it is possible that it was begun in Florence. Since Leonardo completed very few pictures and was notorious for beginning projects that he never brought to completion, it seems difficult to explain the existence of two similar but not identical pictures, and no satisfactory explanation has ever been suggested. One of the reasons for Leonardo's presence in Milan was the commission given him by the Sforza duke to make a large equestrian statue in memory of his father. This monument never progressed beyond a large clay model of the horse—the rider was never even begun—and even the model itself was destroyed early in the 16th century.

By 1497 Leonardo had almost completed his most famous work, the fresco of *The Last Supper* in the refectory of S. Maria delle Grazie in Milan. This is a masterpiece of psychological penetration, and is in many ways the first work of the High Renaissance style. Unfortunately it had begun to deteriorate even in Leonardo's own lifetime because he refused to use the normal fresco technique, which required rapid execution, and employed instead an oil technique on the plaster of the wall.

Study for the Madonna with a Cat
about 1480   *London, B. M.*

The Adoration of the Magi, about 1482
Florence, Uffizi

An Antique Warrior, about 1475
London, B. M.

This allowed him great deliberation and permitted him to put the maximum expressiveness into the faces of the individual Apostles. The painting began to deteriorate almost at once, and the composition is now very difficult to appreciate in detail. Something of his concern with subtlety of expression and with tightly knit composition can be seen in the tempera cartoon that has been acquired by the National Gallery in London.

During the sixteen or seventeen years Leonardo spent in Milan he also worked as an architect and engineer and made anatomical studies which established him as indisputably the greatest anatomist in the world. He also planned a treatise on architecture and worked on a number of scientific problems. The results of these studies are known in the thousands of pages in his notebooks, many of which contain extraordinarily prophetic drawings and notes: for example, Leonardo anticipated many later discoveries in aeronautics and almost discovered the circulation of the blood. For some reason he never quite pushed these discoveries to a conclusion and to many of his contemporaries he seemed to be frittering away his time in a variety of pursuits.

The French invasion of 1499 led to the fall of the Sforzas, and Leonardo went to Venice and Mantua in 1500. He then returned to his native Florence, where in 1503 he was commissioned to paint a gigantic fresco in the new council chamber in direct competition with one commissioned from Michelangelo. Both were battle pieces and neither was ever completed, but both left an indelible mark on the character of Florentine art in the 16th century. Leonardo's represented an incident

St. Jerome, about 1483
Rome, Vatican Gall.

The Last Supper, about 1497
Milan, S. Maria delle Grazie, Refectory

St. John the Baptist, 1503-13
Paris, Louvre

Ginevra de'Benci, about 1474
Washington, D. C., N. G.

Study for the Virgin and Child
with St. Anne and St. John the Baptist
(detail) about 1501
London, N. G.

in the *Battle of Anghiari.* It is clear that for him the interest of the group of soldiers fighting for possession of a standard centered in the expression of extreme fury, illustrating his own remark that war is a form of bestial madness. During his years in Florence Leonardo continued his anatomical studies and painted the *Mona Lisa.* He probably also began the *Virgin and Child with St. Anne,* now in the Louvre. In 1506 he was back in Milan, working for the French king, and in the next few years Leonardo traveled a great deal before settling in France in 1516. The French king, Francis I, was eagerly welcoming representatives of the Italian Renaissance, and Leonardo remained in France until his death in 1519.

Leonardo's genius is perhaps most fully appreciated through the study of his

Landscape: The Arno Valley, 1473
Florence, Uffizi

Studies for Military Machinery, about 1485
London, B. M.

Study for the Adoration of the Magi   *Florence, Uffizi*

Study of Drapery
Rome, Gall. Naz. d'Arte Antica

drawings. Thousands of these exist, the majority of them in the Royal Library at Windsor. They represent the whole of the range of his interests, and illustrate the way in which in his hands science became art and art science. He wrote several drafts of a treatise on painting which was never completed, but it is clear that for him the painter's business was the faithful representation of human emotions in terms of facial expressions or gestures. Thus he began the study of anatomy in order to represent the human body more accurately, but very soon found himself pursuing it for its own sake. In the same way he made scores of elaborate drawings for his treatise on architecture, but as far as is known never completed it.

K. Clark   Leonardo da Vinci   Cambridge, 1939
L. Douglas   Leonardo da Vinci, his Life and his Pictures   Chicago, 1944
H. L. Heydenreich   Leonardo da Vinci   London, 1954
A. E. Popham   The Drawings of Leonardo da Vinci   London, 1946

HIS WORKS INCLUDE

The Benois Madonna, about 1478
Leningrad, Hermitage
Ginevra de'Benci, about 1474
Washington, D. C., N. G.
The Adoration of the Magi
about 1482
Florence, Uffizi
The Virgin of the Rocks, before 1483
Paris, Louvre
The Last Supper, about 1497
Milan, S. Maria delle Grazie, Refectory
St. John the Baptist, 1503-13
Paris, Louvre

See also pages 227, 228, 229, 230, 328, 329, 330

Self-portrait (?), about 1484
Florence, S. Maria del Carmine,
Brancacci Chapel

FILIPPINO LIPPI

1457/8-1504

The painter son of a famous artist

Filippino Lippi, a Florentine painter of frescoes and altarpieces, was the son of Fra Filippo Lippi and Lucrezia Buti, a nun, and was born possibly at Prato in about 1457. He could not have learned very much directly from his father, who died when he was only twelve years old; he was trained by his tutor, Fra Diamante, and by Botticelli. When Filippino completed Masaccio's unfinished frescoes in the Brancacci Chapel, he was captured by that artist's enduring fascination, even though this was expressed through the medium of the most topical narrative subjects in 15th-century Florence. He was in Rome between 1488 and 1493, but died in 1504 in Florence, where he had lived and worked.

K. B. Neilson   Filippino Lippi   Cambridge, Mass., 1938

The Assumption, about 1489
Rome, S. Maria sopra Minerva

The Virgin and Child
with St. Jerome and
St. Dominic
London, N. G.

HIS WORKS INCLUDE

Frescoes, about 1484
Florence, S. Maria del Carmine,
Brancacci Chapel

The Madonna Appearing to
St. Bernard, about 1486
Florence, Badia

The Annunciation, about 1493
Rome, S. Maria sopra Minerva

Frescoes, 1502
Florence, S. Maria Novella, Strozzi Chapel

See also page 231

MASACCIO AND FILIPPINO LIPPI
St. Peter Restores the King's Son to Life, about 1484 *Florence, S. Maria del Carmine, Brancacci Chapel*

FRA FILIPPO LIPPI

about 1406-1469

A reluctant monk who was the foremost Florentine painter of his day

Filippo Lippi was born in Florence in about 1406; when his parents died an aunt sent him to the Carmine Monastery. Here he saw the creation of the frescoes of the Brancacci Chapel, with the result that Masolino, and still more Masaccio, made an early and deep impression on him.

There are no records of Filippo between 1431 and 1437, and it can only be supposed that he went to Padua with the exiled Cosimo de' Medici. During his early life he must have studied Fra Angelico's work, and from it inherited a tendency to make his colors lighter and more delicate, while retaining a firm architectural composition which he merged with the contemporary Florentine ideas about form. After returning to Florence, Filippo brought to maturity a style of his own that was closely allied to, and even more advanced than, contemporary achievements in form and expression. Perspective became more and more important to him, while his colors heightened and became increasingly harmonious. The generous curves and inflated lines of his youthful manner became lithe and graceful. It is easy to see in him the beginnings of the naturalistic hedonism that found its climax in the art of Botticelli.

Filippo Lippi worked for a long time at Prato, engaged on other important tasks. From 1456 to 1461 he was chaplain of the convent of S. Margherita at Prato, from which he abducted Lucrezia Buti, a nun. Filippino Lippi the painter was their son. The last days of Filippo's life were spent painting the frescoes in the apse of the cathedral at Spoleto.

Portrait of Francesco Maringhi, from the Coronation of the Virgin, 1441-47
Florence, Uffizi

The Adoration of the Magi,
Washington, D. C., N. G.

The Trivulzio Madonna, about 1434
Milan, Mus. del Castello Sforzesco

HIS WORKS INCLUDE

The Trivulzio Madonna, about 1434
Milan, Mus. del Castello Sforzesco

The Barbadori Altarpiece, 1438
Paris, Louvre

The Coronation of the Virgin, 1441-47
Florence, Uffizi

The Annunciation
Rome, Pal. Venezia

The Madonna, about 1452
Florence, Pal. Pitti

Frescoes, 1452-64
Prato, Cath.

See also pages 198, 310

95

Figures
London, B. M.

HIS WORKS INCLUDE

The Dancing Lesson, about 1741
Venice, Accad.

Family Concert
Milan, Brera

The Sagredo Family, about 1742
Venice, Pin. Querini Stampalia

Hunt in a Valley, about 1765
Venice, Pin. Querini Stampalia

See also pages 300, 363

PIETRO LONGHI

1702-1785

An elegant and fashionable painter of everyday life in Venice

The name of the comic dramatist Carlo Goldoni has often been mentioned in connection with Pietro Longhi because there is a certain affinity of ideas in their two worlds. Both were concerned with portraying reality at first hand, transforming any small incident into poetry.

Pietro Falca, known by the name of Longhi, was born in Venice in 1702 and studied under the Academician Antonio Balestra. However, his training at Bologna under Giuseppe Maria Crespi was more important to his artistic development. His favorite subjects were *vignettes* taken straight from the daily life of the middle and working classes. He painted these with an astonishing freshness, in which humor, candor, wit, and warm-heartedness are mixed. His coloring is extremely subtle, and his delicate handling of light conceals the painstaking care put into the detailed design. In his typical little scenes of everyday patrician life in Venice, the triviality of subject matter is outweighed by the purely lyrical values they assume through the exquisite finesse of their execution.

Pietro Longhi, who died in Venice in 1785, had one son, Alessandro, who made a name for himself as a portrait painter in the second half of the 18th century.

M. Levey   Painting in 18th-Century Venice   London, 1959

Exhibition of a Rhinoceros at Venice,
after 1751   *London, N. G.*

The Dancing Lesson, about 1741
Venice, Accad.

AMBROGIO LORENZETTI

active 1319-1348

A pioneer of the concepts of perspective and realism

Ambrogio Lorenzetti's elder brother Pietro was also a painter, and some art historians prefer to write of the "Lorenzetti Brothers" and of "their" role in the development of Sienese painting. Actually, their roles were different, and Ambrogio's was probably the more important. The brothers are known to have collaborated in 1335 on frescoes, now lost, in the Hospital of the Scala in Siena. This is the only universally accepted instance of collaboration between them. Since there is no record of either brother after 1348, it is supposed that they both died when the Black Death struck Siena in 1348-49.

It is thought by some that Ambrogio was a pupil of his older brother, but the influence of such painters as Cimabue, Giotto, and Simone Martini was obviously more decisive than that of Pietro Lorenzetti. Apart from all such influences, Ambrogio Lorenzetti is noted for his depiction of everyday life and characters, his subtle use of color, and his feeling for landscape.

In the frescoes depicting *The Effects of Good and Bad Government on the Town and on the Country*, 1337-39, in the Palazzo Pubblico in Siena, he found his main opportunity to portray the daily life of his time. In contrast to most Sienese paintings of the time, these frescoes convey the illusion of three dimensions. Ambrogio's excellence as both colorist and draftsman is well demonstrated in these frescoes. This impressive work, and Ambrogio's other paintings, influenced Sienese artists well into the 15th century.

G. Rowley   Ambrogio Lorenzetti   Princeton, 1958

A Group of Poor Clares
London, N. G.

The Annunciation, 1344
Siena, Pin.

The Effects of Good Government, about 1337
Siena, Pal. Pubblico

HIS WORKS INCLUDE

The Madonna and Child
Siena, S. Francesco

The Madonna and Child, 1319
Milan, Brera

The Ordination of St. Louis,
about 1326
Siena, S. Francesco

The Madonna and Child, about 1330
Siena, Pal. Pubblico

The Annunciation, 1344
Siena, Pin.

The Effects of Good and Bad
Government on the Town and on
the Country, 1337-39
Siena, Pal. Pubblico

See also pages 177, 178

The Birth of the Virgin, 1342
Siena, Mus. dell'Opera del Duomo

PIETRO LORENZETTI

about 1280-1348

A fresco painter who fell under the influence of Giotto

Little is known about Pietro Lorenzetti, except that he was Ambrogio's brother, and probably older than he. It is thought that he was born in Siena about 1280, and it may be that he was working there on a picture for the Palazzo Pubblico in 1306. He studied with Duccio at the time when Simone Martini was Duccio's pupil, but he was also influenced by the dramatic and powerful style of Giovanni Pisano, who, in about 1290, was carving many of the figures on the façade of the cathedral in Siena. This influence predisposed Pietro to be receptive to the art of Giotto. He himself painted frescoes at Assisi, from which one can see the impression Giotto had made on him; his vision had become severe and monumental, while he came close to his brother Ambrogio's subtle sense of color.

Pietro Lorenzetti died in Siena, probably during the plague of 1348-49.

E. T. De Wald   Pietro Lorenzetti   Cambridge, Mass., 1930

HIS WORKS INCLUDE

Polyptych, 1320
Arezzo, S. Maria

The Altarpiece of the Carmelites, 1328
Siena, Pin.

The Madonna and Child with Angels 1340
Florence, Uffizi

Altarpiece, 1316 or 1341
Florence, Uffizi

The Madonna and Child with Angels about 1341
Cortona, Cath.

The Birth of the Virgin, 1342
Siena, Mus. dell'Opera del Duomo

See also page 180

Predella panels from the Altarpiece of the Carmelites, 1328   *Siena, Pin.*

The Madonna and Child with Saints and Donor, about 1330
Assisi, S. Francesco

The Deposition, about 1337
Assisi, S. Francesco

LORENZO LOTTO

about 1480-1556

A Venetian painter of portraits and religious works

Lorenzo Lotto was born probably in Venice about 1480. His development is obscure, his early work showing recollections of Antonello da Messina, Giorgione, and Giovanni Bellini. His roving spirit, which had taken him, when still a youth but already a painter, to Recanati, impelled him to find out everything that was happening in the field of art, both in Italy and beyond the Alps. Thus from time to time he saw the works of Raphael, Correggio, and Leonardo, and even those of Grünewald, Altdorfer, and Dürer. Out of this there emerged a fascinating, versatile and restless personality, apparently shy but with unusual depth. In his permanent exile in the provinces of the Marches, Lotto successfully avoided Titian's powerful influence. He expressed the ideas of Mannerism in an ecstasy of devotion and humanity, conveyed in bold splashes of color, dazzling reflections of light, and, later on, in the distortion of form and substance in a subtle, and surprisingly modern way.

In 1508 Lotto was working under Raphael in Rome on the Vatican apartments. From there he went to Jesi, and from 1513 to 1525 was in Venice and in Bergamo. He also made various other journeys. After a lifetime of traveling, he finally went to Loreto, where he was admitted as an oblate friar in the Santa Casa, and remained there until his death in 1556.

B. Berenson   Lorenzo Lotto   London and New York, 1955

Portrait of a Young Man, about 1510
Vienna. Kunsthist. Mus.

HIS WORKS INCLUDE

The Mystical Marriage of St. Catherine, 1523
Bergamo, S. Bernardino
Andrea Odoni, 1527
Hampton Court, Royal Coll.
The Presentation in the Temple, 1554
Loreto, Pal. Apostolico

See also pages 244, 245, 332

A Lady as Lucretia, about 1530
London, N. G.

Portrait of a Man
Milan, Brera

99

The Madonna of the Roses
Milan, Brera

HIS WORKS INCLUDE

The Madonna and Child
with Saints, 1507
Paris, Mus. Jacquemart-André

The Passion of Christ, 1516
Milan, S. Giorgio al Palazzo

The Madonna and Child
with St. John, after 1516
London, N. G.

Frescoes (formerly in the Villa
Pelucca), about 1523
Milan, Brera

Frescoes, 1522-1524 and 1530
Milan, S. Maurizio

The Madonna and Child
with Saints and a Donor, 1526
London, Courtauld Inst. Gall.

See also pages 246, 333

BERNARDINO LUINI   about 1481/2-1532

A Lombard painter deeply affected by the stylistic revival of the early 16th century

Neither the date nor the place of Luini's birth is known, but he certainly came from Lombardy, perhaps from Milan itself. He was probably born about 1481. There is a picture dated 1507 that is attributed to him, and he was definitely active as a painter by 1512. From that time there are numerous dated works, mostly fresco cycles, in Lombardy. He died in July, 1532.

Like every other Lombard artist of his generation, Luini was profoundly influenced by Leonardo da Vinci, and this influence remained the strongest throughout his entire career. It is also possible to distinguish other elements in his style, of which the most important reflects the work of the Milanese painter Bramantino.

The Death of the Firstborn
about 1525   *Milan, Brera*

Christ among the Doctors
London, N. G.

HIS WORKS INCLUDE

Landscape with Fleeing Monks
Milan, Brera

St. Charles Borromeo Receiving the
Lay Brothers
Milan, Mus. Poldi-Pezzoli

The Refectory
Bassano, Mus. Civico

Carpenters
Venice, I. Brass Coll.

The Family of Pulcinella
New York, Kress Coll.

See also pages 293, 367, 368

ALESSANDRO MAGNASCO   1677-1749

A painter of melodramatic landscapes peopled by small figures

Alessandro Magnasco, also known as Lissandrino, was born at Genoa in 1677 and died there in 1749. He probably went to Milan at an early age, and it was there that he developed a bent for fantasy and learned a peculiarly free handling of paint that derived ultimately from Rubens. Almost all his pictures represent wild landscapes of a type similar to Salvator Rosa's, and they are nearly all populated with small and savagely gesticulating figures of friars, bandits, or beggars. He frequently collaborated with other painters. It is very difficult to attribute works to him with any certainty, since landscapes and extravagant scenes of this type have tended to be ascribed to him indiscriminately.

R. Wittkower   Art and Architecture in Italy   London, 1958

ANDREA MANTEGNA

about 1431-1506

A painter of austere frescoes who late in life painted more fanciful easel pictures

Andrea Mantegna was born the son of a carpenter in Isola di Carturo, a village of the Venetian plain, in about 1431. When he was ten years old, he was taken to Padua to the teacher Francesco Squarcione, who took him in with his boarders and enrolled him as his adopted son in the guild of Paduan painters. Andrea soon emerged as an amazing prodigy in Padua, where humanist ideas brought in by the Tuscan artists, especially by Donatello, were superseding the last traces of the International Gothic style. In addition, there was a growing fashion for archaeological learning encouraged by the Paduan University. As early as 1448 Mantegna was commissioned to paint some of the frescoes in the Ovetari Chapel in the church of the Eremitani, and his work there finally dominated the whole scheme. Except for the *Martyrdom of St. Christopher* these frescoes were destroyed in World War II. Having extricated himself with great difficulty from his association with Squarcione, he turned instead to the Bellini family and married Jacopo's daughter Niccolosa in 1454.

Portrait of Andrea Mantegna
(probably by the artist)
Mantua, S. Andrea

Mantegna's impressive power of giving the effect of depth, and his doctrinaire humanism, were gradually enriched by subtler vibrations of color. The great altarpiece in S. Zeno at Verona (1457-59) became the model for all North Italian painters who longed for novelty. Having long admired Piero della Francesca's frescoes at Ferrara, Mantegna arrived in 1460 in Mantua at the court of the Marchese Ludovico Gonzaga. Here he continued to experiment, his experience enlarged by travels in Tuscany and to Rome.

It was during this period at Mantua that Mantegna decorated the *Camera Picta*,

Samson and Delilah, about 1495
London, N. G.

Altarpiece of the Virgin and Saints, 1457-59
Verona, S. Zeno

The Ascension, about 1468
Florence, Uffizi

later called *Camera degli Sposi*, with frescoes that constitute his greatest masterpieces. They were finished in 1474. Based on his complex humanist culture, they unite the artist's austere composition, his feeling for space, and his color so refined that in smaller works it develops into over-subtle tonal gradations. Another impressive group of works, in which he gives full proof of his powers to reconstruct the ancient world, are the cartoons showing the *Triumph of Caesar*. These, originally designed for the decoration of a theater in the Gonzaga palace, are now in the Royal Collection at Hampton Court, London.

In his later years the favor of the lords of Mantua was not enough to relieve Mantegna's financial difficulties. In addition to spectacularly effective works, such as the allegorical paintings for Isabella d'Este's "little study" and the *Madonna of Victory*, he began to paint some intimate and painstakingly worked out canvases. In these the artist appears to have rediscovered secret feelings which had lain hidden beneath the heroic indifference of his unemotional style. In fact, Mantegna had always harbored a profound sense of pathos which is conveyed even through his severe manner of expression. The lesson he gave was one of the most fruitful, and all the painters of North Italy were indebted to him for his revelations, which finally freed the region from the last shackles of the International Gothic style. He died at Mantua on September 13, 1506.

P. Kristeller Andrea Mantegna London, 1901
M. Meiss Andrea Mantegna as Illuminator New York, 1957
E. Tietze-Conrat Andrea Mantegna London, 1955

HIS WORKS INCLUDE

The Story of St. James and
St. Christopher, 1448-53
Padua, Eremitani Church, Ovetari Chapel

The Madonna and Child
with Saints, about 1459
Verona, S. Zeno

The Agony in the Garden, about 1460-70
London, N. G.

The Death of the Virgin, 1464
Madrid, Prado

Frescoes, 1474
Mantua, Castello, Camera degli Sposi

The Triumph of Caesar, about 1486
Hampton Court, Royal Coll.

The Madonna of Victory, 1496
Paris, Louvre

The Dead Christ, about 1506
Milan, Brera

Isabella d'Este's Studiolo
(partly by Mantegna)
Paris, Louvre

See also pages 213, 214, 215, 315

The Martyrdom of St. Sebastian
about 1459 *Vienna Kunsthist. Mus.*

The Martyrdom of St. James, 1448-53
Padua, Eremitani Church, Ovetari Chapel (destroyed 1944)

SIMONE MARTINI

about 1284-1344

An important Sienese painter of the 14th century

Simone Martini was the pupil of the first great Sienese painter, Duccio di Buoninsegna, who influenced his style. This is apparent in the *Maestà*, which Simone
painted for the Palazzo Pubblico at Siena shortly after his master had painted an
altarpiece with the same subject for the cathedral of Siena.

In certain respects Duccio overcame the prevailing Byzantine style, but Simone

St. Louis of Toulouse Crowning
Robert of Anjou, King of
Naples, 1317
Naples, Gall. Naz.

Maestà (detail) 1315
Siena, Pal. Pubblico

Crucifixion (detail)
Antwerp, Mus. Royal des B-A.

103

Christ Discovered in the Temple, 1342
Liverpool, England, Walker Art Gall.

HIS WORKS INCLUDE

The Maestà, 1315
Siena, Pal. Pubblico

The Annunciation, 1333
Florence, Uffizi

The Deposition, about 1341
Antwerp, Mus. Royal des B.-A.

The Annunciation, about 1341
Antwerp, Mus. Royal des B.-A.

The Road to Calvary, about 1341
Paris, Louvre

See also pages 174, 175

did so to a still greater degree. The Oriental influences that he retained were of a different kind, manifesting themselves in the love of exoticism that was to become typical of the International Gothic style.

After painting the *Maestà* in Siena, Simone went to Naples, where at the French court of Robert of Anjou he came into contact with the Gothic style. At Naples, in 1317, he painted the *St. Louis of Toulouse*, and on returning to Tuscany executed a polyptych for the Church of S. Catherina at Pisa in 1319. Probably about 1321-26 he painted frescoes in the Lower Church of St. Francis at Assisi, and in 1328 he produced another masterpiece for the Palazzo Pubblico at Siena, *Guidoriccio da Fogliano*.

Simone constantly refined the elegance of his line, his rhythm of composition, and the nuances of his color. The *Annunciation* of 1333 shows his later style, although his brother-in-law and pupil, Lippo Memmi, collaborated with him in painting the saints on the side panels and the roundels above.

Simone ended his career at Avignon, where he died in 1344 while painting frescoes in the papal palace. Through painters who came to the papal court, these frescoes, which have unfortunately disappeared, had a great influence on French art, and on the formation of the International Gothic style.

G. Paccagnini Simone Martini London, 1957
E. Sandberg-Vavala Sienese Studies Florence, 1953

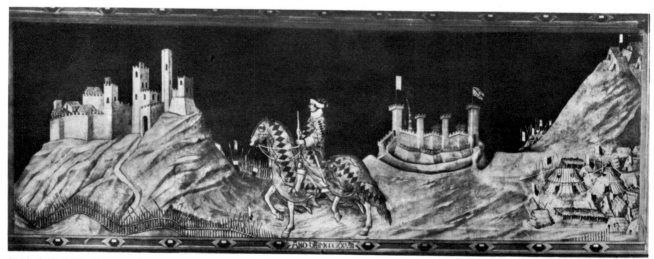

Guidoriccio da Fogliano, 1328
Siena, Pal. Pubblico

MASACCIO

The first and probably the most outstanding of the great masters of 15th-century Florence.

Son of Giovanni di Mone and Jacopa di Martinozzo, Tommaso was generally known by his nickname Masaccio, "Hulking Tom." He was born at San Giovanni Valdarno, half way between Florence and Arezzo, on December 21, 1401. His father died when he was very young, but he had a brother Giovanni, nicknamed lo Scheggia, "the Splinter," who was also a painter. Masaccio was traditionally believed to have been a pupil of Masolino, but this was not so. It is not altogether impossible, however, that Masolino, who also originated from Valdarno, did give his young fellow citizen some ideas on technique. There are no more records of Masaccio until January 7, 1422, when he enrolled at Florence in the Guild of Doctors and Apothecaries, to which painters were attached.

It is possible that Masaccio had previously studied the work of Gentile da Fabriano, yet he shows a feeling for volume and a way of coordinating his composition which are entirely original. This is true even in the earliest works ascribed to him. The fact that he was already enrolled in the Guild in Florence by 1422 is proof that a very young man could be recognized as an independent artist. Besides, he had at that time already started to collaborate with Masolino, as in the altar-

Self-portrait(?), about 1427
*Florence, S. Maria del Carmine,
Brancacci Chapel*

Adam and Eve, about 1426
*Florence, S. Maria del Carmine,
Brancacci Chapel*

The Brancacci Chapel, about 1425-28
Florence, S. Maria del Carmine

piece in the Uffizi. This partnership lasted until Masaccio's death, but he was never dependent upon his elder colleague. On February 19, 1426, he received a commission for an altarpiece for the Carmelite church at Pisa, which must have been completed by December 26th of the same year. Directly after this he succeeded Masolino in continuing the frescoes in the Brancacci Chapel of the Carmine Church at Florence. In the meantime he completed the *Trinity* fresco in the Church of S. Maria Novella. Before interrupting his work in the Brancacci Chapel he may have gone to Rome to begin other fescoes in S. Clemente; these were later continued by Masolino. Masaccio set off for Rome probably early in 1428 and died before he was 27, perhaps of the plague.

Now that modern critics have analyzed and compared Masolino and Masaccio, it appears ever more obvious that Masaccio was the true founder of Renaissance painting. He succeeded in expressing in his own art the new feeling for space that Brunelleschi and Donatello were developing in architecture and sculpture. This feeling for space also indicated a new conception of man and the importance he claimed in his own right, in an art which for centuries had seemed to be solely concerned with the mystical and abstract celebration of the divine. Masaccio is therefore outstanding for his different approach to reality. He carried out Giotto's latent suggestions, and paved the way for all future discoveries in 15th-century Florentine painting

U. Procacci   Masaccio   London, 1962

The Trinity, about 1427
Florence, S. Maria Novella

The Crucifixion, 1426
Naples, Mus. Naz.

MASO DI BANCO

active about 1325-1350

A Giottesque painter of frescoes

The life of this 14th-century Florentine painter, Maso di Banco, is obscure; indeed, he has at times been confused with Giottino. Documented information about him dates from about 1325 to 1350, and about 1341 he achieved his masterpiece in S. Croce—frescoes of the life of St Sylvester. It is also likely that he went with Giotto to Naples, and before 1332 had worked in the church at Castelnuovo there. It may therefore be assumed that he was born about 1310. Maso was one of the greatest of Giotto's pupils, and to the master's ideas of form and space he added a feeling for landscape like that of Ambrogio Lorenzetti.

MASOLINO

about 1383/4-1447

A fresco painter of the Florentine school

Tommaso di Cristoforo Fini, called Masolino, was probably born at San Giovanni Valdarno in 1383. The date of his death is tentatively put at 1447. He appears a rather complex artistic figure, not only because of the confusion which has existed over his relationship with Masaccio, but also because of the uncertain order of his paintings. According to recent opinion, his early work was in the Late Gothic tradition, and he was in touch with Masaccio in 1420-21, though the relationship was not one of master and pupil. On the contrary, it was the elder of the two, Masolino, who felt the other's influence more.

The faintly lyrical touch which distinguishes Masolino's early works changed noticeably into more ambitious expressions of space and volume. These can be seen in parts of the frescoes in the Brancacci Chapel of the Carmine church at Florence, where he worked alongside Masaccio, possibly in about 1426. Masolino painted there *Adam and Eve in the Garden of Eden* and *The Healing of the Cripple and The*

St. Peter Healing the Sick (detail)
about 1424-26
Florence, S. Maria del Carmine, Brancacci Chapel

The Feast of Herod (detail) about 1435
Castiglione d'Olona, Baptistery

The Baptism of Christ, about 1435
Castiglione d'Olona, Baptistery

Raising of Tabitha, in which Masaccio cooperated on the background architecture. In fact, here, and even more in the S. Clemente frescoes in Rome, Masolino added Masaccio's influence to his own International Gothic taste for story-telling. He imitated Masaccio's style less in the last works attributed to him, those painted after 1435 at Castiglione d'Olona in the baptistery, church, and the palace of his patron, Cardinal Branda Castiglione.

H. Lindberg   *To the Problem of Masolino and Masaccio   London, 1931*

LIPPO MEMMI

died 1356

A devoted imitator of Simone Martini

The Sienese fresco painter Lippo Memmi was the son of Memmo di Filippuccio, also a painter. Lippo became the pupil and collaborator of Simone Martini, who married his sister in 1324. His earliest known work is the *Maestà* painted in 1317 for the great hall of the Palazzo Pubblico in his home town, San Gimignano. His main period of activity, however, was between 1332 and 1351, during which he painted the fresco over the door of the convent of the Servites at Siena and a *Madonna*, now in Berlin.

MICHELANGELO

Sculptor, architect, poet, and painter

Michelangelo Buonarroti was the greatest artist of the 16th century. He was supreme as a sculptor, and as a painter and architect his achievements were at least equal to the greatest creators in these fields. In addition to this, he wrote a considerable quantity of poetry of a very high order.

Michelangelo was born in 1475 at Caprese in the Florentine state where his father was a government official. As a youth he was first apprenticed to Ghirlandaio, and it was probably in the workshop of that excellent technician that he acquired his mastery of fresco painting. Soon after this his apprenticeship was canceled, and he went to work in a sculpture studio patronized by Lorenzo de' Medici. Here Michelangelo not only worked under Bertoldo, who had been a pupil of Donatello, but, what was more important, he came into contact with Lorenzo the Magnificent and his circle.

From then on Michelangelo regarded himself as equal to the philosophers and writers who surrounded Lorenzo, and much later he even tried to suppress the fact that he had had an ordinary training as a craftsman under Ghirlandaio. Before Michelangelo, the painter or sculptor was regarded as a rather inferior craftsman, by no means equal to the poet, but Michelangelo's own life wrought such a change in the status of the artist that when he was an old man the epithet "divine" could be applied to him without shocking anyone.

ARTIST UNKNOWN
Portrait of Michelangelo (detail)
Florence, Uffizi

HIS WORKS INCLUDE

PAINTINGS

The Doni Tondo, about 1504
Florence Uffizi

Frescoes on the Ceiling of the
Sistine Chapel, 1508-12
Rome, Vatican

The Last Judgment, 1536-41
Rome, Vatican, Sistine Chapel

The Conversion of St. Paul, 1542-50
Rome, Vatican, Pauline Chapel

The Crucifixion of St. Peter, 1542-50
Rome, Vatican, Pauline Chapel

See also pages 235, 236, 237, 238, 331

SCULPTURE

Bacchus, about 1499
Florence, Mus. Naz. del Bargello

Pietà, about 1500
Rome, St. Peter's

David, 1501-4
Florence, Accad.

The Madonna, about 1504
Bruges, Cath.

Moses, about 1515
Rome, S. Pietro in Vincoli

The Rondanini Pietà, about 1564
Milan, Mus. del Castello Sforzesco

See also pages 388, 389

The Battle of the Lapiths and Centaurs, about 1493
Florence, Casa Buonarroti

St. Peter's, 1548-64
Rome

The Pietà, about 1500
Rome, St. Peter's

The Palazzo Farnese (upper section)
1546 *Rome*

Michelangelo's first great work was the *Pietà*, now in St. Peter's, which was executed during his first stay in Rome, 1496-1501. The sheer mastery of this composition at once established him as the leading sculptor of the day, when he was only 25 years old. On his return to Florence, he painted the *Doni Tondo* and began to carve a series of the twelve apostles, but the two major works of the period are the so-called *Bruges Madonna* and the gigantic marble *David*, completed in 1504. The huge marble statue of David represents Michelangelo's ideal, the heroic male nude. The subject would have been realized on an even greater scale had he ever completed the fresco which was commissioned along with one by Leonardo da Vinci for the Council Hall of the Florentine Republic. Nothing now remains of this project except a few copies of some drawings by Michelangelo himself, but, while it existed, the full scale cartoon was studied by every artist in Florence. It had an incalculable influence, its mastery of anatomy and the use of difficult and complicated poses to express temporary emotions seducing many painters of later generations into thinking that a twisted pose was in itself a form of art.

Michelangelo's reputation was so great that in 1505 Pope Julius II employed him in Rome on the grandiose tomb which he had decided to have made in his own lifetime. This originally large commission was enlarged even more by Michelangelo, who conceived a project which would have had 40 life-size figures. In fact, the *Julius Monument* became for Michelangelo the tragedy of his life. The two men were too similar in temperament, and soon quarreled, but after the death of Julius in 1513, Michelangelo was constantly under pressure from the heirs to carry out his contract, while on the other hand each successive pope wished to employ him on new and grand tasks. The tomb as it now exists was not completed until 1545 and contains only one of the figures originally designed by Michelangelo and actually executed by him. This is the huge *Moses*, which may be taken as symbolizing Julius II. Some other figures, for example, the *Slaves*, now in the Louvre, were originally designed for the tomb but were abandoned between 1508 and 1513.

Julius II took Michelangelo off the work for the tomb and commissioned him in 1508 to decorate the vault of the Sistine Chapel, which is perhaps the greatest of his achievements. He undertook it with great reluctance, and then became impatient with the traditional methods of work and the skill of the assistants he had engaged. Eventually he painted virtually the whole ceiling himself under very arduous conditions, and constantly modifying his original plans. The work not only glorifies the human body, but has profound theological implications, and is generally held to express Neo-platonic philosophical ideas. The various parts of the ceiling are subject to different systems of perspective, with the later panels apparently open to the sky. It had a profound influence on the development of ceiling painting of the illusionist type practiced in the 16th and 17th centuries.

When the ceiling was completed in 1512, it seems to have been realized generally that Michelangelo was the supreme artist of the period, and in all probability the greatest since classical times. From then until his death in 1564 he was treated with a veneration accorded to few men before or since. Nevertheless, many of his undertakings came to nothing. For the new Pope, Leo X, Michelangelo worked in Florence, where his major works are the Medici tombs in the New Sacristy of the Church of S. Lorenzo, with the symbolic figures of *Day* and *Night*, *Dawn* and *Evening*. He also built the adjoining library and wasted many years on a project for the façade of S. Lorenzo. These were his first major works in architecture, but were never completed. In 1534 Michelangelo left Florence for good.

From 1536 to 1541 he was at work on the vast fresco of *The Last Judgment* which occupies the entire altar wall of the Sistine Chapel. The spirit of *The Last Judgment* is profoundly pessimistic, and totally at variance with the ceiling. The style is also much heavier and entirely lacking in the grace and joy of the earlier work. The spiritual anguish of *The Last Judgment* is continued in the frescoes he painted in the adjoining Pauline Chapel, completed in 1550. In this and above all in his work from 1547 onwards, as architect in charge of the rebuilding of St. Peter's, may be seen the gloomy but deeply devout expression of the age of the Council of Trent. His last great statues concentrate on the theme of the *Pietà*. One intended for his own tomb is now in the cathedral in Florence in a fragmentary and mutilated state. Another, the *Rondanini Pietà*, is almost abstract, and it might be compared with a late Beethoven quartet in its complexity and depth of feeling. It was

A Slave, about 1510
Paris, Louvre

The Prisoner, about 1534
Florence, Accad.

The Virgin and Child with the Infant St. John, about 1506
London, R. A.

111

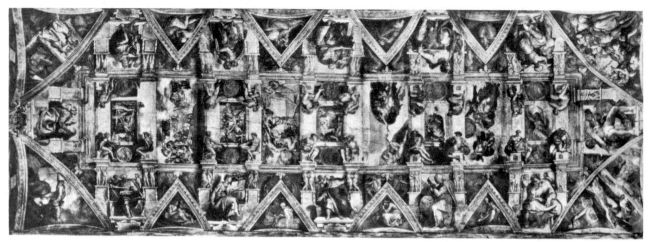

The Sistine Ceiling, 1508-12
Rome, Vatican, Sistine Chapel

M.A.B.

The Conversion of St. Paul, 1542-50
Rome, Vatican, Pauline Chapel

Jeremiah, from the Sistine Ceiling, 1508-12
Rome, Vatican, Sistine Chapel

The Last Judgment, 1536-41
Rome, Vatican, Sistine Chapel

The Capitol (detail) begun 1546
Rome

Fragment of the cartoon for
The Crucifixion of St. Peter
Naples, Mus. Naz.

The Rondanini Pietà, about 1564
Milan, Mus. del Castello Sforzesco

probably this statue on which he was working within a week of his death in his eighty-ninth year.

Michelangelo's immense importance to his contemporaries is attested by the fact that his style dominated Italian art for generations, and he was the first modern artist to have two biographies written in his own lifetime. The earlier of these, written in 1550, is included in the first edition of Vasari's "Lives" and was reprinted with extensive alterations and additions in the second edition of 1568. Between these dates came the "Life" by Michelangelo's pupil Condivi, which is to a large extent the authorized version brought out by Michelangelo himself. These early biographies help us to appreciate the astonishment with which his contemporaries regarded him, and the spell cast not only by his prodigious skill but also by his conviction that the human body is not only capable of expressing every emotion, but is the only real subject of the visual arts.

L. Goldscheider Michelangelo: painting, sculpture, architecture London, 1953
J. A. Symonds Michelangelo London, 1893
C. de Tolnay Michelangelo (5 vols.) Princeton, 1943-1960

LORENZO MONACO

about 1370/2-1422/5

A monk who painted manuscript illuminations, altarpieces, and frescoes

Although Lorenzo di Giovanni, known as Lorenzo Monaco, was born at Siena he is considered one of the most interesting representatives of Florentine painting immediately prior to Masaccio. The initial formative period in his native city, with its consequent impressions left by Simone Martini and the Lorenzetti, was followed by the influence of the Florentine painters Orcagna and Agnolo Gaddi. This enabled him to create a style of his own. At times, his work foreshadows that of Masolino and Fra Angelico. He was a monk of the Camaldolensian order from 1390. Most of his work was done in Florence and its surroundings, but records of him cease in 1422, which is probably the date of his *Adoration of the Magi*. This work shows a marked difference in his manner due to the influence of the International Gothic style, probably imported into Florence by Gentile da Fabriano.

The Adoration of the Magi,
about 1422
Florence, Uffizi

Incidents from the Life of St. Benedict
of Nursia, about 1414
London, N. G.

HIS WORKS INCLUDE

The Madonna with St. Peter
and St. Paul
Baltimore, Walters Art Gall.

The Coronation of the Virgin, 1414
Florence, Uffizi

The Coronation of the Virgin
about 1414
London, N. G.

See also page 185

PIER FRANCESCO MAZZUCCHELLI called MORAZZONE

1571-1626

The most dramatic painter of the Milanese school

Pier Francesco de' Mazzucchi or Mazzucchelli was born on August 3, 1571, at Morazzone near Venice, and was known by the nickname taken from his birthplace. He was in Rome shortly before 1592 and stayed there until about 1597, maintaining contact with the Sienese Mannerist Ventura Salimbeni and academic painters like the Cavaliere d'Arpino. He was also acquainted with the Venetian school of painting through Titian and Tintoretto, and from it derived a much more intense quality of color than that of his Lombard contemporaries. He worked in his native district and in Piedmont. Allying himself with the decorative tradition set by Gaudenzio Ferrari, he revealed an artistic temperament that was inclined both to fiery impetuosity and to the expression of pathetic sentiments. Because of this he was able to bring a greater dramatic tension into his art, which was mainly eclectic in style. He died at Piacenza in 1626, while engaged on the frescoes for the cupola of the cathedral.

HIS WORKS INCLUDE

Frescoes, 1602-12
Varallo, Sacro Monte

Jacob Wrestling with the Angel
about 1610
Milan, Arcivescovado

Scenes from the life of S. Rocco
about 1612
Borgomanero, S. Bartolommeo

See also page 274

An Italian Nobleman (detail)
London, N. G.

ALESSANDRO BONVICINO called IL MORETTO

about 1498-1554

Painter of altarpieces and distinguished portraits

Alessandro Bonvicino, called il Moretto, "little darkie," was born probably at Brescia in about 1498. He would therefore have known Vincenzo Foppa in his early adolescence. Soon afterwards he was working alongside the local artist, Floriano Ferramola. Most of his works were done for churches in his home town. He made a visit to Venice in 1544. Records show that he died in Brescia on December 22, 1554.

Moretto is one of those artists who contrived to merge Lombard and Venetian naturalism in an individual way. His light, although rather cold and metallic, contains echoes of Giorgione, and in his realism as well as his adherence to the poetry found in nature, he may be considered a forerunner of Caravaggio.

HIS WORKS INCLUDE

Count Sciarra Martinengo Cesaresco
about 1530
London, N. G.

The Adoration of the Child
Brescia, Pin. Tosio Martinengo

The Conversion of St. Paul
Milan, S. Maria presso S. Celso

Christ with the Angel
Brescia, Pin. Tosio Martinengo

Christ in the House of the Pharisee
1544
Venice, S. Maria della Pietà

See also page 261

Christ Blessing St. John the Baptist
early work   *London, N. G.*

GIOVANNI BATTISTA MORONI

about 1525-1578

A master of realistic portraiture

Very little is known about Giovanni Battista Moroni, who was born at Albino near Bergamo between 1525 and 1530, and who died on February 5, 1578. The information that does exist concerns only his paintings and his artistic training which,

HIS WORKS INCLUDE

Prioress Alardi, 1553
New York, Met. Mus.

The Unknown Poet, 1560
Brescia, Pin. Tosio Martinengo

Portrait of a Widow
Dublin, N. G.

Portrait of a Member of the Albani
Family
Bergamo, coll. Roncalli

Old Gentleman, after 1570
Bergamo, Accad. Carrara

Portrait of a Horseman, 1576
Boston, Isabella Stewart Gardner Mus.

See also page 268

Portrait of
Bernardo Spini (detail)
Bergamo, Accad. Carrara

Titian's Schoolmaster
*Washington, D. C.,
N. G., Widener Coll.*

The Tailor
London, N. G.

Portrait of a Lawyer
London, N. G.

according to one plausible tradition, he received at Brescia under Moretto's guidance. As Moroni lived in a region that was part of the Venetian Republic, he was somewhat influenced by Venetian art, but he was content to follow Lotto's naturalistic lead, rather than Titian's official one. He found his inspiration in a more strictly realistic type of painting favoured in Brescia or Cremona. Thus he became an exceptionally fine portrait painter, and in some respects heralded the advent of the great Caravaggio.

An Italian Nobleman
London, N. G.

FRANCESCO PARMIGIANINO · 1503-1540

An outstanding early Mannerist

Parmigianino, whose real name was Francesco Mazzola, was born at Parma into a family of not very important painters. He started to paint under Correggio's beneficial influence. Through it he learned how to obtain those particular shades of color which had had their origin much earlier in Ferrara. He used these in his own elegant and sensitive interpretation of Mannerism. He knew the work of

Self-portrait, about 1527
Vienna, Kunsthist. Mus.

Study for Ceiling in S. Giovanni
Evangelista, about 1522
London, B. M.

117

Cupid and Putti
Città di Castello, Pal. Mancini

The Madonna and Child with St. John
the Baptist and St. Jerome, about 1527
London, N. G.

Michelangelo and Raphael, and was acquainted, through prints, with German painting.

From 1523 Parmigianino was in Rome, but left in 1527 following the Sack of Rome. He returned to Emilia, staying first at Bologna, where he evolved an abstract and intellectual conception of form. This he developed in a polished, intellectual style that verged on the surrealistic, characterized by subtle, cool lights and the toning down of color almost to a monochrome. His figures had long necks and hands, and were placed in sinuous, graceful attitudes.

On his return to Parma, Parmigianino worked on his fresco masterpieces in the Church of S. Maria della Steccata, and in the castle at Fontanellato near by. He was an odd, turbulent character who practiced alchemy; this brought suspicion on him and he was obliged to leave the Farnese capital. He spent the last years of his short life at Casalmaggiore, where, according to the biographer Vasari, he lived in eccentric seclusion, giving way eventually to melancholic madness.

PIETRO VANNUCCI called IL PERUGINO

about 1445/50-1523

A fresco painter, who was a pupil of Piero della Francesca

Pietro Vannucci, called Il Perugino, was born in Città della Pieve near Perugia. He seems to have been a pupil of Piero della Francesca at about the same time as Signorelli, but as he wanted to learn Florentine ideas he also worked for Verrocchio. His reputation was such that he was invited to paint several frescoes in the Sistine Chapel in Rome in 1480. Some of this work was destroyed to make way for Michelangelo's *Last Judgment* but the *Christ Giving the Keys to St. Peter* is an excellent example of his calm and serene art, lucid in composition and with the figures harmoniously disposed.

The last years of the 15th century saw Perugino active both in Florence and in Perugia, and his style forms a notable contrast with the agitated manner then prevalent in Florentine circles. By about 1500, however, his art was already deteriorating into a superficial sentimentality, and his compositions became repetitive. In the very last years of the 15th century he achieved the climax of his career in frescoes at Perugia, on which he was almost certainly assisted by the young

Self-portrait, from Christ giving the Keys to St. Peter, about 1482
Rome, Vatican, Sistine Chapel

The Baptism of Christ, about 1517
Perugia, Gall. Naz. dell'Umbria

The Crucifixion, about 1480
Florence, Uffizi

Tobias and the Angel, right panel of The Virgin and Child with St. Michael and St. Raphael, about 1500 *London, N.G.*

119

The Crucifixion, 1496
Florence, S. Maria Maddalena dei Pazzi

Raphael. Raphael himself learned much from this contact, although by 1505 he
had already gone far beyond Perugino. Perugino continued to work until his death
in 1523, by which time he was regarded as long out of date.

Self-portrait
Venice, Accad.

J3 Piazetta

GIAMBATTISTA PIAZZETTA

1683-1754

A Venetian genre painter who had great influence on Tiepolo

Son of an obscure sculptor in marble and wood, the painter Giambattista Piazzetta
was born in Venice on February 13, 1683, and was initiated into his art by
Molinari, a painter who was fond of strong contrasts that took the form of dark,
shadowy *tenebroso* effects. When he was about 20 years old, Piazzetta abandoned
this provincial style to tap a much richer source, that of Giuseppe Maria Crespi in
Bologna. Although he did not abandon the interplay of contrasting light and
shadow, he enriched it with a softer color and a greater variety of tone.

Piazzetta progressed beyond the pedantic naturalism of the 17th-century Venetian painters in the modeling of form, and also evolved a greater freedom in
projecting figures apparently into open space. During the 1720's his style took on
very definite characteristics: the realistic, well-drawn heads that are typical of him
and are repeated in many of his fine drawings, and his color, which became ever
more luminous and subtle in a way that emphasized the pathos he wished to
create. Furthermore, Piazzetta managed to achieve a fully-rounded, three-dimensional quality in his forms, with the bulk of the object bathed in a clear sunny light.

In spite of his election as President of the Venetian Academy in 1750, Piazzetta
led a life of considerable hardship. He worked on his paintings with scrupulous

Cow at the Seashore,
about 1740
Cologne, Wallraf-Richartz-Mus.

The Fortune Teller
Venice, Accad.

Rebecca at the Well, about 1745
Milan, Brera

care, even repeating them several times; this was the cause of his slow production, which certainly did not help him financially. He died a poor man in 1754 in Venice, never having moved from there since his youthful period in Bologna. His family petitioned the State for a pension, claiming that "his constant studies and pursuit of glory rather than gain had reduced him to poverty and hastened his death."

Piazzetta played an important role in 18th-century Venetian painting, as it recovered from the crisis that had hindered its development in the previous century. Tiepolo found in him a starting point, for he drew his first direct inspiration from Piazzetta's fresh coloring, flooded with the light of the last glorious phase of Venetian art.

M. Levey Painting in 18th-century Venice London, 1959

HIS WORKS INCLUDE

St. James Martyr, 1717
Venice, S. Stae

The Madonna, about 1727
Venice, S. Maria della Fava

The Glory of St. Dominic
about 1727
Venice, S. Giovanni e S. Paolo

Ecstasy of St. Francis, about 1732
Vicenza, Pin.

The Assumption, 1735
Lille, Mus. des B-A.

Pastoral Scene
Chicago, Art Inst.

See also pages 294, 361

PIERO DELLA FRANCESCA   1410/20-1492

A great painter influenced by the scientific discoveries of his time

Piero della Francesca is today reckoned one of the greatest Italian painters. Comparatively little is known about him, since he worked very little in Florence and was therefore not much regarded by the Florentines themselves. He was born at Borgo San Sepolcro in the neighborhood of Siena, almost on the borders of Tuscany and Umbria. He is first recorded in 1439 when he was working with Domenico Veneziano on some frescoes, which have since perished. This was in Florence, so he may have had some early training there. It is certain that Veneziano, himself not a typical Florentine, was one of the most important influences on Piero's early development.

Sienese art was probably the most important single inspiration of the beginning of Piero's career. In his earliest works he shows a solidity of color and line that entirely disregard the dramatic representation of his Florentine contemporaries. The only interest he shared with the Florentines was perspective, and he was later

ANONYMOUS Portrait of
Piero della Francesca
Paris, Bibl. Nat.

to devote a great deal of his time to the mathematical basis of this scientific aid to representation. Indeed, at the end of his life he wrote a treatise on the subject, and another on pure mathematics.

From 1442 Piero worked in his native village, and in 1445 he was commissioned

The Legend of the True Cross, 1452-64
Arezzo, S. Francesco

St. Michael, 1454-69
London, N. G.

The Finding and Verification of the True Cross, 1452-64
Arezzo, S. Francesco

to paint a polyptych that was to be delivered in three years. In fact, the final payments were not made until 1462, and it is therefore not a certainly dateable work. This polyptych is still in Borgo San Sepolcro and has the static calm of Piero's mature works. The picture of the *Baptism of Christ* in London, with its rigid symmetry and pale bright color, shows stronger Sienese influence and is usually regarded as his earliest extant work.

In 1449 Piero is known to have painted some frescoes in Ferrara. These seem to have been the foundation of the Ferrarese school, but are no longer known. About this time he was probably also working in Urbino, where he came in contact with the architect and theorist Alberti, and where he probably also saw some Flemish paintings from which he may have learned technique. The palace at Urbino, one of the most beautiful creations of Italian Renaissance architecture, has been attributed to Piero, but there is no evidence that he ever practiced as an architect. It is certainly true, however, that the sense of interval which is so marked in the palace is also characteristic of Piero's paintings.

In 1451 Piero painted a fresco at Rimini, in the church that Alberti was then rebuilding. In the following year he began his most important surviving work—the cycle of frescoes in the Church of St. Francis at Arezzo. This cycle, now rather damaged, is undoubtedly his masterpiece, but because of its relatively obscure situation it remained almost unknown until the late 19th century. The cycle represents *The Legend of the True Cross*, and the scenes are carefully arranged to form balanced compositions on either side of the choir. In 1459 Piero was in Rome working in the Vatican, but these works are also lost. In the next few years he painted a pair of portraits of the Duke of Urbino and his Duchess, and probably in

Battista Sforza, probably about 1466
Florence, Uffizi

The Transportation of the True Cross, 1452-64
Arezzo, S. Francesco

The Resurrection, about 1463
Borgo San Sepolcro, Pin. Civica

The Madonna and Child with Saints and Federico da Montefeltro, Duke of Urbino (The Brera Madonna) about 1476 *Milan, Brera*

the 1470's a number of other works, including the altarpiece now in the Brera, Milan, which represents the Duke of Urbino as donor. This altarpiece may be dated about 1476, and is precisely contemporary with altarpieces by Giovanni Bellini and Antonello da Messina that tackled the same problem—the representation of picture space as a continuation of the church which housed the altarpiece.

Piero's last years are somewhat mysterious. He died in 1492, but seems to have ceased to paint in about 1480, his last important work being the unfinished *Nativity* in London. In his last years he seems to have devoted himself to his treatises on mathematics and on perspective, and it is probable that he died blind. The simplicity and calm of his compositions, together with his pale flat colors and the immobility of his figures, have caused his work to be greatly appreciated in modern times, although these qualities were precisely the opposite to those striven for by most of his contemporaries. Piero's pupils included Perugino and Signorelli, both of whom soon abandoned his principles and adapted themselves to a more Florentine taste.

K. Clark Piero della Francesca London, 1951

The Nativity, about 1475
London, N. G.

The Nativity (detail) about 1475
London, N. G.

PIETRO DA CORTONA   1596-1669

A painter and architect

Pietro Berrettini, called da Cortona from his birth place, was a decorative painter of great repute who had a very considerable following during the 17th century. Having received his first education in his native Tuscany, he arrived in Rome in

The Dome, 1647-51
Rome, S. Maria in Vallicella

Allegory of Divine Providence and
Barberini Power, 1633-39
Rome, Pal. Barberini

HIS WORKS INCLUDE

The Triumph of Bacchus, about 1652
Rome, Gall. Capitolina

Allegory of Divine Providence
and Barberini Power, 1633-39
Rome, Pal. Barberini

Frescoes, finished 1647
Florence, Pal. Pitti

See also page 285

1612, and was deeply impressed by the work of the Carracci family. He also had a great admiration for Titian, which enlivened and enriched his color.

Through the decorative works of Agostino Carracci's pupil, Lanfranco, Pietro found his way back to Correggio, and from this point he began to develop a scenic style of painting, with bold illusionist perspective and a strong sense of form and movement derived from his contemporary Rubens.

Pietro's patron was Pope Urban VIII of the Barberini family, who secured for him important commissions. These included his masterpiece, the huge fresco representing an allegory of *Divine Providence and Barberini Power*, painted on a ceiling in the Barberini Palace in Rome between 1633 and 1639. He visited Venice, and worked for a long time in Florence on a series of similar frescoes, before returning to Rome, where he died on May 16, 1669.

Pietro da Cortona is perhaps the most typical exponent of the spectacular Baroque style in decorative painting. He was extremely skillful, and possessed a rare pictorial fluency, achieving his most powerful effects with vibrant colors and daring composition.

E. Waterhouse Italian Baroque Painting London, 1962
R. Wittkower Art and Architecture in Italy, 1600-1750 London, 1958

Sala della Stufa (detail) about 1637
Florence, Pal. Pitti

125

Detail from the Borgia Apartments
about 1495
Rome, Vatican

BERNARDINO PINTURICCHIO

about 1454-1513

A decorator of apartments in the Vatican

Bernardino Pinturicchio's training took place partly in the workshop of Perugino, whom he assisted on the frescoes in the Sistine Chapel in Rome in 1481 and 1482. He painted another series of frescoes in the Vatican for Pope Alexander VI which although accomplished show the fundamental frivolity of his mind. His best known work is his fresco cycle in the library of the cathedral at Siena, showing scenes from the life of the humanist Pope, Pius II. These were painted between 1503 and 1508 and show his powers as an illustrator. He died in Siena in 1513.

C. Ricci *Pinturicchio* London, 1902
M. Phillips *Pinturicchio* London, 1908

BERNARDINVS.

HIS WORKS INCLUDE

Frescoes of the Borgia Apartments
about 1495
Rome, Vatican
Scenes from the Life of Pope Pius II,
1503-8
Siena, Cath.

See also page 324

Scenes from The Odyssey, about 1509
London, N. G.

126

GIOVANNI BATTISTA PIRANESI   1720-1778

An artist who recorded Roman antiquities

Piranesi was a practicing architect but is best known as one of the greatest of all etchers. He was born in 1720 at Moiano di Mestre near Venice, but he went to Rome at the age of 20 and lived there until his death in 1778. It was the experience of seeing the great Roman ruins that determined his choice of career, and from 1745 he began the great series of views of Rome for which he is famous, 137 in all. He was a bitter opponent of the idea that Greek architecture was better than Roman. The strict delineation of the antique ruins gave his prints an authenticity that made them immensely popular, but at the same time the views are colored by a touch of romantic fantasy. His work was especially popular among English visitors. The series of imaginary prisons, the *Carceri d'Invenzione*, shows his romantic bent most clearly.

A. Hind G. B. Piranesi London, 1922
A. H. Mayor G. B. Piranesi New York, 1952
T. H. Thomas G. B. Piranesi London, 1960

HIS WORKS INCLUDE
Views of Ancient Rome, 1745-65
The Prisons, 1745-61
Views of Rome, 1770-78
London, B.M.

See also page 366

The column of Marcus Aurelius, Rome
London, British Museum

Hadrian's Villa, Tivoli
London, B. M.

Ancient sepulchre (la Conocchia), Rome
London, British Museum

Self-portrait
Florence, Mus. Naz. del Bargello

Portrait of Margherita Gonzaga,
about 1438
Paris, Louvre

HIS WORKS INCLUDE

The Madonna with the Quail
about 1420
Verona, Mus. di Castelvecchio

The Annunciation, 1423
Verona, S. Fermo Maggiore

St. George and the Princess, 1433-38
Verona, S. Anastasia

The Vision of St. Eustace, about 1438
London, N. G.

Lionello d'Este, about 1441
Bergamo, Accad. Carrara

See also pages 190, 307

PISANELLO
probably 1395 - about 1455

An artist famous for his portrait medallions

The successor of Gentile da Fabriano, Antonio Pisano, known as Pisanello, was born in or before 1395, probably at Pisa. His mother was from Verona and re-married twice after her first husband died, returning to her native city at the beginning of the 15th century. Thus Antonio grew up in the artistic surroundings of Verona. Soon after 1415 he was invited to take part (with Gentile da Fabriano) in decorating the Greater Council Chamber of the Venetian Ducal Palace. Gentile was largely responsible for the design, which was partly inspired by the 14th-century style of Altichiero, and also showed a tendency toward the detail and realism of International Gothic style, particularly in Pisanello's wonderful studies of animals.

Pisanello's earliest major work is *The Annunciation* of 1423. He was at Florence, perhaps with Gentile, in 1422 and 1423, at Pavia a year later, and then at Mantua. He returned to Verona in 1426, and worked in Ferrara in 1431 and in Rome in the following year. For six years he was court artist to the Lords of Ferrara, Mantua, and Milan, and acquired a unique reputation for portrait medallions. The last clear references to him reveal that he went to Alfonso of Aragon at Naples in 1449. The date of his death is established as about 1455.

Pisanello's art—from the first intermingled with Gothic elements and very sensi-tive to Northern influences—shows an interest in psychology, and an effort to pene-

The Vision of St. Eustace, about 1438
London, N. G.

The Madonna and Child with
St. George and St. Anthony Abbot
London, N. G.

trate deeply into nature, as well as a vague awareness of the fashion for archaeology that had spread from Padua. All these give Pisanello a special place of honor in the transition from the International Gothic style to the humanist era. The romantic atmosphere that seems to pervade the isolated and aristocratic world of his art is shown to perfection in *St. George and the Princess*, where with a striking boldness of line and a tendency to surrealistic coloring Pisanello achieves the heights of poetry.

G. F. Hill Pisanello London, 1905

ANDREA PISANO   about 1290-1349

A goldsmith and sculptor in bronze

Andrea, generally known as "Pisano," is more correctly called "da Pontedera," after the town where he was born, the son of a notary, Ser Ugolino. He was not related in any way to Nicola or Giovanni Pisano. Nothing is known about his training, since he was already well-known as a goldsmith when he came to Florence in 1330, and was given the commission for the first pair of Baptistery doors, which he carried out superbly. He collaborated with Giotto, adopting his balanced composition and converting it into an elegant, lyrical style.

After Giotto died, Andrea succeeded him for a short time as director of works at the cathedral. On leaving this position, he took up a similar one at Orvieto, where he died in 1349. His two sons were both sculptors, and one of them, Nino, produced some excellent work that shows increasingly close affinities with the highly elaborate French fashion in ivory carving.

J. Pope-Hennessy Italian Gothic Sculpture London, 1955

The South Doors (detail) 1330-36
Florence, Baptistery

The South Doors, 1330-36
Florence, Baptistery

HIS WORKS INCLUDE

The South Doors, 1330-36
Florence, Baptistery
The Arts, 1334-43
Florence, Cath. Campanile

See also page 374

GIOVANNI PISANO

about 1248 - after 1314

With his father, the creator of modern sculpture

Giovanni was the son of Nicola Pisano, under whom he received his early training in Pisa. The great pulpit in Siena Cathedral was the work of Nicola between 1265 and 1268, but it is known that his assistants included Giovanni as well as Arnolfo di Cambio. There has been some dispute concerning the share taken by Giovanni in this and in a fountain at Perugia, which is signed by both father and son and dated 1278. In both cases there is a marked influence from contemporary French Gothic art, and it has been suggested that Giovanni actually went to France. Certainly his work has an intense emotionalism lacking in the more classic style of his father. The pulpit at Pistoia, by Giovanni alone and completed in 1301, shows the combination of his father's style with the more emotional Gothic manner.

Giovanni also practiced as an architect, working on the façade of Siena Cathedral from 1284 to 1296. The sculpture that he executed in Siena is of great importance in the development of Sienese painting, while the *Madonna* which he made for the Arena Chapel at Padua has a marked similarity to the monumental art of Giotto, whose frescoes in the chapel are contemporary with it. Giovanni Pisano's great masterpiece is the pulpit in Pisa Cathedral, commissioned in 1302 and signed and dated 1311, with a curious inscription that seems to be a long string of complaints about the difficulties experienced in the course of the work. Giovanni is last recorded in 1314.

J. Pope-Hennessy   Italian Gothic Sculpture   London, 1955

The Madonna and Child, about 1305
Padua, Arena Chapel

Pulpit, 1311
Pisa, Cath.

Pulpit (detail) 1311
Pisa, Cath.

Pulpit, 1297-1301
Pistoia, S. Andrea

The Fonte Maggiore (detail) 1278
Perugia

NICOLA PISANO   about 1220/5 - probably 1284

The artist who has provided much inspiration for modern sculpture

Nicola Pisano, the father of Giovanni Pisano, is one of the most important of 13th-century artists, since he revived the forms of Greco-Roman classicism many years before Cavallini and Giotto introduced similar motives in painting. Nicola's origins are obscure and neither the date nor the place of his birth are known. The name Pisano certainly implies that he was born in Pisa, but there is considerable evidence for the belief that he was born in Apulia in southern Italy in about 1220. This would certainly account for the fact that the earliest deliberate revival of Roman art took place under Emperor Frederick II, partly from political motives, in the south of Italy.

Nicola Pisano must have been in Pisa before 1260, since his great pulpit in the baptistery there is signed and dated 1260. This is his masterpiece and shows very clearly how he used the forms of classicism in preference to the more slender and remote figures characteristic of northern art. In turn these had great influence on the work of his son. Giovanni worked with him between 1265 and 1268 on a pulpit for Siena Cathedral. Other works by Nicola are known, and he again collaborated with his son on the great fountain outside the cathedral at Perugia. He seems also to have been active as an architect, in which once more his son followed his lead. Arnolfo di Cambio was Nicola's pupil both in sculpture and in architecture. The date of Nicola's death is not certain, but was probably in 1284.

G. H. and E. R. Crichton *Nicola Pisano and the Revival of Sculpture* Cambridge, *1938*
J. Pope-Hennessy *Italian Gothic Sculpture* London, *1955*

Massacre of the Innocents, from the Pulpit, 1265-68
Siena, Cath.

131

Geometry, from the tomb of
Pope Sixtus IV, 1493
Rome, St. Peter's

HIS WORKS INCLUDE

Dance of Nudes
Arcetri, Torre del Gallo
David
West Berlin, Staatl. Mus.
Woman in Profile
Milan, Mus. Poldi Pezzoli
The Rape of Deianira
New Haven, Conn., Yale Univ. Art Gall.
The Martyrdom of St. Sebastian
about 1475
London, N. G.

See also pages 216, 313, 383

ANTONIO POLLAIUOLO

about 1432-1498

An artist noted as a draftsman and anatomist

Antonio Pollaiuolo and his younger brother, Piero, were versatile artists and craftsmen who ran one of the most successful workshops in late 15th-century Florence. Antonio was born in very humble circumstances in Florence between 1426 and 1433, the son of Jacopo Benci. At first he worked as a goldsmith, assisted by his brother, who was often also his competent collaborator as a painter. Antonio made his greatest reputation in painting and sculpture, to which he brought entirely personal and original qualities. The example of Donatello inspired him with an enthusiasm for expressing movement, from which he evolved a style of tension and violent action. At the same time Pollaiuolo gave prominence to contour lines, in order to express energy, though not allowing this to detract from the elaborate refinement of form that he had also acquired during his initial development. He was therefore one of the most typical representatives of 15th-century Florentine humanism, bringing to his art a natural good taste, a refined culture, and an inborn elegance.

As a painter Pollaiuolo certainly studied Andrea del Castagno's work with great interest, and this familiarized him with the current tendency to emphasize the three-dimensional quality of form to its fullest extent. With Andrea this tended to peter out on the level of dramatic pathos, but Antonio developed it, showing to advantage his extraordinary skill in drawing, by which he could convey the idea of substance by contour alone.

Pollaiuolo worked for the Medici family, executing the pictures showing the *Labours of Hercules*. He undertook a variety of commissions for Florentine churches, and finally went to Rome to carry out some sculptural works. There he died, two years after his brother Piero, and was buried in the Church of S. Pietro in Vincoli.

Hercules Slaying Hydra
Florence, Uffizi

The Battle of Nude Warriors
Florence, Uffizi

Attrib. to Piero and
Antonio Pollaiuolo
Apollo and Daphne
London, N. G.

JACOPO CARUCCI DA PONTORMO 1494-1556

One of the greatest Tuscan Mannerists

Jacopo Carucci was born at Pontormo near Empoli, and went to Florence as a child. There he was a pupil of Andrea del Sarto from 1512 to 1515.

Pontormo was an early exponent of the style known as Mannerism. This resulted from the reaction of artists against the rules that had been deduced from classical art and established during the Renaissance. Feelings of futility were expressed in their paintings by exaggerations that contorted the attitudes and lent affected expressions to the features. Pontormo's *Deposition from the Cross*, in its theatrical atmosphere, the paganism of the youthful figures, and the involved disposition of the forms, demonstrates this style. The drawing in this work shows the influence of Michelangelo.

As a portraitist, Pontormo was a subtle draftsman with pen or chalk. His talent also extended to decoration, as attested by his work in the villa at Poggio a Caiano in 1521. His most original works are frescoes in the Medici Villa at Careggi.

Pontormo made early contact with the Medici when he painted a *Madonna*,

The Holy Family and Saints, 1518
Florence, S. Michele Visdomini

Joseph in Egypt, about 1519
London, N. G.

The Deposition, about 1528
Florence, S. Felicita

133

which was one of the first Mannerist pictures. He continued to work for the Medici at intervals throughout his life. Not much is known of the work of his later years, which were overshadowed by increasing pessimism and neurosis.

F. Mortimer Clapp Jacopo Carucci da Pontormo *New Haven, 1916*
S. J. Freedberg Painting in the High Renaissance in Rome and Florence *Cambridge, Mass., 1961*

Decorative fresco, 1521
Poggio a Caiano, Villa Medici

JACOPO DELLA QUERCIA 1371/74-1438

The most important Sienese artist of his time

Jacopo della Quercia was born the son of a sculptor in Siena between 1371 and 1374. The first work attributed to him is the *Tomb of Ilaria del Carretto* at Lucca. This has traditionally been dated 1406, but it was more probably made somewhat later. It is now in a fragmentary state, but it seems to show that della Quercia was aware of northern European sculpture. Before this he had taken part in the competition for the second Baptistery doors in Florence, but his entry is now lost.

Between 1408 and 1419 Jacopo was in Siena working on a public fountain that now exists, in a dismembered state, in the Palazzo Pubblico there. The graceful figures from this fountain have a classical quality that sets them apart from contemporary Sienese sculpture. Jacopo was always a slow worker, and his other work for the Baptistery of Siena Cathedral was so delayed that the commission for a *Salome* was taken away from him and given to Donatello. From 1425 almost until his death in 1438 he worked on the reliefs for the doorway of S. Petronio in Bologna, but these were left unfinished at his death. They have a pure solemnity that perhaps owed something to Donatello. These reliefs make della Quercia the forerunner of Michelangelo.

J. Pope-Hennessy Italian Gothic Sculpture *London, 1955*

RAPHAEL

The youngest of the three greatest artists of the Renaissance

Raphael was the son of a local painter of Urbino, who probably lived just long enough to give his son a first grounding as a painter. There is a fresco of the *Madonna and Child* in a house at Urbino that is traditionally regarded as a very early work by Raphael but it may in fact be by his father, who died in 1494. The next years of Raphael's life are obscure. He is first documented in 1500 when he received a part share in a commission for a picture now lost. By this time he had almost certainly worked with Perugino on the frescoes in Perugia, and although he was only 17 his style seems already to have been in advance of Perugino's art.

Two early works, which probably date from 1500 or very shortly after, are the large *Crucifixion* and tiny *Knight's Dream*, both in London. The first signed and dated picture by him is *The Marriage of the Virgin* of 1504. This picture shows that at the age of 21 Raphael was still profoundly influenced by Perugino, although already a more subtle artist. The next few years mark the first of the decisive changes in Raphael's style. This was due to his stay in Florence, where he at once realized that Florentine art under the leadership of Leonardo and Michelangelo was something entirely different from that produced in a provincial backwater like Perugia. For the next three or four years Raphael set himself to learn everything he could from the Florentines, and there is a series of Madonnas which documents his progress. The influence of Michelangelo is particularly noticeable in the *Deposition* of 1507. Michelangelo's influence at that time and again about

Self-portrait, about 1506
Florence, Uffizi

HIS WORKS INCLUDE

The Crucifixion, about 1500
London, N. G.

The Knight's Dream, about 1500
London, N. G.

The Three Graces, about 1500
Chantilly, Mus. Condé

The Marriage of the Virgin, 1504
Milan, Brera

The Madonna of the Goldfinch, 1506
Florence, Uffizi

The Deposition, 1507
Rome, Gall. Borghese

La Belle Jardinière, 1507
Paris, Louvre

The Stanze, 1509-15
Rome, Vatican

A Cardinal, about 1511
Madrid, Prado

Pope Julius II, 1512
Florence, Uffizi

Baldassare Castiglione, 1519
Paris, Louvre

St. Cecilia, about 1516
Bologna, Pin.

Loggia, about 1516
Rome, Villa Farnesina

The Sistine Madonna
Dresden, Gemäldegal.

Leo X and Two Cardinals, 1518
Florence, Uffizi

The Transfiguration, about 1520
Rome, Vatican, Pin.

See also pages 247, 248, 249, 250, 251, 334, 335, 336, 337

Angelo Doni, about 1504
Florence, Pal. Pitti

St. Catherine of Alexandria
London, N. G.

135

The School of Athens, 1509-12
Rome, Vatican, Stanza della Segnatura

The Disputà, *or* Disputation Concerning the Blessed Sacrament, about 1509
Rome, Vatican, Stanza della Segnatura

The Ansidei Madonna, about 1506
London, N. G.

Parnassus, 1509-12
Rome, Vatican, Stanza della Segnatura

The Miracle of the Mass at Bolsena (detail) 1511-14
Rome, Vatican, Stanza d'Eliodoro

The Expulsion of Heliodorus (detail)
about 1511
Rome, Vatican, Stanza d'Eliodoro

The Crucifixion, about 1500
London, N.G.

six years later was only temporary, since it is evident that Raphael realized that he could not compete with Michelangelo on his own ground.

The *Cowper Madonna* in Washington is signed and dated 1508, and is probably the last picture Raphael painted in Florence, since he is known to have been in Rome early in January, 1509, where he remained until his early death in 1520. The journey to Rome was his reward for the years of apprenticeship in Florence. The hitherto obscure provincial painter was given the splendid commission for the frescoes in four state rooms of the Vatican, known as the Stanze. Pope Julius II was the most enlightened patron of the age, and must have detected Raphael's powers, since the commission placed him on a level with Michelangelo, then working in the Sistine Chapel. The last twelve years of Raphael's life saw the full development of his style and can be taken to typify the High Renaissance in Rome. The earlier frescoes in the Stanze, such as the *School of Athens* and the so-called *Disputà*, are perhaps the most characteristic examples of a fully classical style.

The later works vary slightly, as Raphael began to employ large numbers of assistants to get through the enormous commissions that constantly showered on him. It is also true that his own style in his last works seems to have altered. This may be seen in some of the later frescoes such as the *Liberation of St. Peter* and the *Expulsion of Heliodorus*, both of which are richer in color and far more dramatic in feeling than the earlier frescoes.

From 1515 to 1516 Raphael was employed on a series of designs for tapestries to hang in the Sistine Chapel. Seven of the original cartoons still exist, and ten tapestries are in the Vatican. Some of these are calm and classical in design, in a style similar to that of the earlier frescoes, but in one or two cases the figures are represented in violent action and somewhat crowded together. This tendency toward violent muscular contractions and slightly theatrical gestures is one of the hallmarks of the style known as Mannerism, which derives at least partly from Michelangelo.

Galatea, 1511
Rome, Villa Farnesina

Ceiling of the Stanza della Segnatura
about 1509   *Rome, Vatican*

The Deposition, 1507
Rome, Gall. Borghese

Whether Raphael was also one of the creators of the Mannerist style is a question still much debated. The principal evidence for it is to be found in his last major work, the altarpiece of *The Transfiguration*, now in the Vatican. Cardinal Giulio de' Medici, later Pope Clement VII, was Bishop of Narbonne in France, and commissioned two very large altarpieces for his cathedral there. One was the *Raising of Lazarus* by Sebastiano del Piombo, and the other was Raphael's *Transfiguration*, which was left unfinished at his death. There can be no doubt that to some extent contemporaries regarded Sebastiano as Michelangelo's creature, and the commission was therefore a direct confrontation of the two greatest living artists, who were known to be personally antipathetic. It seems possible therefore that Raphael was deliberately challenging Michelangelo and that the rather melodramatic quality of *The Transfiguration* and similar later works must be due to Raphael himself. For many years critics have tended to play down Raphael's last works, and to stress that *The Transfiguration* was unfinished at his death, and was completed by Giulio Romano and others. This explanation overlooks the fact that Raphael must have been responsible for the basic design, representing a boy possessed by a devil. These elements in his style were taken up and developed into a fully Mannerist art by Giulio Romano. As Raphael died at 37 it is impossible to say whether he would have developed further along the same lines. It was the classical aspect of his style that was revived by the Carracci at the beginning of the 17th century, and by the Neoclassic artists of the early 18th century.

St. Cecilia, about 1516
Bologna, Pin.

O. Fischel Raphael London, 1948
U. Middeldorf Raphael's Drawings New York, 1949
A. P. Oppé Raphael London, 1909
W. E. Suida Raphael London, 1941

The Transfiguration, about 1520
Rome, Vatican

The Miraculous Draught of Fishes (detail) 1515
London, V. and A.

The Veiled Woman
Florence, Pal. Pitti

SIMONE CANTARINI
Portrait of Guido Reni, about 1640
Bologna, Pin.

HIS WORKS INCLUDE

The Annunciation, 1610
Rome, Quirinale Pal.

Pietà, 1613
Bologna, Pin.

Atalanta and Hippomene, about 1620
Naples, Mus. Naz.

Self-portrait, about 1630
Florence, Uffizi

Cleopatra, 1638-39
Florence, Pal. Pitti

St. John the Baptist in the Desert
1640-42
London, Dulwich College Art Gall.

See also pages 281, 359

A painter important to the development of the Baroque style

Guido Reni was born near Bologna, where he worked as a pupil of the Flemish painter Calvaert until 1593. In about 1593 he moved into the Carracci academy. He followed Annibale Carracci to Rome, together with his fellow pupil Albani, and worked there between periods in Bologna, where he ran one of the largest and most famous workshops for the production of altarpieces.

In his early days Reni had been influenced by Caravaggio. His close imitations of that master's strong effects of light and shade and realistic presentation led to threats of murder, so that he reverted to a tamer and more sentimental style. He was a gambler, and his enormous production was necessary to pay off his heavy losses. His best work in Rome is the ceiling fresco of the *Aurora*, painted about 1613/14, in the Casino Rospigliosi. This makes no attempt to create the effect of illusionism, as did Guercino's contemporary fresco of the same subject. After his initial essay in Caravaggism, Reni settled down to a style based upon the antique, and such models of classical perfection as Raphael. This enabled him to produce paintings of great serenity, but they are marred by an affected sentiment and the mannered and artificial nature of the gestures and facial expressions.

E. Waterhouse   Italian Baroque Painting   London, 1962
R. Wittkower   Art and Architecture in Italy, 1600-1750   London, 1958

Aurora, 1613/14
Rome, Casino Rospigliosi

Lot and his Daughters Leaving Sodom
London, N. G.

MARCO RICCI

1676-1730

MR

A romantic landscape painter

Marco Ricci was born at Belluno in June, 1676, the son of a landscape painter, Girolamo. He was the nephew of the artist Sebastiano Ricci, under whom he received his training as a painter in Venice. Marco Ricci's was a brilliant but somewhat stormy temperament, and after wounding a rival in a brawl, he was forced to flee to Split for four years.

There followed a period when he probably collaborated with Magnasco, or was at least influenced by him. Later on, in about 1710 and 1714, he twice visited England. This experience fostered his interest in landscape, as well as a romantic tendency derived perhaps from Salvator Rosa and Magnasco. However, his uncle Sebastiano's good influence gave his work a solidity and strength, both in color and composition.

Toward the end of his life Ricci executed a series of tempera paintings on leather, that were bought by the English Consul in Venice, Joseph Smith, and later passed to the Royal Collection at Windsor Castle. One important group of his drawings may be found in the Bassano Museum. The artist's violent nature led him first to crime and then probably to suicide, in Venice on January 21, 1730.

HIS WORKS INCLUDE

Landscape with Waterfall
Venice, Accad.

The Miracle of Moses
(in collaboration with
Sebastiano Ricci)
Venice, SS. Cosmas e Damiano

Ruins
Vicenza, Gall.

See also page 360

LUCA DELLA ROBBIA

1399/1400-1482

The founder of a flourishing business in colored terracotta

Luca della Robbia is famous for the invention of glazed and painted terracotta. After his death this invention was exploited by his nephew Andrea and other members of the family, but Luca himself was originally more famous as a sculptor in marble.

Luca was born at Florence in 1399 or 1400 and died there in 1482. His first great

A Child, 1466
Florence, Spedale degli Innocenti

Cantoria, 1431-38
Florence, Mus. dell'Opera del Duomo

HIS WORKS INCLUDE

Cantoria, 1431-38
Florence, Mus. dell'Opera del Duomo

Reliefs, about 1439
Florence, Campanile

The Sacristy Door, about 1447
Florence, Cath.

See also page 382

St. Mathias, about 1440-50
Florence, S. Croce, Pazzi Chapel

work was the cantoria or musicians' gallery in Florence Cathedral, the commission for which was given to him in 1431. The work, completed in 1438, was a pendant to the gallery of Donatello. Both are now reconstructed in the cathedral museum. The reliefs of music-making angels on the cantoria are gay and charming but at the same time have a classical solidity of structure; this work is the foundation of Luca's fame. His works in blue and white terracotta are very numerous and are mostly of a simple devotional type, which was continued by the later members of the studio.

J. Pope-Hennessy   Italian Renaissance Sculpture   London, 1958

Attrib. to Ercole Roberti
The Last Supper
London, N. G.

HIS WORKS INCLUDE

September, 1470
Ferrara, Pal. Schifanoia

The Altarpiece of S. Lazzaro
about 1475
West Berlin, Staatl. Mus.

The Madonna and Child with Saints
about 1481
Milan, Brera

Pietà
Liverpool, England, Walker Art Gall.

The Ascent to Calvary, about 1481
Dresden, Gemäldegal.

See also page 224

ERCOLE ROBERTI

about 1450-1496

A pupil of Francesco del Cossa, best known for his altarpieces

Ercole Roberti was probably born in about 1450. It is known for certain that in about 1470 Ercole was working in the Schifanoia Palace at Ferrara, probably as Francesco del Cossa's assistant. He joined his master at Bologna in 1475. After that, his activities alternated between the two cities, except for a period in Venice and Mantua, in 1489 and 1490. In 1486 Ercole succeeded the then elderly Cosimo Tura as court painter to the Este family. He also turned his attention to architecture, producing plans for the projected Church of S. Maria in Vado at Ferrara for Biagio Rossetti.

Ercole Roberti drew his first inspiration from Cosimo Tura, though he also followed Francesco del Cossa. However, he succeeded in interpreting the ideas of Piero della Francesca, as well as those of Antonello da Messina and the Venetians, in a personal way, merging them in a vision of intensely vibrant color and soft flickers of light. This personal style is easily recognized by its deep pathos and its sensibility. Ercole's experiments in 15th-century Ferrara ended on a note that was still romantic.

B. Nicolson   The Painters of Ferrara   London, 1951

The Israelites
Gathering Manna
London, N. G.

GIULIO PIPPI called GIULIO ROMANO   about 1492-1546

A pupil and heir of Raphael

Giulio Pippi called Romano was, as his name implies, a painter from Rome. He was a very precocious assistant to Raphael on the Vatican frescoes. It seems certain that Giulio executed a considerable part of the later frescoes under Raphael's general supervision, and it was Giulio who was Raphael's artistic executor in 1520.

Giulio died in Mantua in 1546, and the records of the hospital imply that he had been born in 1499. This would make him so youthful when he was working with Raphael, however, that it is more probable that he was born about 1492.

Giulio left Rome rather hastily before the Sack in 1527 and spent the rest of his life working for the Gonzaga Duke of Mantua. His greatest work was the building and decoration of the Palazzo del Tè just outside Mantua, which both in its architecture and in its painting is one of the first masterpieces of the Mannerist style. The *Hall of Giants* in the Palazzo del Tè is technically extremely accomplished, but is marred by the brutal melodrama which underlies many of Giulio's works.

F. Hartt   Giulio Romano   Yale, 1958

HIS WORKS INCLUDE
The Martyrdom of St. Stephen
about 1523
Genoa, S. Stefano
Frescoes of the Stanza of Constantine
1524
Rome, Vatican
The Hall of Giants, 1532-34
Mantua, Pal. del Tè

See also page 345

Julius Roma.

Ceiling of the Hall of Giants, 1532-34
Mantua, Pal. del Tè

The Hall of Giants (detail) 1532-34
Mantua, Pal. del Tè

SALVATOR ROSA   1615-1673

A spirited romantic painter

Rosa was one of the most dashing and versatile artists of his century, a painter, poet, musician, and writer of comedies. Many romantic stories have been told about him and he has even been described as a professional bandit, although there appears to be an element of exaggeration in this. He was born near Naples and was largely self-taught. His favorite subjects were battle pieces, tempests, and romantic landscapes. He also painted a few more conventional religious pictures.

HIS WORKS INCLUDE
The Martyrdom of St. Cosmas and
St. Damian, about 1661
Rome, S. Giovanni dei Fiorentini
The Virgin of Intercession
Milan, Brera
Seascape
Florence, Uffizi
Sea-battle
Florence, Pal. Pitti

See also page 287

143

Self-portrait (detail) about 1640
London, N. G.

Landscape with a Hermit
Liverpool, England, Walker of Art Gall.

Rosa worked in Rome and also at Viterbo and Florence, but he settled finally in Rome and died there in 1673. His Arcadian landscapes were much admired in the 18th century, particularly in England, where he had a great influence on the idea of the picturesque.

E. Waterhouse   *Italian Baroque Painting*   London, 1962
R. Wittkower   *Art and Architecture in Italy, 1600-1750*   London, 1958

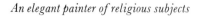

Self-portrait
London, B. M.

HIS WORKS INCLUDE

Frescoes, 1604
Siena, S. Caterina

The Martyrdom of St. Cecilia, 1607
Pisa, S. Cecilia

Angels, 1609
Pisa, Cath.

See also page 358

VENTURA SALIMBENI   about 1567 - about 1615

An elegant painter of religious subjects

Ventura Salimbeni was born at Siena in about 1567 and is a typical representative of the last phase of Mannerism in central Italian painting. He may be considered a true descendant of Domenico Beccafumi, but he also incorporated some ingredients of Federico Barocci's style in his pale, clear colors. He worked in his native town and the surrounding district, and in Rome, Pisa, Lucca, Florence, and Genoa. Salimbeni was an elegant painter, though rather lacking in warmth of feeling. His best qualities shine through in his drawings, which are more spontaneous than his paintings.

The Adoration of the Magi (detail)
London, B. M.

JACOPO TATTI called SANSOVINO

1486-1570

Architect and sculptor, who designed the Library of St. Mark

Jacopo Tatti, called Sansovino, was a Florentine architect and sculptor whose best work was done in Venice. He took his name from his master, Andrea Sansovino, who taught him sculpture and took him to Rome. There Jacopo was deeply influenced by Michelangelo and at the same time began to work as an architect in Bramante's circle.

Jacopo left Rome at the time of the Sack in 1527 and went to Venice, where he became city architect. His masterpiece is the Library of St. Mark facing the Doge's Palace. As a sculptor he continued in Venice in a style comparable to that of Tintoretto's paintings, and his best-known works are the gigantic statues of *Mars* and *Neptune* in the courtyard of the Doge's Palace. Sansovino died at a great age at Venice in 1570.

J. Pope-Hennessy Italian Renaissance Sculpture London, 1958

HIS WORKS INCLUDE

The Evangelists, 1547-56
Venice, St. Mark's

The Madonna and Child, 1562
Venice, Loggia of the Doge's Palace

Porta della Sagrestia, 1562-63
Venice, St. Mark's

See also page 391

ANDREA DEL SARTO

1486-1531

An important Florentine painter contemporary with Raphael and Michelangelo

Andrea del Sarto was born in Florence in 1486, and there he had his first lessons in the rudiments of art from a modest painter, Andrea Barile. He then studied under Piero di Cosimo, and established a partnership with his fellow pupil Franciabigio. He was little influenced by his master's art, which still belonged to the 15th century. Andrea preferred to study Leonardo, whom he was fully capable of

Portrait of a Sculptor
(detail) 1525
London, N. G.

The Madonna and Child with St. Elizabeth
and St. John the Baptist *London, N. G.*

Madonna del Sacco (detail) 1525
Florence, SS. Annunziata

appreciating, and he adopted the subtle shading of Leonardo's *sfumato* technique. He was also mindful of Raphael's harmonious composition, and of the strength of Michelangelo's forms. In his works the whole scene is always bathed in a soft light, and the sinuous line of an intellectual Mannerism can be discerned. This is chiefly apparent in his exquisite drawings.

From 1508 Andrea was a member of the Guild of Doctors and Apothecaries, to which painters were attached. In 1517 he married a beautiful widow, Lucrezia del Fede, who was often his model. Between 1518 and 1519 Andrea went to France at the invitation of Francis I. In 1530 during the siege of Florence he was commissioned to paint the portraits of the mutinous captains and traitors hanged in effigy. Andrea del Sarto died prematurely on January 22, 1531, at a time when Florence was in the grip of panic because of the plague. His death may have been due to this disease.

A. Guinness   Andrea del Sarto   London, 1899

The Last Supper, 1527
Florence, S. Salvi

SASSETTA

about 1392-1450

A great Sienese painter

One of the major painters of 15th-century Siena, Stefano di Giovanni di Consolo da Cortona, known as Sassetta, was probably born about 1392. Little is known of his life, except that he figures in the Sienese "list of painters" only after 1428, and that he married in 1440. On April 1, 1450, he died of pneumonia.

Sassetta was the most exquisite Sienese painter of the first half of the 15th century. Although he worked in the tradition of his 14th-century masters Simone Martini and the Lorenzetti, the International Gothic style is evident in his work. The best example of this, showing both his power of blending tradition and modernity and his essentially mystic nature, is the St. Francis altarpiece that he painted about 1440. Some works once attributed to Sassetta, notably an altarpiece in the church of the Osservanza, near Siena, are now thought to be by an anonymous imitator. As a result, Sassetta's own artistic personality has emerged more clearly.

The Funeral of St. Francis
London, N. G.

J. Pope-Hennessy   Sassetta   London, 1939

Attrib. to Sassetta
Heads of Angels (fragment)
London, N. G.

HIS WORKS INCLUDE

Stories of Saints, about 1426
(parts of the polyptych of the
Arte della Cana)
Siena, Pin.

The Journey of the Magi, about 1429
New York, coll. Maitland Griggs

The Madonna of the Snow, about 1432
Florence, coll. Count Contini-Bonacossi

Scenes from the Life of St. Francis
between 1437 and 1444 (parts of
the San Sepolcro Altarpiece)
London, N. G.

See also page 191

GIAN GIROLAMO SAVOLDO

about 1480 - about 1550

A pupil of Giorgione who foreshadowed the realism of Caravaggio

Gian Girolamo Savoldo was born at Brescia in about 1480, and he was received into the Painters' Guild at Florence on December 2, 1508. Little is known about his early artistic development, which may have taken place in his native town. He seems to have come from a prosperous family, and to have pursued his art without having to earn his living by it. A decisive factor in his painting was his long period in Venice, where he had settled by 1510. There are frequent references to him at Venice and at Treviso until his death in about 1550.

HIS WORKS INCLUDE

Tobias and the Angel, 1540
Rome, Gall. Borghese

The Adoration
Brescia, Pin. Tosio Martinengo

The Pesaro Altarpiece
Milan, Brera

Mary Magdalen Approaching
the Sepulchre
London, N. G.

See also pages 243, 332

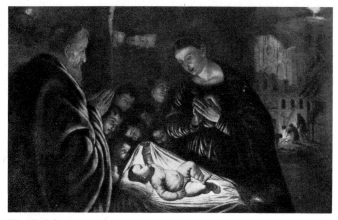

The Nativity
Milan, coll. Aldo Crespi

St. Jerome
London, N.G.

Savoldo was strongly influenced by Giorgione, but his work also displays certain similarities to the Flemish painters in his representation of light, for their naturalism had affected Lombard artists since the time of Vincenzo Foppa. In his adherence to this tradition, Savoldo was a forerunner of Caravaggio, the most vividly realistic of Italian painters.

HIS WORKS INCLUDE

St. Sebastian, about 1509
Venice, S. Bartolommeo a Rialto

Pietà, about 1517
Viterbo, Mus. Civico

Pope Clement VII, about 1532
Naples, Mus. Naz.

See also pages 252, 338

SEBASTIANO LUCIANI called DEL PIOMBO   about 1485-1547

A Venetian painter deeply influenced by Giorgione and Michelangelo

Sebastiano Luciani, called del Piombo, was born in Venice probably in 1485. He was one of the group of young men who received their first training under Giovanni Bellini, but who were far more deeply influenced by Giorgione, who was so much nearer their own age. Giorgione died young, and there is a small group of

The Raising of Lazarus, about 1519
London, N.G.

The Death of Adonis
Florence, Uffizi

148

Salome, 1510
London, N. G.

Portrait of a Lady as St. Agatha
London, N. G.

Andrea Doria, 1526
Rome, Gall. Doria

pictures that may be unfinished works by Giorgione completed by Sebastiano, or by Titian, or by both.

Early in his career Sebastiano left Venice, having absorbed Giorgione's technique. He went to Rome in 1511 and at once came under the influence of Raphael and Michelangelo. Both inspired him to give greater importance to draftsmanship. He soon quarreled with Raphael and as a result he fell more and more under the influence of Michelangelo, who actually provided him with a number of drawings for various compositions, such as *The Raising of Lazarus* and *The Flagellation*.

The nickname del Piombo derives from a sinecure in the Vatican Chancery which was given to Sebastiano in 1531. As a result he painted fewer works in his last years. Among them, however, were a number of admirable portraits in which the old Venetian feeling for color is still obvious, whereas his other works tended to be dominated by Michelangelo's ideas and many of them are not even pleasing in color.

S. J. Freedberg   Painting of the High Renaissance in Rome and Florence   Cambridge, Mass., 1961

The Flagellation, 1517-24
Rome, S. Pietro in Montorio

GIACOMO SERPOTTA   1656-1732

One of the greatest Baroque artists of Southern Italy and Sicily

Serpotta was born at Palermo in 1656 into a family of engravers and stucco workers, and very early showed an unusual aptitude for modeling. After going to Rome, he returned to Sicily, where he executed all his sculptural works, mostly in stucco. In addition to Palermo, where he left behind his real masterpieces, in the Oratorio di S. Lorenzo, he worked at Alcamo, Messina, and other places on the island. His modeling is smooth, polished, fully rounded and graceful, full of light and life. He died at Palermo in 1732.

HIS WORKS INCLUDE

Charity, 1690-96
Palermo, Oratory of S. Lorenzo
The Crucifixion
Alcamo, S. Francesco da Paola
Stucco decorations, 1710-17
Palermo, S. Domenico

See also page 396

Self-portrait, about 1503
Orvieto, Cath.

LUCA SIGNORELLI

about 1441/50-1523

One of a group of painters chosen to decorate the Sistine Chapel

Luca Signorelli was born at Cortona some time between 1441 and 1450. Vasari says he was 82 at his death, and therefore puts his birth at 1439, but he was mistaken about the date of death. Even if the mistake is corrected, changing the birth date to 1441, it is still difficult to trace the full course of his artistic development. From this point of view, it would be more expedient to put the date of his birth between 1445 and 1450. Thus it would be possible for him to have completed his early and profitable training under Piero della Francesca in nearby Borgo San Sepolcro, which, like Cortona, is situated on the borders of Tuscany and Umbria.

Piero della Francesca's influence, which can be found in Signorelli's early paintings, is especially noticeable in the carefully arranged construction of his composition and in the crystalline clarity of his colors. His work also shows important features in common with the Florentine School, such as the dramatic qualities of Andrea del Castagno and, in particular, Antonio Pollaiuolo's explosive energy, expressed by the tension in his outline.

Signorelli soon received important commissions, such as the one Pope Sixtus IV gave him in 1481 for the Sistine Chapel where he executed the *Testament of Moses*. Later he was at Loreto, Monte Oliveto Maggiore near Siena, and Orvieto, and in the meantime completed numerous Madonnas and various altarpieces. In all these his style became more and more clearly defined. He sometimes showed himself to

The Madonna and Child with Saints, 1515
London, N.G.

The Triumph of Chastity: Love Disarmed and Bound, about 1509
London, N.G.

be very observant of life around him, and he possessed the ability to catch both physical and psychological features with a frankness that could be a harsh judgment of the people whose portraits he painted. An example of this is the detail in which he portrays himself beside Fra Angelico in the chapel of S. Brizio in the cathedral at Orvieto.

Piero della Francesca's abstract yet powerful forms, when submitted to the Florentine conventions of plasticity, influenced Signorelli in distorting the human figure and exaggerating its anatomy, which he studied with almost fanatical care. Thus he is considered a kind of prophetic anticipator of Michelangelo in his work for the Sistine Chapel.

The powerful plasticity of his forms makes its greatest impact in his frescoes in Orvieto Cathedral, painted between 1499 and 1503. During the following years the artist, who lost two sons in 1502 and 1506, appeared to moderate the violence of his vision, which was also characterized by a dense color scheme. A tendency to pathos can be detected, almost a reflection of the traditional Umbrian mysticism that had reached him through the art of Perugino, or, more likely, through Raphael's great revelations.

In the last years of his life, Luca Signorelli again undertook public commissions of major importance in his home town, and was greatly respected and admired.

M. Cruttwell Signorelli London, 1899

HIS WORKS INCLUDE

The Flagellation, about 1480
Milan, Brera

The Madonna and Child with Angels and Saints, 1484
Perugia, Cath.

Frescoes, 1491-96
Loreto, Casa Santa

Scenes from the Life of St. Benedict from 1497
Monte Oliveto Maggiore, Monastery

The Holy Family, 1495-1500
Florence, Uffizi

Deeds of The Antichrist and The Last Judgment, about 1503
Orvieto, Cath.

The Madonna and Child with Saints 1508
Milan, Brera

See also pages 219, 317

GIOVANNI ANTONIO BAZZI called IL SODOMA   1477-1549

One of the best-known Sienese painters of the 16th century

Although Giovanni Antonio Bazzi, called Il Sodoma, was born at Vercelli in Piedmont in 1477, he is thought of as a Tuscan by adoption since he did most of his work at Siena. In fact, after an apprenticeship under Martino Spanzotti, he left his home town when barely 25 years of age to work in the neighborhood of Pienza. Leonardo and Raphael became the masters he idolized, and he interpreted them with a certain sweetness. However, he was not oblivious, especially in his landscape backgrounds, to the northern influences that were widespread in Italy. He continued Signorelli's frescoes in the cloister of the Monte Oliveto Maggiore Monastery, and in 1508 and 1512 he went to Rome to execute works in the Stanza della Segnatura of the Vatican and in the Villa Farnesina. He was also at San Gimignano, Pisa, Florence, Lucca, and Piombino, but he spent most of his life at Siena, where he died in 1549. Sodoma established a personal note of his own within the framework of Mannerism—immediacy and a frankly sentimental appeal. Even in the themes taken from Raphael's and Leonardo's works, he reveals the same qualities of fresh spontaneity in his numerous and excellent drawings.

H. Cust G. A. Bazzi London, 1906

The Marriage of Alexander and Roxana (detail) 1512
Rome, Villa Farnesina

HIS WORKS INCLUDE

Story of St. Benedict, about 1508
Monte Oliveto Maggiore, Monastery

The Ecstasy of St. Catherine, 1526
Siena, S. Domenico

St. Sebastian, about 1531
Florence, Pal. Pitti

The Epiphany, about 1530
Siena, S. Agostino

The Sacrific of Isaac, about 1542
Pisa, Cath.

See also page 339

An Allegory of Fame, about 1635
London, N. G.

HIS WORKS INCLUDE

The Cook
Genoa, Pal. Rosso

Altarpiece of the Deaf-mutes, 1629
Genoa, Church of the Deaf-mutes

St. Sebastian and St. Irene, after 1630
Venice, S. Benedetto

St. Lawrence Distributing Alms
New York, Kress Coll.

See also page 283

BERNARDO STROZZI — 1581-1644

A Rubenesque painter

Bernardo Strozzi was born in 1581 at Genoa, where he received a good classical education as a child, and was left an orphan at 15 years old. He devoted himself to painting, entering the order of the Capuchins in 1598. The monastic rules irked him so much that he became a priest, and got the nickname of "Il Prete Genovese." However, he always showed a certain intolerance of the priestly robe, which perhaps played its part in his reputation for romantic adventures, such as that of his arrest on September 3, 1630, and subsequent flight to Venice.

Whatever the reason for his abrupt flight, Strozzi reached Venice that year, and stayed there until his death in 1644. His artistic formation was very complex, including characteristics of extreme Mannerism, as well as the influence of Barocci, the Lombards of Cerano's school, Caravaggio and his followers, and the Flemish painters, especially Rubens. Through his lively and good-natured temperament—not without its streak of sensuality—he integrated these influences in his own way. He developed his manner in Venice, incorporating the local traditions in color.

E. Waterhouse   Italian Baroque Painting   London, 1962
R. Wittkower   Art and Architecture in Italy, 1600-1750   London, 1958

Portrait of G. B. Tiepolo from the
"Compendio delle Vite," 1762
by Alessandro Longhi
Paris, Bibl. Nat., et al.

GIOVANNI BATTISTA TIEPOLO — 1696-1770

The last of the great Venetian fresco painters

Giovanni Battista Tiepolo represents the last magnificent phase of the 18th-century grand decorative manner, and summarizes the ideals of his age: in fact, the last lingering laments for the classical culture which had been Veronese's chief source of inspiration, the Arcadian gallantry and the superficial but enchanting elegance of the Rococo, are united in his work.

Tiepolo was born in Venice in 1696, and after an indifferent training under the minor painter Gregorio Lazzarini, he drew from Piazzetta inspiration for the forms of his later work. He had already been received into the guild of Venetian painters in 1717. Two years later he married Cecilia, Francesco Guardi's sister, by whom he had nine children. Of these, Gian Domenico and Lorenzo did credit to their father as artists.

In the frescoes Tiepolo executed at Udine in 1725 and 1726 there emerged a new sense of light, which had the general effect of brightening his color. His design became looser, with violently receding figures flung from an exploding center, and his use of space seems to defy all laws of gravity. These features appear again in his frescoes painted at Milan in 1731 in the Archinti and Casati palaces, and in the Colleoni Chapel at Bergamo. Between 1735 and 1740, he also completed two huge

The Banquet of Anthony and Cleopatra
1745-50
Venice, Pal. Labia

St. Simon Stock
Milan, Brera

GIOVANNI BATTISTA and GIAN DOMENICO TIEPOLO
The Minuet, about 1754
Paris, Louvre

A Seated Man and a Girl
with a Pitcher (detail)
1750-59   *London, N. G.*

153

Henry IV of Germany at Canossa (?)
London, N.G.

paintings of biblical subjects for the parish church of Verolanuova near Brescia. Their size is their most striking feature. At this time his painting became still more airy and artificial.

Tiepolo was next occupied on large altarpieces and imposing decorative works —for instance, those done for the Palazzo Labia in Venice and the Palazzo Clerici in Milan—until he was invited to paint the frescoes in the Residenz at Würzburg in Germany. The palace itself is a superb example of German Rococo architecture, and Tiepolo wedded painting and architecture into one huge, yet airy, allegory of German history, with special reference to the prince-bishop as a patron. This work, probably his most successful, took him from 1750 to 1753. His sons Domenico and Lorenzo assisted him.

In 1756 Tiepolo was made president of the newly founded Academy in Venice. After completing the decoration of the Villa Valmarana, near Vicenza, he went to Madrid at the request of the Spanish king, taking his sons with him. The Spanish works were a swan song both for Tiepolo and for the resplendent decorative painting of the 18th century. Yet the luminous tones of his color were not forgotten by Goya, who found in this last flicker of Venetian light a starting point for his own achievements. Tiepolo died suddenly in Madrid on March 27, 1770. His sons attempted to follow their father's footsteps in religious works, Gian Domenico with considerable skill, but they were more successful in drawing and engraving. In these media, as in some of their decorative paintings, they reveal realistic and sometimes grotesque elements.

M. Levey   Painting in 18th-century Venice   London, 1959
A. Morassi   A complete Catalogue of the Paintings of G. B. Tiepolo   London, 1962

Self-portrait (detail) 1588
Paris, Louvre

JACOPO ROBUSTI called TINTORETTO   1518-1594

A Venetian painter of mythological and religious subjects

The date of Tintoretto's birth, which at one time was thought to be as early as 1512, has however been fixed at 1518; there is no doubt at all that the place was Venice. Jacopo Robusti was the son of a dyer—hence his nickname. He was already working in 1539 as a master painter, and had served his apprenticeship under Bonifacio Veronese and Andrea Schiavone, artists who because of their Mannerist tendencies must have been even more sympathetic to him than Titian. Tintoretto, because of his Mannerist inclinations, must also have studied Lorenzo Lotto with great interest, and thus drew on the provincial source which had given life to the art of Bassano and impetus to that of El Greco.

Tintoretto set himself a goal that gave rise to the tale credited by all the earlier historians: that of attempting to combine Venetian color with the drawing of the Roman and Florentine schools. It is said that he wrote on his workshop wall "The drawing of Michelangelo and the color of Titian." However, he was never a member of Titian's group, and although some of his particular problems regarding light seemed to be the logical result of lessons learned from Titian, Jacopo maintained an absolutely individual style of expression. This individuality is definitely one of his greatest virtues. He lived his whole life in Venice, leaving it for only two journeys: the first about 1545 or 1546 to Rome (this is not unanimously accepted) and the other to Mantua. Apart from these two journeys, there is little to record of his life, which ended on May 31, 1594.

There are, however, intriguing details, such as the occasion when he managed to get for himself a commission announced for public competition. He did this by impertinently painting the *S. Rocco in Glory* directly on to the ceiling in question in the Scuola di S. Rocco. Contemporary writers also describe the jealousy of Titian when faced with Tintoretto's exceptional ability. This is an indication of the great reputation he acquired even during his lifetime, which is also borne out by the importance of the commissions entrusted to him.

Even in his first experiments Tintoretto displayed an agility of composition that forecast the dramatic power he later achieved by creating tension in his use of light. This power is already apparent in *The Miracle of St. Mark*, the work that made his reputation; it then appears to slacken over a period in which he was searching for a closer unity between emotion and imagination, light and shadow. He eventually evolved an excited, turbulent style. His effects are sometimes taken to extremes, so that the lighting destroys the impression of three-dimensional form.

After the great compositions executed for the Venetian Ducal Palace, Tintoretto's chief cycle of work was done for the Scuola di S. Rocco. This kept him

Christ before Pilate, about 1566
Venice, Scuola di S. Rocco

Susannah and the Elders, 1555-60
Vienna, Kunsthist. Mus.

Portrait of a Young Man (detail)
Milan, Brera

155

Sketch for Paradise in Ducal Palace, about 1587
Paris, Louvre

occupied at various intervals between 1564 and 1587. He gradually reached the supreme sacrifice of color in the clash of flaring illumination. In these last works— and in the *Last Supper* for the Church of S. Giorgio Maggiore—Tintoretto abandoned Renaissance ideals and threw himself into the spirit of the Baroque age, in which form and movement are identified in a tumultuous outburst of the imagination.

H. Tietze   Tintoretto, the Paintings and Drawings   London, 1948

Self-portrait (detail) about 1570
Madrid, Prado

TITIANVS·F.

TITIAN   about 1485/90-1576

One of the painters who approached most nearly the ideals of the High Renaissance

Titian, whose real name was Tiziano Vecelli, was born at Pieve di Cadore in the Alpine foothills north of Venice. It was long believed that the date of his birth was 1477, and this date was established through letters which he himself wrote to his patron, Philip II of Spain, in his extreme old age. In the letters, which were written in order to obtain more rapid payment for his works, he made himself out to be increasingly old and infirm. However, the course of his career and the very early age at which an artist of his quality can be expected to develop, suggest that the date of his birth may be more reasonably fixed between 1485 and 1490. It is most unlikely that he was older than Giorgione, under whom he was working in 1508.

   Titian's first training in Venice was with a minor designer of mosaics, then with Gentile Bellini, and afterwards with Giovanni Bellini. The decisive influence, however, was that of Giorgione, with whom he worked on frescoes, now entirely lost, on the outside walls of the Palazzo Fondaco dei Tedeschi in 1508. His contact with Giorgione broadened his style, so that his forms became larger, and his treatment of light more subtle. He reflects the more generalized vision of the 16th century rather than the narrower, more detailed approach to form of the 15th century. Giorgione's early death in 1510 led to a number of his works being completed by

The Pardo Venus, about 1535-40 *Paris, Louvre*

Francis I (detail) about 1539
Paris, Louvre

Titian and Sebastiano del Piombo, and this has not only bedeviled the attributions to Giorgione, but has also obscured Titian's early development.

In 1511 Titian was working in Padua on frescoes in the Scuola del Santo. In the same year when Sebastiano del Piombo left Venice for Rome, Titian returned to Venice, where he was then the only serious rival to the aged Giovanni Bellini. In 1516 he succeeded Bellini as painter to the State. His own enormous reputation may be said to have begun with the *Assumption* painted for the Frari Church in 1516-18. The work contains a new feeling for breadth and for brilliance of color. It emphasizes dramatic movement and splendor of gesture, which excel even the grandest aspects of Bellini. In 1532 he painted a portrait of the Emperor Charles V at Bologna, which despite its being a copy of a full length portrait by the German painter Seisenegger, made so great an impact on the emperor that Titian was made court painter in 1534 and ennobled. His friendly relation with his imperial patron is paralleled only by the position held by Leonardo in the court of France, and Raphael and Michelangelo in the Vatican.

Philip II, who in 1555 succeeded Charles V as king of Spain, continued his

Portrait of a Man (detail) about 1508
London, N. G.

The Presentation of the Virgin, 1534-38
Venice, Accad.

The Emperor Charles V on
Horseback, 1548 *Madrid, Prado*

157

patronage and was the greatest collector of Titian's works. During the 1540's Titian underwent some slight influence from Michelangelo, and his only documented visit to Rome in 1545 certainly had the effect of increasing the Mannerist inclinations in his work. He tended toward a more acid color scheme and to more involved and complicated compositions. It was during the years 1547 to 1550 that he developed, chiefly as a result of his imperial patronage, the sort of portrait —noble, simple, and direct—which became the very type of the Grand Manner portrait. It was later exploited by Rubens, van Dyck, and by almost every other great painter.

During his later years Titian produced a great many mythological subjects (which he himself described as "poesie"), largely for Philip II, which show the Spanish king as a collector well able to move outside the narrower confines of Counter-Reformation art. In these works Titian developed a freedom of handling that almost anticipated Impressionism in its use of patches of color and of light and shadow. At the end of his life Titian painted works which on close inspection appear to be a mass of unformed blobs, thumb marks, and brush scratches, and which at a distance reveal the most magical combinations of form and color. This strange style caused him to be accused of failing powers. It was Palma Giovane who described his method of work, saying that he regarded his paintings almost as enemies, left them for months face to the wall, and then with ruthless determination corrected, repainted, softened, and strengthened, using his fingers far more than his brush.

H. Tietze   Titian Paintings and Drawings   London, 1950
L. Venturi   Titian   New York, 1954

Bacchus and Ariadne, about 1523
London, N. G.

The Madonna and Child with St. Catherine and St. John
about 1530   *London, N. G.*

COSIMO TURA

before 1431-1495

The first great painter of Ferrara

Cosimo, colloquially called Cosmè, Tura, was the founder of the 15th-century humanist school of painting at Ferrara, even though reminiscences of the Gothic tradition lingered in his style, especially in his early work. However, he strove toward new, individual interpretations, through the influences exerted by the Paduan group, which included Mantegna and Crivelli, and through the compelling fascination of Piero della Francesca and his assistants working at Ferrara. Later, he came close to the pathos of Roger van der Weyden, though he tended to contruct his works according to a rational pattern typical of the early Renaissance. Before 1474 he went to Venice and drew from that visit the inspiration for more luminous coloring.

In his later years, after he had become court painter to the Este family and was harassed by financial difficulties because of his patron's meanness, Tura realized that the younger Francesco del Cossa and Ercole Roberti had already superseded him. He therefore tried to bring himself up to date by incorporating their themes. He died at Ferrara in 1495, having given up his position as court painter in 1486.

B. Nicolson   The Painters of Ferrara   London, 1951
E. Ruhmer   Cosimo Tura   London, 1958

HIS WORKS INCLUDE

Allegorical Figure, about 1463
London, N. G.

Pietà, about 1468
Venice, Mus. Correr

The Annunciation, 1469
Ferrara, Mus. del Duomo

St. George, 1469
Ferrara, Mus. del Duomo

The Virgin and Child Enthroned, 1474
London, N. G.

S. Maurelio, after 1480
Milan, Mus. Poldi Pezzoli

Giacomo della Masca, 1484
Modeno Gall. Estense

See also page 212

PAOLO UCCELLO

1396/7-1475

A painter of romantic fancy and narrative skill

The Florentine painter Paolo Uccello was not, as has been supposed, born at Pratovecchio, but in Florence. When he was only ten years old, Uccello was apprenticed to the sculptor Ghiberti, whose workshop was then engaged on the North Doors of the Baptistery at Florence. Possibly he was also influenced by Lorenzo Monaco, whose painting introduced him to the romantic and narrative propensities of the International Gothic style.

In 1425 Uccello went to Venice. Here he apparently spent five years working on mosaics for the façade of the Cathedral of St. Mark's. On his return to Florence he painted about 1431 the Genesis frescoes in the Chiostro Verde (Green Cloister) of S. Maria Novella. In 1436 he executed in the cathedral at Florence the *Monument to Giovanni Acuto*. Sir John Hawkwood was an English mercenary captain who had served under the Florentines, and was called by them Giovanni Acuto. After this work Uccello appears to have followed Donatello's theories about perspective, while placing great importance on outline. When he had finished cartoons for the windows of the cathedral at Florence, he visited Padua in 1445. Two new frescoes in the Chiostro Verde of S. Maria Novella, which show scenes of the Flood, belong to this period. He later painted the *Rout of San Romano*, three panels originally intended for a room in the Medici palace. His last known works, *The Hunt in a*

Self-portrait (?) (detail) 1455-65
Paris, Louvre

Forest and *The Legend of the Host*, show that he kept to an irrational, whimsical style, full of poetry, in which the humanist rules of painting were freely adapted. He was therefore considered an old-fashioned outsider by his contemporaries. He died in poverty in Florence on December 10, 1475.

J. Pope-Hennessy Paolo Uccello London, 1950

A Hunt in a Forest, about 1460
Oxford, Ashmolean

Self-portrait
(detail from the Feast in the
House of Levi), 1573
Venice, Accad.

PAOLO CALIARI called VERONESE   about 1528-1588

A painter of huge and sumptuous decorations for great palaces

The decorative painter Paolo Caliari was born about 1528 in Verona, from which his name Veronese is taken, and was taught by Antonio Badile, a local painter. The problem of his training is interesting, since he stayed in his native province until 1551 and for several years afterwards continued to keep in touch with the group at Verona. He soon developed a free handling of Mannerist techniques which he derived from Giulio Romano, Primaticcio, and in particular Parmigia-

The Marriage at Cana, about 1571
Paris, Louvre

The Family of Darius before Alexander, 1575-80
London, N. G.

The Finding of Moses
Madrid, Prado

nino. A few echoes of the Brescians Moretto and Lorenzo Lotto are also seen in his style. In addition, he aimed at rediscovering the effect of a serenely triumphant classicism.

As soon as he had settled in Venice, shortly after the mid-century, Veronese transmuted Titian's glowing fiery tones into a clear and luminous expanse of color, intensely pure, and softening into a faint iridescence. The first great cycle of paintings he undertook was the decoration of the Church of St. Sebastian in Venice. From this moment Veronese set against Tintoretto's sense of drama and Jacopo Bassano's rural realism a joyous vision extolling the beauty of life. His color sur-

The Adoration of the Magi, 1573
London, N. G.

Love Conquering Strength
Vicenzo, Villa Maser

faces seem almost to be divided into different facets as they reflect the light, and he thus anticipated the modern theory of Impressionism.

Veronese's classicism had its perfect complement in Palladio's style of architecture. The painter revealed his noblest decorative genius in the frescoes destined for the Palladian villas of the Veneto. After 1560 he painted stupendous views of the countryside for the Villa Maser, near Vicenza, built by Palladio.

When in 1573 he had completed a painting of *The Last Supper* he had to submit to a trial by the Inquisition for certain alleged liberties he had taken in placing the figures of clowns and Moors near that of Christ. He replied that painters, like poets and madmen, were sometimes entitled to take poetic licence, but changed the title to *Feast in the House of Levi*, which gave less offence. Apart from this brush with the Inquisitors, his life proceeded serenely and productively. From 1575 to 1577 he was occupied with decorating the Sala del Collegio in the Doge's Palace in Venice. He later completed a series of *Allegories* for the Emperor Rudolf II. In his last works his researches into the qualities of light became more and more apparent. He died in Venice in 1588.

Putto with a Dolphin, about 1480
Florence, Pal. del Signoria

ANDREA DEL VERROCCHIO   about 1435-1488

A great sculptor who ran a famous workshop of young painters

Andrea di Michele Cioni, called del Verrocchio from the name of the goldsmith under whom he learned his art, is known chiefly as a sculptor, above all for the equestrian monument at Venice to the memory of the *condottiere* Bartolommeo Colleoni. As a sculptor he is one of the greatest Florentine artists of the generation following Donatello. Information about his activities as a painter is more complicated and contradictory. Verrocchio ran a workshop in Florence that was extremely

Attrib. to Verrocchio
Head of an Angel   *Florence, Uffizi*

well known and through which passed Leonardo, Perugino, Botticelli, and Ghirlandaio, as well as others of lesser fame.

Andrea was born in Florence probably in 1435, though the less plausible dates of 1432 and 1436 have also been suggested. He lived almost all his life in his native city, and the strands of his biography are interwoven with information concerning his contracts. The execution of the *Baptism of Christ*, a painting destined for the Church of S. Salvi and now in the Uffizi Gallery, is placed at around 1470. In this the angel seen in profile and part of the surrounding landscape have been justifiably ascribed to Leonardo. On the other hand, Ragghianti has pointed out stylistic details that coincide convincingly with Botticelli's youthful work, so that the authorship of this painting still poses a difficult problem. What is known for

Attrib. to Verrocchio
The Madonna and Child with
Two Angels   *London, N. G.*

The Monument to Bartolommeo Colleoni,
about 1479-90   *Venice*

Giuliano de' Medici, about 1475
Washington, D.C., N.G., Mellon Coll.

163

Attrib. to Verrocchio
Tobias and the Angel (detail)
London, N. G.

certain of Verrocchio therefore pertains rather to his sculptures. In 1465 a commission for an *Incredulity of St. Thomas* was given him, in 1472 he completed the tomb of Cosimo de' Medici in S. Lorenzo in Florence, and later his *David*. In 1479 he was invited by the Republic of Venice to submit a study for the Colleoni monument, which was to be his masterpiece. Two years later he dispatched a model of the horse and himself went to Venice in 1483. Verrocchio died in 1488 leaving the monument unfinished.

Verrocchio's paintings, reduced to an extremely limited and uncertain number, are attributed to him chiefly on the basis of certain stylistic similarities to his sculptures and drawings. Nevertheless their identity is verified by things other than tradition. Their quality and spirit are the same as those which emanate from work definitely known to be his. He possessed an inspired and aristocratic naturalism, in which the humanist tradition, expert craftsmanship, and rapturous emotion were harmonized through a skillful interplay of light and shade. This softened the tension that Donatello gave to form, and graced his movement with a refined elegance. From 1470 to 1480 Verrocchio was justifiably the most fashionable and highly praised artist in the Florence of Lorenzo the Magnificent.

M. Cruttwell   Verrocchio   London, 1904
J. Pope-Hennessy   Italian Renaissance Sculpture   London, 1958

FRANCESCO ZUCCARELLI   1702-1788

A Florentine who worked in England

There are innumerable pastoral landscapes by Zuccarelli, examples of which are to be found in many public galleries in Europe and America.

See also page 363

Francesco Zuccarelli was born near Florence in 1702, and died there in 1788, but the greater part of his long life was spent in Venice and in England. He was one of the most popular landscape painters of the 18th century. He went to London in 1752 for the first time. On his second visit he was elected a founder member of the Royal Academy in 1768. His landscapes are elegant and charming, but they lack the solidity of those by his English friend, Richard Wilson. Zuccarelli is a typical Arcadian artist—his softly colored, gentle landscapes are filled with prettily pastoral scenes, in which he tends to place more importance on a vaguely rustic lyricism than on realistic details.

The Rest on the Flight into Egypt
Venice, Accad.

Landscape with Cattle and Figures
London, N. G.

CIMABUE The Virgin and Child Enthroned,
with Angels and Prophets (The Santa
Trinità Madonna) about 1285
tempera on panel 151⅞ × 87¾ in.
Florence, Uffizi

PIETRO CAVALLINI The Last Judgment - detail of St. John the Baptist, about 1293 *fresco*
Rome, S. Cecilia

DUCCIO DI BUONINSEGNA The Crucifixion - panel from the Maestà, 1308-11
tempera on panel
Siena, Museo dell'Opera del Duomo

DUCCIO DI BUONINSEGNA The Virgin and Child with Saints and Prophets,
after 1311   *tempera on panel   66⅞ × 93¼ in.*
Siena, Pinacoteca

GIOTTO The Miracle of the Spring, about 1297-1300 *fresco*
Assisi, S. Francesco

GIOTTO The Last Judgment, about 1305 *fresco*
Padua, Arena Chapel

GIOTTO   The Annunciation to St. Anne, about 1305   *fresco*
Padua, Arena Chapel

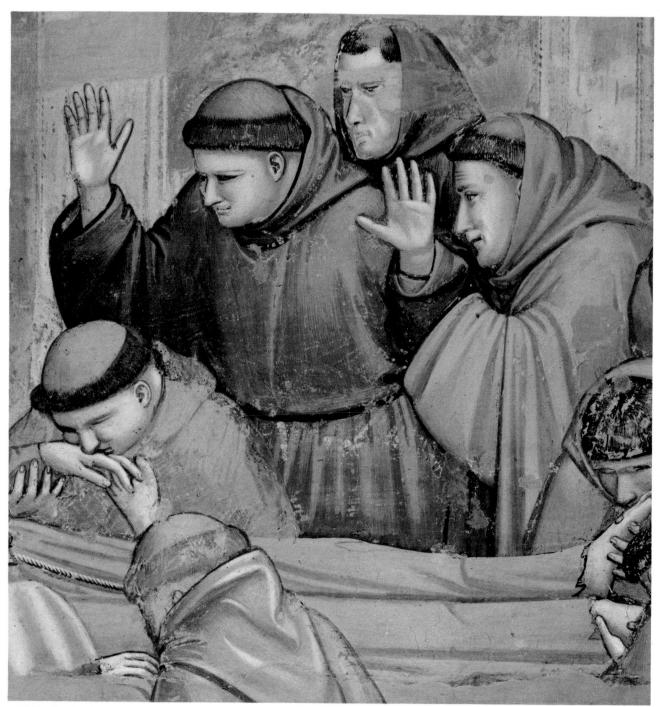

GIOTTO   The Death of St. Francis (detail) about 1325   *fresco*
Florence, S. Croce, Bardi Chapel

GIOTTO The Madonna Enthroned with Angels (the Ognissanti Madonna) about 1310
tempera on panel 128 × 80¼ in.
Florence, Uffizi

SIMONE MARTINI Guidoriccio da Fogliano (detail) 1328 *fresco*
Siena, Palazzo Pubblico

SIMONE MARTINI The Annunciation, 1333 *tempera on panel 100⅜ × 113 in.*
Florence, Uffizi

BERNARDO DADDI The Annunciation, about 1334 *tempera on panel* $16\frac{7}{8} \times 27\frac{1}{8}$ *in.*
Paris, Louvre

AMBROGIO LORENZETTI The Effects of Good Government (detail) about 1337 *fresco*
Siena, Palazzo Pubblico

AMBROGIO LORENZETTI The Madonna and Child, 1319
tempera on panel $33\frac{1}{4} \times 22\frac{1}{4}$ in.
Milan, Brera

MASO DI BANCO   The Resurrection of the Magi, about 1341   *fresco*
Florence, S. Croce

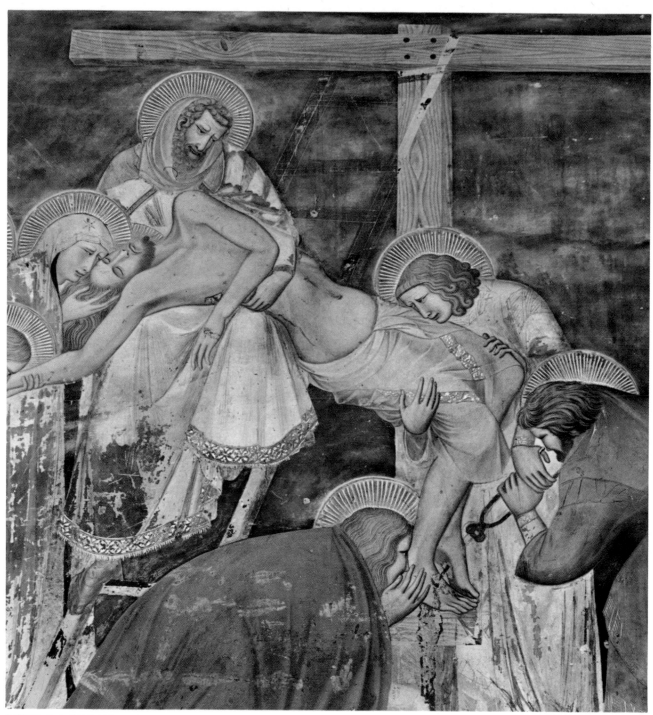

PIETRO LORENZETTI The Deposition (detail) about 1337 *fresco*
Assisi, S. Francesco

TADDEO GADDI   The Meeting at the Golden Gate, 1332-38   *fresco*
Florence, S. Croce

ALTICHIERO   Madonna, Saints, and Warriors of the Cavalli Family (detail) about 1365-70   *fresco*
Verona, S. Anastasia

GIOVANNI DA MILANO The Martyrdom of St. Catherine of Alexandria, about 1354 *tempera on panel* *12¾ × 8⅝ in.*
Prato, Pinacoteca

GENTILE DA FABRIANO The Adoration of the Magi, 1423 *tempera on panel* *112 × 107 in.*
Florence, Uffizi

LORENZO MONACO The Coronation of the Virgin, about 1414 *tempera on panel* *$85\frac{1}{2} \times 127$ in.*
London, National Gallery

MASOLINO The Baptism of Christ (detail) about 1435 *fresco*
Castiglione d'Olona, Baptistery

FRA ANGELICO   The Martyrdom of St. Cosmas and St. Damian,
from predella panel, about 1438-45   *tempera on panel   15 × 18⅞ in.*
Paris, Louvre

ECCE VIRGO CONCIPIET 7 PARIET FILIVM 7 VOCABIT NOMEN EIVS EMANVL. YSA. VI. C

FRA ANGELICO The Annunciation, 1440-47 *fresco*
Florence, Convent of S. Marco

FRA ANGELICO Sixtus II Giving the Treasures of the Church to St. Lawrence, about 1448 *fresco*
Rome, Vatican

PISANELLO   The Vision of St. Eustace (detail) about 1438   *tempera on panel* $21\frac{1}{2} \times 25\frac{3}{4}$ *in.*
London, National Gallery

SASSETTA Scene from The Story of St. Francis, about 1437-44 *tempera on panel $34\frac{1}{4} \times 20\frac{5}{8}$ in.*
London, National Gallery

DOMENICO VENEZIANO   The Madonna Enthroned with Saints (detail from the St. Lucy
Altarpiece) about 1444   *tempera on panel $83\frac{7}{8} \times 82\frac{1}{4}$ in.*
Florence, Uffizi

PAOLO UCCELLO St. George and the Dragon, about 1460 *oil on panel* *23 × 30 in.*
London, National Gallery

PAOLO UCCELLO   The Rout of San Romano, about 1452-57   *tempera on panel*   *72 × 125¾ in.*
London, National Gallery

JACOPO BELLINI The Madonna and Child *tempera on panel* $32\frac{5}{8} \times 26$ *in.*
Bergamo, Accademia Carrara

MASACCIO   The Tribute Money, about 1427   *fresco*
Florence, S. Maria del Carmine, Brancacci Chapel

MASACCIO   St. Peter Distributing Alms, about 1427   *part of a fresco*
Florence, S. Maria del Carmine, Brancacci Chapel

FRA FILIPPO LIPPI The Trivulzio Madonna (detail) about 1434 *tempera on panel*
Milan, Museo del Castello Sforzesco

PIERO DELLA FRANCESCA The Baptism of Christ, 1445-50 *tempera on panel* *66 × 45¾ in.*
London, National Gallery

PIERO DELLA FRANCESCA Triumph of Battista Sforza, Duchess of Urbino, about 1466 *tempera on panel* *13 in. wide*
Florence, Uffizi

PIERO DELLA FRANCESCA The Victory of Constantine (detail): from The Legend of the True Cross, 1452-64 *fresco*
Arezzo, S. Francesco

PIERO DELLA FRANCESCA The Flagellation, about 1451   *tempera on panel* $22\frac{7}{8} \times 31\frac{7}{8}$ *in.*
Urbino, Ducal Palace, Gallery of the Marches

BENOZZO GOZZOLI Procession of the Magi — detail of The Youngest of the Magi and his Page, 1459 *fresco*
Florence, Palazzo Medici-Riccardi

ANDREA DEL CASTAGNO   Christ and St. Julian (detail) about 1455   *fresco*
Florence, SS. Annunziata

VINCENZO FOPPA The Adoration of the Kings: altarpiece, about 1502 *oil on wood 94×83 in.*
London, National Gallery

GIOVANNI and GENTILE BELLINI St. Mark Preaching in Alexandria, about 1506 *oil on canvas* $136\frac{5}{8} \times 303\frac{5}{8}$ *in.*
Milan, Brera

ANTONELLO DA MESSINA   The Annunciation, 1474   *oil on wood $17\frac{3}{4} \times 13\frac{5}{8}$ in.*
Palermo, Galleria Nazionale

CARLO CRIVELLI   The Annunciation: altarpiece, 1486   *oil on canvas* $81\frac{1}{2} \times 57\frac{3}{4}$ *in.*
London. National Gallery

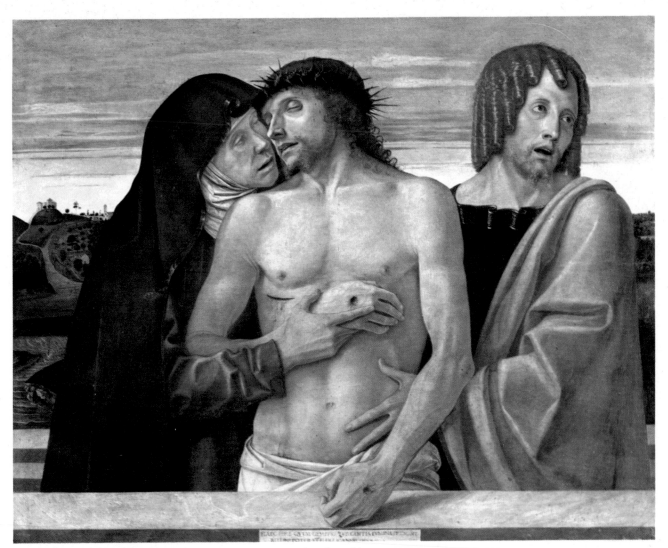

GIOVANNI BELLINI Pietà, about 1470 *tempera on panel* $33\frac{7}{8} \times 42\frac{1}{8}$ *in.*
Milan, Brera

GIOVANNI BELLINI St. Francis in Ecstasy, about 1480 *oil and tempera on wood* $49 \times 55\frac{7}{8}$ *in.*
New York, Frick Collection

GIOVANNI BELLINI The Madonna Adoring the Sleeping Child, about 1465
tempera on wood 28¼ × 18¼ in.
New York, Metropolitan Museum of Art

COSIMO TURA   Allegorical Figure, about 1463   *tempera on panel* $45\frac{3}{4} \times 28$ *in.*
London, National Gallery

ANDREA MANTEGNA   The Agony in the Garden, about 1460-70   *tempera on panel* $24\frac{3}{4} \times 31\frac{1}{2}$ *in.*
London, National Gallery

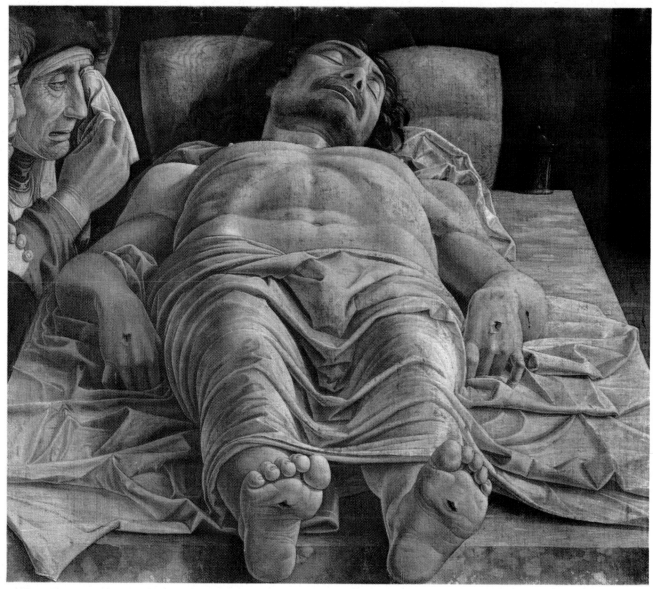

ANDREA MANTEGNA   The Dead Christ, about 1506   *tempera on canvas* $26\frac{3}{4} \times 31\frac{7}{8}$ *in.*
Milan, Brera

ANDREA MANTEGNA   The Gonzaga Family, 1474   *part of a fresco*
Mantua, Castello, Camera degli Sposi

ANTONIO and PIERO POLLAIUOLO The Martyrdom of St. Sebastian, about 1475
tempera on panel 114¾ × 79¾ *in.*
London, National Gallery

ANDREA DEL VERROCCHIO   The Baptism of Christ, about 1470   *tempera on panel*   69⅝ × 61 *in.*
Florence, Uffizi

FRANCESCO DEL COSSA St. Lucy, 1470-75 (slightly trimmed at top and bottom) *tempera on panel* $31\frac{1}{4} \times 21\frac{5}{8}$ *in.*
Washington, D.C., National Gallery

LUCA SIGNORELLI The Flagellation, about 1480 *tempera on panel* *33⅛ × 23⅝ in.*
Milan, Brera

SANDRO BOTTICELLI The Birth of Venus, 1486 *tempera on panel* $68\frac{7}{8} \times 109\frac{1}{2}$ *in.*
Florence, Uffizi

SANDRO BOTTICELLI   The Mystic Nativity, about 1500   *tempera on panel* $42\frac{3}{4} \times 29\frac{1}{2}$ *in.*
London, National Gallery

SANDRO BOTTICELLI Woman Receiving Allegorical Figures, 1484 *part of a fresco*
Paris. Louvre

PERUGINO Christ Giving the Keys of the Church to St. Peter, about 1482 *fresco*
Rome, Vatican, Sistine Chapel

ERCOLE ROBERTI Pietà *tempera on panel* $13\frac{1}{2} \times 12\frac{1}{4}$ *in.*
Liverpool, England, Walker Art Gallery

DOMENICO GHIRLANDAIO   The Birth of St. John the Baptist (detail) about 1490   *fresco*
Florence, S. Maria Novella

BRAMANTINO   The Adoration of the Kings, 1500   *oil on panel* $22\frac{3}{8} \times 21\frac{5}{8}$ *in.*
London, National Gallery

LEONARDO DA VINCI The Annunciation, 1470-75   *oil on panel*   *38¾ × 86 in.*
Florence, Uffizi

LEONARDO DA VINCI   The Virgin of the Rocks, before 1483
oil on panel   78¾ × 48 in.
Paris, Louvre

LEONARDO DA VINCI Mona Lisa, about 1504 *oil on panel 30¼ × 21 in.*
Paris, Louvre

LEONARDO DA VINCI The Virgin and Child with St. Anne, about 1516
oil on panel 67 × 51 in.
Paris, Louvre

FILIPPINO LIPPI The Madonna Appearing to St. Bernard, about 1486   *oil on panel* $82\frac{5}{8} \times 76\frac{3}{4}$ *in.*
Florence, Badia

VITTORE CARPACCIO The Arrival of the Ambassadors (detail) about 1498 *oil on canvas* *108×231⅞ in.*
Venice, Accademia

GAUDENZIO FERRARI The Birth of the Virgin, about 1534 *part of a fresco*
Vercelli, S. Cristoforo

FRA BARTOLOMMEO The Madonna Appearing to St. Bernard, about 1507 *tempera on panel* *82⅞ × 86⅜ in.*
Florence, Accademia

MICHELANGELO The Holy Family (the Doni Tondo) about 1504 *oil on panel diameter 47¼ in.*
Florence, Uffizi

MICHELANGELO The Creation of Adam (detail) 1508-12 *ceiling fresco*
Rome, Vatican, Sistine Chapel

MICHELANGELO The Delphic Sibyl, 1508-12 *ceiling fresco*
Rome, Vatican, Sistine Chapel

MICHELANGELO The Last Judgment (detail) 1536-41 *fresco*
Rome, Vatican, Sistine Chapel

GIORGIONE The Tempest, about 1505 *oil on canvas* $32\frac{1}{4} \times 28\frac{3}{4}$ *in.*
Venice, Accademia

GIORGIONE The Three Philosophers (detail) begun about 1501 *oil on canvas 48⅜ × 56¼ in.*
Vienna, Kunsthistorisches Museum

GIORGIONE Fête Champêtre, about 1510   *oil on canvas* $43\frac{1}{4} \times 54\frac{1}{4}$ *in.*
Paris, Louvre

DOSSO DOSSI Circe, about 1530 *oil on canvas 69¼ × 68¼ in.*
Rome, Borghese Gallery

GIAN GIROLAMO SAVOLDO Tobias and the Angel, 1540 *oil on canvas* $37\frac{3}{4} \times 48\frac{7}{8}$ *in.*
Rome, Borghese Gallery

243

LORENZO LOTTO Portrait of Bishop Bernardo de Rossi *oil on panel 21¼ × 16⅞ in.*
Naples, Museo di Capodimonte

LORENZO LOTTO   The Madonna and Child with Saints, 1533   *oil on canvas* $31\frac{7}{8} \times 45\frac{1}{4}$ *in.*
Bergamo, Accademia Carrara

245

BERNARDINO LUINI The Gathering of the Manna, about 1523 *fresco* $78 \times 59\frac{7}{8}$ *in.*
Milan, Brera

RAPHAEL   The Marriage of the Virgin, 1504   *oil on panel $66\frac{7}{8} \times 46\frac{1}{2}$ in.*
Milan, Brera

RAPHAEL   The Madonna of the Goldfinch, about 1506   *oil on panel   42⅛ × 30¼ in.*
Florence, Uffizi

RAPHAEL The School of Athens (detail) 1509-12 *fresco*
Rome, Vatican, Stanza della Segnatura

RAPHAEL   Count Baldassare Castiglione, 1519   *oil on canvas   32¼ × 26⅜ in.*
Paris, Louvre

RAPHAEL The Transfiguration (detail) about 1520 *oil on panel* *159½ × 109½ in.*
Rome, Vatican, Pinacoteca

SEBASTIANO DEL PIOMBO The Holy Family, about 1517 *oil on wood* $38\frac{3}{4} \times 42\frac{1}{2}$ *in.*
London, National Gallery

ANDREA DEL SARTO   The Madonna of the Harpies, 1517   *oil on panel* $81\frac{1}{2} \times 70\frac{1}{2}$ *in.*
Florence, Uffizi

TITIAN Sacred and Profane Love, about 1515   *oil on canvas*   *46¼ × 109⅞ in.*
Rome, Borghese Gallery

TITIAN The Presentation of the Virgin (detail) 1534-38 *oil on canvas* *131⅞×305⅛ in.*
Venice, Accademia

TITIAN   The Vendramin Family, about 1543   *oil on canvas   81 × 118½ in.*
London, National Gallery

TITIAN Shepherd and Nymph, about 1570 *oil on canvas $58\frac{5}{8} \times 73\frac{5}{8}$ in.*
Vienna, Kunsthistorisches Museum

CORREGGIO Danaë, about 1530   *oil on canvas   63 × 76 in.*
Rome, Borghese Gallery

CORREGGIO The Apostles Philip and Jude - detail from Christ in Glory, 1520-23 *dome fresco*
Parma, S. Giovanni Evangelista

JACOPO PONTORMO   The Deposition (detail) about 1528   *oil on panel*   *123¼ × 75⅜ in.*
Florence, S. Felicita

MORETTO   Count Sciarra Martinengo Cesaresco, about 1530   *oil on canvas   44.×37 in.*
London, National Gallery

AGNOLO BRONZINO   Eleonora of Toledo and her Son Giovanni de' Medici, about 1546   *oil on canvas*   *43¼ × 37¾ in.*
Florence, Uffizi

FRANCESCO PARMIGIANINO The Madonna of the Long Neck,
1534-40 *oil on panel 85 × 25 in.*
Florence, Uffizi

563

JACOPO BASSANO The Good Samaritan, 1540-50 *oil on canvas* *25 × 33 in.*
London, Hampton Court, Royal Collection

264

TINTORETTO The Miracle of St. Mark, about 1548   *oil on canvas* $163\frac{3}{8} \times 213$ *in.*
Venice, Accademia

TINTORETTO Bacchus and Ariadne, 1578 *oil on canvas 57½ × 61¾ in.*
Venice, Palazzo Ducale

TINTORETTO Portrait of Vincenzo Morosini, about 1580-85
oil on canvas $33\frac{1}{4} \times 20\frac{3}{8}$ in.
London, National Gallery

GIOVANNI BATTISTA MORONI Portrait of a Child, about 1567 *oil on canvas* $16\frac{1}{2} \times 12\frac{5}{8}$ *in.*
Bergamo, Accademia Carrara

PAOLO VERONESE Feast in the House of Levi (centre section) 1573   *oil on canvas   218¼ × 504 in.*
Venice, Accademia

PAOLO VERONESE The Crucifixion, about 1575 *oil on canvas 40⅜ × 40⅜ in.*
Paris, Louvre

PAOLO VERONESE The Martyrdom of St. Justina, about 1575 *oil on canvas* $30\frac{3}{4} \times 40\frac{3}{4}$ *in.*
Padua, Museo Civico

LUDOVICO CARRACCI The Annunciation, about 1585 *oil on canvas* *82⅝ × 90¼ in.*
Bologna, Pinacoteca

AGOSTINO CARRACCI   The Last Communion of St. Jerome, about 1593
oil on canvas   148 × 88⅛ in.
Bologna, Pinacoteca

CERANO, MORAZZONE and PROCACCINI The Martyrdom of St. Rufina and St. Secunda, about 1625 *oil on canvas* 75⅜ × 75⅜ in.
Milan, Brera

ANNIBALE CARRACCI St. Anthony Tempted by Devils, about 1597 *oil on canvas* *19¼ × 13¼ in.*
London, National Gallery

ORAZIO GENTILESCHI St. Valerian, St. Tiburzio, and St. Cecilia (detail) 1620   *oil on canvas* $137\frac{3}{4} \times 85\frac{7}{8}$ *in.*
Milan, Brera

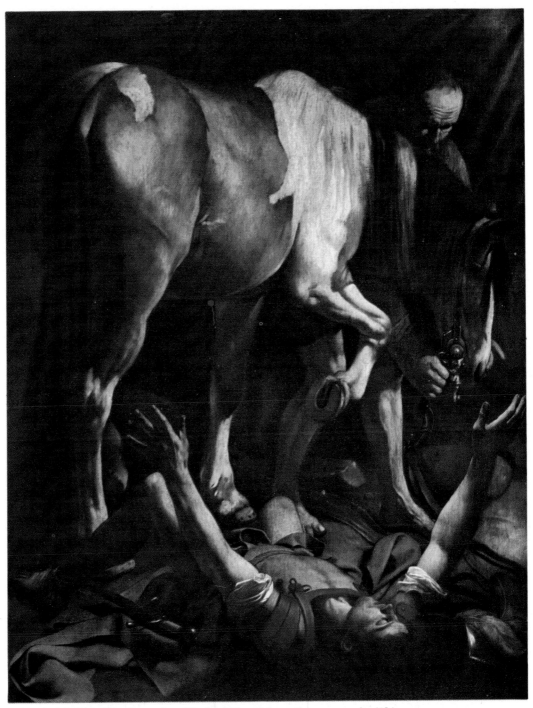

CARAVAGGIO   The Conversion of St. Paul, about 1601   *oil on canvas   90½×68⅞ in.*
Rome, S. Maria del Popolo

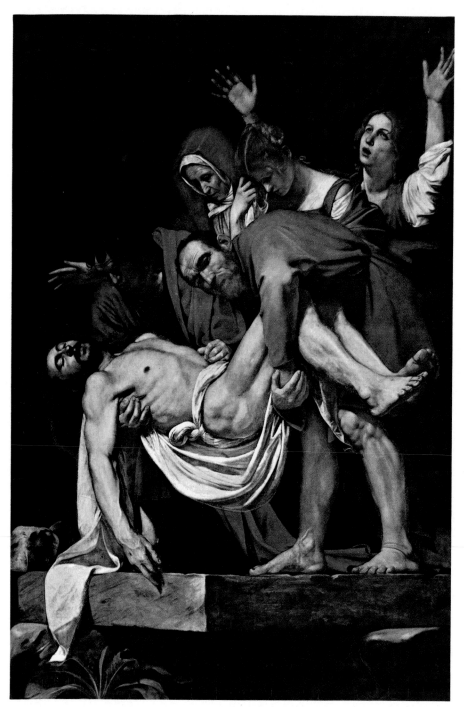

CARAVAGGIO The Deposition, about 1604 *oil on canvas* *118 × 81¼ in.*
Rome, Vatican, Pinacoteca

CARAVAGGIO   The Death of the Virgin (detail) about 1606   *oil on canvas $145\frac{1}{4} \times 96\frac{1}{2}$ in.*
Paris, Louvre

CARAVAGGIO   The Calling of St. Matthew (detail) about 1599   *oil on canvas   129⅛ × 137 in.*
Rome, S. Luigi dei Francesi

GUIDO RENI The Young Bacchus, about 1620   *oil on canvas* $34\frac{1}{2} \times 27\frac{1}{2}$ *in.*
Florence, Pitti Palace

DOMENICHINO The Hunt of Diana, about 1617 *oil on canvas* *88⅝ × 126 in.*
Rome, Borghese Gallery

BERNARDO STROZZI St. Sebastian and St. Irene,
after 1630 *oil on canvas* $171\frac{1}{4} \times 79\frac{1}{2}$ *in.*
Venice, S. Benedetto

GUERCINO   The Bath of Diana, about 1618   *oil on canvas   12½ × 20½ in.*
Bergamo, Accademia Carrara

PIETRO DA CORTONA   The Rape of the Sabine Women, about 1629   *oil on canvas   108¼ × 166½ in.*
Rome, Capitoline Museum

EVARISTO BASCHENIS Musical Instruments, about 1675 *oil on canvas 29½ × 42½ in.*
Bergamo, Accademia Carrara

SALVATOR ROSA Marina, about 1640   *oil on canvas   92⅛ × 155¾ in.*
Florence, Pitti Palace

LUCA GIORDANO The Crucifixion of St. Peter, 1692 *oil on canvas* $77\frac{1}{8} \times 101\frac{5}{8}$ *in.*
Venice, Accademia

BACICCIA   Pope Clement IX, about 1668   *oil on canvas* $29\frac{1}{8} \times 24\frac{3}{8}$ *in.*
Rome, Accademia di S. Luca

VITTORE GHISLANDI called FRA GALGARIO Youth *oil on canvas* $17\frac{3}{4} \times 13$ *in.*
Bergamo, Accademia Carrara

GIUSEPPE MARIA CRESPI The Scullery Maid, about 1710-15 *oil on canvas 29¼ × 16⅞ in.*
Florence, Contini Collection

ROSALBA CARRIERA Self-portrait, about 1730 *pastel on paper* $12\frac{1}{4} \times 9\frac{7}{8}$ *in.*
Venice, Accademia

ALESSANDRO MAGNASCO Landscape with Fleeing Monks *oil on canvas $92\frac{1}{2} \times 68\frac{7}{8}$ in.*
Milan, Brera

GIAMBATTISTA PIAZZETTA Rebecca at the Well (detail) about 1745 *oil on canvas 40⅛ × 53⅞ in.*
Milan, Brera

GIOVANNI BATTISTA TIEPOLO The Trinity Appearing to St. Clement, about 1735
oil on canvas 27¼ × 21¾ in.
London, National Gallery

GIOVANNI BATTISTA TIEPOLO   The Emperor Frederick Invests Bishop Arnolfo, 1752   *part of a fresco*
Würzburg, Residenz

GIOVANNI BATTISTA and GIAN DOMENICO TIEPOLO The Minuet (detail) about 1754 *oil on canvas* $31\frac{1}{8} \times 39\frac{3}{8}$ *in.*
Paris, Louvre

CANALETTO The Stonemason's Yard, about 1730 *oil on canvas* *48¾ × 64⅛ in.*
London, National Gallery

CANALETTO   The Reception of Count Bolagnos at the Ducal Palace, after 1729   *oil on canvas   71⅝ × 103⅜ in.*
Milan, Collection Aldo Crespi

PIETRO LONGHI Family Concert *oil on canvas* $19\frac{5}{8} \times 24\frac{3}{8}$ *in.*
Milan, Brera

FRANCESCO GUARDI The Dogana and the Salute, Venice *oil on canvas* *18⅛ × 26 in.*
Milan, Collection Aldo Crespi

FRANCESCO GUARDI The Doge's Procession to S. Zaccaria, about 1763   *oil on canvas $26\frac{3}{8} \times 38\frac{5}{8}$ in.*
Paris, Louvre

BERNARDO BELLOTTO Gazzada, near Varese *oil on canvas* $25\frac{5}{8} \times 39\frac{3}{8}$ *in.*
Milan, Brera

GIACOMO CERUTI The Laundress *oil on canvas 47⅞ × 56¾ in.*
Brescia, Pinacoteca Tosio Martinengo

Drawings

TADDEO GADDI   The Presentation in the Temple, about 1338
brush, terre verte and white lead $14\frac{1}{8} \times 11\frac{1}{4}$ in.
Paris, Louvre

GIOVANNINO DE' GRASSI Hunting the Wild Boar; and a Leopard in a Garden
(study for a crest), about 1370-80 $10\frac{1}{4} \times 6\frac{7}{8}$ in.
Bergamo, Biblioteca Civica

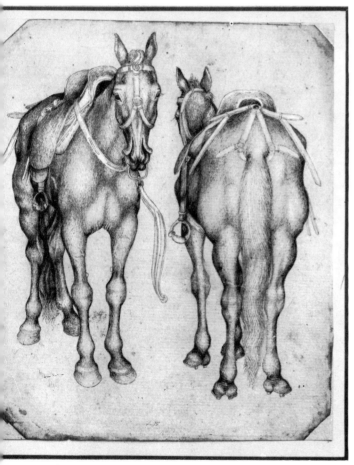

NELLO   Studies of a Horse, about 1435   *pen and ink on paper   6½ × 5⅝ in.*
Louvre

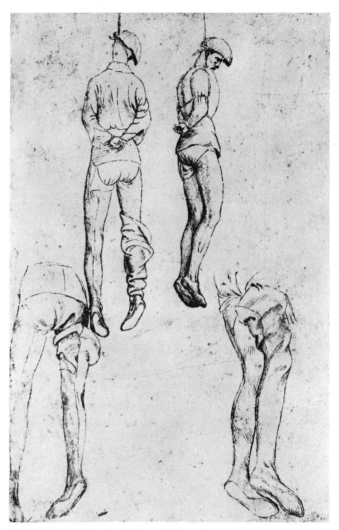

PISANELLO   Study of Hanged Men, about 1435
pen and ink on paper
London, private collection

MICHELINO DA BESOZZO The Adoration of the Magi, and other figure studies, about 1402
silverpoint, with pen and bistre $11\frac{1}{4} \times 8\frac{1}{2}$ in.
Vienna, Albertina

JACOPO BELLINI View of a Palace *pen and ink* $11\frac{1}{2} \times 16\frac{3}{4}$ in.
Paris, Louvre

Studio of FRA FILIPPO LIPPI Boy with a Rearing Horse, about 1460
silverpoint with white heightening $14\frac{1}{8} \times 9\frac{3}{4}$ *in.*
London, British Museum

BONIFACIO BEMBO Lancelot of the Lake, 1446 *pen and ink* $7\frac{7}{8} \times 10\frac{3}{4}$ *in.*
Florence, Biblioteca Nazionale

Attributed to PIERO DELLA FRANCESCA The Redeemer $11\frac{7}{8} \times 8\frac{3}{4}$ in.
Milan, Biblioteca Ambrosiana

ANTONIO POLLAIUOLO Eve Spinning, about 1475 *pen and bistre 10⅞ × 7⅞ in.*
Florence, Uffizi

PAOLO UCCELLO   Design for the Monument to Giovanni Acuto (Sir John Hawkwood), 1436
silverpoint with color   18⅜ × 12½ in.
Florence, Uffizi

ANDREA MANTEGNA Judith, 1491
pen, bistre, and white lead on yellow paper $15\frac{3}{8} \times 10\frac{1}{4}$ *in.*
Florence, Uffizi

ANDREA MANTEGNA The Judgment of Solomon, about 1490-1500
tempera on canvas $18\frac{1}{4} \times 14\frac{5}{8}$ *in.*
Paris, Louvre

ANDREA DEL VERROCCHIO Head of a Woman
Paris, Louvre

FRANCESCO DI GIORGIO MARTINI
Two Female Figures
pen and ink
Florence, Uffizi

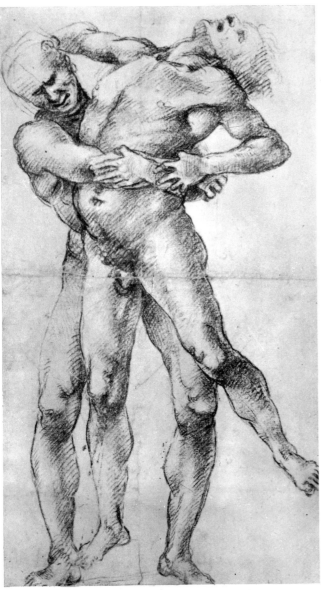

LUCA SIGNORELLI   Hercules and Antaeus, about 1490
gray chalk   11⅛×6¼ in.
Windsor, Royal Collection

317

SANDRO BOTTICELLI   An illustration for Dante's 'Inferno,' Canto XXXI, 1481-1500   *silverpoint with ink*   *12¼ × 18¼ in.*
Rome, Vatican Library

SANDRO BOTTICELLI   Angel in Profile, about 1483
chalk, brush, and sepia   10 × 6¼ in.
Florence, Uffizi

SANDRO BOTTICELLI   Female Figure
Florence, Uffizi

319

PERUGINO Head of a Young Man *silverpoint with white heightening*
Florence, Uffizi

DOMENICO GHIRLANDAIO Head of a Woman
silverpoint with white heightening
Florence, Uffizi

VINCENZO FOPPA The Justice of Trajan, about 1470 *pen and wash* $9\frac{7}{8} \times 15\frac{3}{8}$ *in.*
West Berlin, Staatliche Museen

GIOVANNI BELLINI   Portrait of a Woman, about 1497
silverpoint and white chalk on blue paper   8¼ × 5¼ in.
Venice, Accademia

GIOVANNI BELLINI   Head of a Young Man
black chalk on gray-brown paper   13⅞ × 10 in.
Frankfurt-am-Main, Staedel Institute

BRAMANTINO Two Apostles *brush drawing with white heightening* $12\frac{5}{8} \times 8\frac{5}{8}$ *in.*
Milan, Pinacoteca Ambrosiana

PINTURICCHIO   A Group of Soldiers   *drawing with white heightening* $10\frac{1}{4} \times 6\frac{1}{2}$ *in.*
Venice, Accademia

GAUDENZIO FERRARI Christ among the Doctors, 1510-15 *pen, brush, and wash $17\frac{3}{4} \times 13\frac{3}{4}$ in.*
London, British Museum

VITTORE CARPACCIO   Study for the Legend of St. Ursula,
about 1490
pen and watercolor $4\frac{1}{8} \times 4\frac{5}{8}$ *in.*
Florence, Uffizi

VITTORE CARPACCIO
Study for the Meeting of St. Ursula with the Pope, 1495
brush drawing in gray on green paper with white heightening $7\frac{3}{4} \times 8\frac{5}{8}$ *in.*
London, British Museum

LORENZO DI CREDI Male Head *silverpoint with white heightening* *16 × 15 in.*
Florence, Uffizi

LEONARDO DA VINCI   The Virgin and Child with St. Anne and
St. John the Baptist, about 1501
charcoal heightened with white $55\frac{3}{4} \times 41$ *in.*
London, National Gallery

LEONARDO DA VINCI Isabella d'Este, 1500 *charcoal and chalk 24¾ × 18⅛ in.*
Paris, Louvre

LEONARDO DA VINCI
Studies for the Trivulzio Monument
about 1512   *red chalk*
(*above*) 8⅜ × 6⅞ in.   (*below*) 11 × 7⅞ in.
Windsor, Royal Collection

LEONARDO DA VINCI   Self-portrait, about 1512   *red chalk*   13⅛ × 8¾ in.
Turin, Biblioteca Reale

MICHELANGELO
Pietà, about 1560   *red chalk*
15⅞ × 9¼ in.   Vienna, Albertina

331

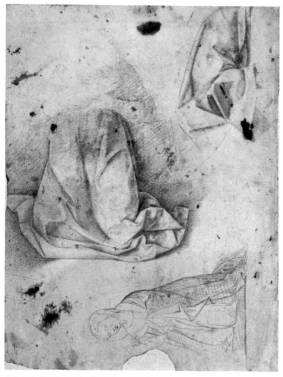

GIORGIONE Praying Madonna and other studies
red chalk 11⅛ × 8⅝ in.
Milan, Pinacoteca Ambrosiana

LORENZO LOTTO Head of a Madonna
about 1508
Rome, Gabinetto Nazionale

GIORGIONE View of Castelfranco, about 1500 *red chalk 7⅞ × 11½ in.*
Rotterdam, Museum Boymans-van Beuningen

GIAN GIROLAMO SAVOLDO
Head of a Woman
charcoal heightened with white wash
Florence, Uffizi

332

BERNARDINO LUINI Head of a Woman $7\frac{1}{4} \times 6\frac{7}{8}$ in.
Milan, Pinacoteca Ambrosiana

RAPHAEL Venus and Psyche, about 1516 *red chalk* *10½ × 7¾ in.*
Paris, Louvre

RAPHAEL Self-portrait (?), about 1504 *gray-black chalk heightened with white   15 × 10¼ in.*
Oxford, Ashmolean Museum

RAPHAEL Study for St. George, about 1504 *pen and ink* $10\frac{1}{4} \times 10\frac{5}{8}$ *in.*
Florence, Uffizi

336

RAPHAEL Woman Kneeling: study for the Mass of Bolsena
about 1517 *red chalk* 11 × 7¼ *in.*
Chatsworth, England, Trustees of the Chatsworth Settlement

RAPHAEL Study of Two Apostles, about 1517
black chalk heightened with white
Oxford, Ashmolean Museum

337

SEBASTIANO DEL PIOMBO Lazarus Rising from the
Tomb (detail) 1517 *red chalk* $9\frac{7}{8} \times 7\frac{1}{8}$ *in.*
London, British Museum

DOMENICO BECCAFUMI Study for a Man
pen and ink $9\frac{7}{8} \times 4\frac{1}{8}$ *in.*
London, British Museum

338

ANDREA DEL SARTO   Head of a Woman
red chalk   8½×6½ in.
Florence, Uffizi

GIOVANNI ANTONIO BOLTRAFFIO   Portrait of a Woman
charcoal and chalk   21¼×16 in.
Milan, Pinacoteca Ambrosiana

SODOMA
Head of a Young Man Crowned with Laurel,
about 1525-30 *black and red chalk on tinted paper   11⅜×9 in.*
Florence, Uffizi

339

FRA BARTOLOMMEO   Study for a Woman of Samaria, about 1505   *pen and ink*
Florence, Uffizi

TITIAN   The Battle of Cadore, about 1525   *chalk* $15\frac{1}{8} \times 17\frac{1}{2}$ *in.*
Paris, Louvre

ANTONIO CORREGGIO Study for the Coronation of the Virgin, about 1520 *red chalk* $9\frac{1}{2} \times 7\frac{1}{8}$ *in.*
Paris, Louvre

ANTONIO CORREGGIO Study for the Annunciation, about 1525 $12\frac{3}{4} \times 9\frac{7}{8}$ in.
Milan, Pinacoteca Ambrosiana

JACOPO PONTORMO Portrait of a Woman *red chalk*
Florence, Uffizi

GIULIO ROMANO Horses and Horsemen
Venice, Museo Correr

POLIDORO CALDARA DA CARAVAGGIO
Study for the Story of Niobe, about 1528 $12\frac{1}{8} \times 22\frac{1}{4}$ in.
Milan, Pinacoteca Ambrosiana

POLIDORO CALDARA DA CARAVAGGIO
Study for the Story of Niobe, about 1528 $12\frac{1}{8} \times 10\frac{5}{8}$ in.
Milan, Pinacoteca Ambrosiana

346

FRANCESCO PARMIGIANINO Study for the Presentation of Our Lord, about 1535 *red chalk*
Florence, Uffizi

TINTORETTO Study for St. George
Paris, Louvre

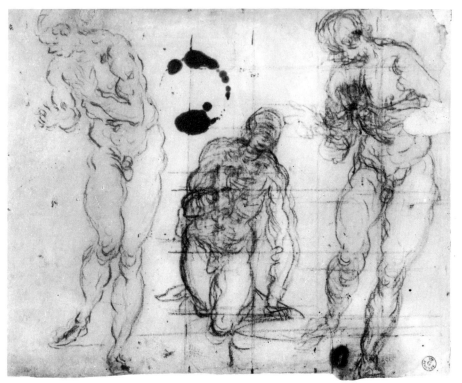

TINTORETTO Male Figures
Florence, Uffizi

TINTORETTO Archer
Florence, Uffizi

JACOPO BASSANO A Hound, about 1575 *chalk on gray paper* *8¼ × 11¾ in.*
Liverpool, England, Walker Art Gallery

FEDERICO BAROCCI   Study of Putto for the Madonna del Popolo   *black and white chalk on brown paper* $17\frac{1}{8} \times 17\frac{1}{8}$ *in.*
Milan, Pinacoteca Ambrosiana

LUCA CAMBIASO   The Elect   *pen and watercolor* $12\frac{5}{8} \times 9$ *in.*
Rome, Gabinetto Nazionale

352

VERONESE   Allegory of Virtue Fleeing Vice   *pen heightened with gouache on blue paper $11\frac{3}{4} \times 10\frac{3}{4}$ in.*
Paris, École des Beaux-Arts

ANNIBALE CARRACCI   Head of St. Anne   *oil sketch on canvas* $14\frac{5}{8} \times 11\frac{1}{4}$ *in.*
Bergamo, Accademia Carrara

LUDOVICO CARRACCI The Dream of Jacob, about 1608 *pen and brown ink* $9\frac{1}{2} \times 7\frac{5}{8}$ *in.*
Windsor, Royal Collection

AGOSTINO CARRACCI Return of the Prodigal Son, about 1590
pen and brown ink, wash, and red chalk $19\frac{5}{8} \times 14\frac{5}{8}$ *in.*
Windsor, Royal Collection

GUERCINO Study for a Decapitation *ink* $7\frac{1}{4} \times 5\frac{5}{8}$ *in.*
Milan, Brera

357

VENTURA SALIMBENI   The Sermon of St. Bernardino   *pen and watercolor*
Rome, Gabinetto Nazionale

GUIDO RENI Study of an Arm Raised across the Breast, after 1620
lead point with red chalk and white heightening $9\frac{1}{4} \times 13\frac{3}{8}$ in.
Milan, Brera

MARCO RICCI Imaginary Landscape
Bassano, Museo Civico

GIAMBATTISTA PIAZZETTA   Head of a Boy
charcoal   16¼ × 12¼ in.
Bergamo, Accademia Carrara

GIAMBATTISTA PIAZZETTA   The Violinist
charcoal and pastel   15 × 11⅜ in.
Milan, Brera

GIOVANNI BATTISTA TIEPOLO
Male Head, about 1770
red chalk with white heightening 17¾ × 11 in.
Venice, Museo Correr

GIOVANNI BATTISTA TIEPOLO   Study of a Man and a Woman
Venice, Museo Correr

PIETRO LONGHI Gondola and Gondoliers *lead point*
Venice, Museo Correr

FRANCESCO ZUCCARELLI Mother and Children Resting
Venice, Museo Correr

FRANCESCO GUARDI   Study for a Battle Scene   *pen and wash* $7\frac{7}{8} \times 10\frac{1}{4}$ *in.*
Milan, Brera

BORROMINI The Painter
Milan, Museo Civico

365

GIOVANNI BATTISTA PIRANESI A Prison, about 1745 *etching* *21⅝ × 16⅛ in.*
London, British Museum

ALESSANDRO MAGNASCO   The Crowning with Thorns $13\frac{3}{8} \times 9\frac{7}{8}$ in.
Milan, collection Saibene

ALESSANDRO MAGNASCO Archer with a Dog *sepia with white heightening* $11\frac{1}{4} \times 8\frac{1}{4}$ *in.*
Genoa, Palazzo Bianco

Sculpture

NICOLA PISANO The Nativity, from the pulpit, 1260 *marble* $33\frac{1}{4} \times 45\frac{1}{4}$ *in.*
Pisa, Baptistery

NICOLA PISANO The Presentation in the Temple (detail) from the pulpit, 1260
marble 33½ × 45¼ in.
Pisa, Baptistery

370

ARNOLFO DI CAMBIO
The Madonna and Child, 1294-1301   *marble   height 68½ in.*
Florence, Museo dell'Opera del Duomo

GIOVANNI PISANO   The Annunciation and Nativity (detail) from the pulpit, 1297-1301   *marble* $31\frac{1}{4} \times 39\frac{3}{8}$ *in.*
Pistoia, S. Andrea

GIOVANNI PISANO
The Madonna and Child, about 1305
marble   height 52 in.
Padua, Arena Chapel

ANDREA PISANO Allegorical Figure of Sculpture, 1334-43 *marble* *height* 30$\frac{3}{4}$ *in.*
Florence, Cathedral Campanile

FILIPPO BRUNELLESCHI Crucifix (detail) about 1410-15 *wood life size*
Florence, S. Maria Novella

LORENZO GHIBERTI The Annunciation, from the North Doors, 1403-24 *bronze relief* $17\frac{3}{4} \times 15\frac{3}{4}$ in.
Florence, Baptistery

LORENZO GHIBERTI The Sacrifice of Isaac, from the East Doors, 1425-52 *bronze relief* *17¾ × 15¾ in.*
Florence, Baptistery

JACOPO DELLA QUERCIA The Tomb of Ilaria del Carretto, 1406 (?)   *marble   length 91⅜ in.*
Lucca, Cathedral

JACOPO DELLA QUERCIA Adam and Eve, from the façade, 1427-37 *marble 39⅜ × 31½ in.*
Bologna, S. Petronio

DONATELLO   The Annunciation, about 1430   *limestone   95 × 74¾ in.*
Florence, S. Croce

DONATELLO Il Gattamelata, 1443-47 *bronze* $133\frac{1}{4} \times 153\frac{3}{4}$ *in.*
Padua

LUCA DELLA ROBBIA   The Madonna of the Rose Garden, about 1430   *glazed terracotta* $32\frac{5}{8} \times 24\frac{3}{4}$ *in.*
Florence, Museo Nazionale del Bargello

ANTONIO POLLAIUOLO Hercules and Antaeus, about 1475-80 *bronze height 17¾ in.*
Florence, Museo Nazionale del Bargello

ANDREA DEL VERROCCHIO
David, before 1476   *bronze   height 46½ in.*
Florence, Museo Nazionale del Bargello

ANDREA DEL VERROCCHIO   Portrait of a Florentine Lady, about 1478   *marble   height 25½ in.*
Florence, Museo Nazionale del Bargello

FRANCESCO LAURANA Battista Sforza, about 1476 *marble*
Florence, Museo Nazionale del Bargello

GIOVANNI ANTONIO AMADEO The Tomb of Medea Colleoni, about 1475 *marble*
Bergamo, Colleoni Chapel

MICHELANGELO   Moses, from the Tomb of Pope Julius II, about 1515   *marble   height 99¼ in.*
Rome, S. Pietro in Vincoli

MICHELANGELO The Tomb of Giuliano de' Medici (detail) 1526-31 *marble*
Florence, S. Lorenzo, Medici Chapel

389

BENVENUTO CELLINI Salt Cellar, about 1540 *gold, enamel and precious stones height 10¼ in.*
Vienna, Kunsthistorisches Museum

JACOPO SANSOVINO St. Mark the Evangelist, 1547-56 *bronze* *height 20½ in.*
Venice, St. Mark's

GIOVANNI DA BOLOGNA Strutting Turkey Cock, about 1567 *bronze height 19¼ in.*
Florence, Museo Nazionale del Bargello

ALESSANDRO ALGARDI Donna Olimpia Maidalchini, about 1650 *marble*
Rome, Doria Gallery

GIAN LORENZO BERNINI   Ecstasy of St. Theresa, 1645-52   *marble   life size*
Rome, S. Maria della Vittoria

GIAN LORENZO BERNINI Francesco I d'Este, about 1651 *marble slightly over life size*
Modena, Museo Estense

GIACOMO SERPOTTA
Charity, 1690-96   *stucco*
Palermo, Oratory of S. Lorenzo

ANTONIO CANOVA Pauline Bonaparte Borghese, about 1808 *marble* *length 78¾ in.*
Rome, Borghese Gallery

Influences and Developments

The Architecture of the 14th Century

In the time of Giotto and Giovanni Pisano 14th-century Italian art provided a stage for the creation of vast buildings that interpreted the Gothic themes evolved in France, Germany and England. In works such as Florence Cathedral (left), the small and ornate S. Maria della Spina at Pisa (b) and Orvieto Cathedral (a), and in civic buildings such as the Palazzo Pubblico in Siena (c), the Palazzo Vecchio in Florence, and the Palazzo dei Priori in Perugia, is seen a transformation of the imaginative and dynamic aspects of the true Gothic style. Although the principles of that style are not altogether abandoned, the decoration is more restrained and these buildings retain a sense of stability derived from the classical Roman tradition. A search for order, balance, and harmony prevailed, revealing an underlying rationalism that gave a foretaste of the Renaissance themes of the early 15th century. Milan Cathedral (d) is an exception to this, since it was started at the end of the century and shows a closer affinity to the cathedrals of the North, where the Flamboyant Gothic style was already established. At Venice, on the other hand, Gothic ornamentation and sumptuous oriental decoration balance each other in a synthesis of elegance, lightness, and fantasy. At the same time, there was a great increase in the demand for miniatures, goldsmith's work, and ivory carving, which demonstrates the taste for elaborate but refined decoration.

Filippo Brunelleschi
The Dome, 1420-36
Florence, Cathedral

398

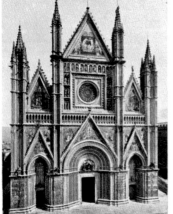

a

b

c

d

e

f

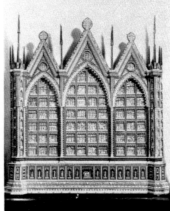

g

a Lorenzo Maitani
The Façade, about 1310
Orvieto, Cathedral

b S. Maria della Spina, begun 1230
Pisa

c Palazzo Pubblico, begun 1298
Siena

d The Interior of the Cathedral,
begun 1386
Milan

e Simone Martini
Miniature from the Virgil Codex
about 1344   *vellum   11 × 8½ in.
Milan, Biblioteca Ambrosiana*

f Reliquary, 15th century
*copper and gilded bronze
Bologna, S. Domenico*

g Triptych
*ivory
Pavia, Certosa*

a Martino Spanzotti
(Piedmontese school)
The Madonna and Child, about
1490
*tempera on panel 47¼ × 25⅝ in.
Turin, Galleria Sabauda*

b Ambrogio Bergognone
(Lombard school)
The Madonna of the Carthusian
Monk, 1483-94
*oil on panel 17¾ × 15⅜ in.
Milan, Brera*

c Francesco Squarcione
(Paduan school)
Polyptych of Lazara (detail)
about 1452
*tempera on panel 68⅞ × 86⅝ in.
Padua, Museo Civico*

d Alvise Vivarini
(Venetian school)
St. Anthony of Padua
*tempera on panel 11¼ × 8⅝ in.
Venice, Museo Correr*

e Marco Zoppo
(Emilian school)
Christ between Two Angels
*tempera on panel 40¼ × 30¼ in.
Pesaro, Museo Civico*

The 15th Century — the Development of Regional Schools

A characteristic of Italian painting in the Renaissance period was the formation of regional schools, in which each artist clearly established his own personality, but incorporated themes common to a whole area, so giving his work a "family" air which related it to that of his colleagues.

It is therefore possible to follow a geographical sequence and outline the characteristics of the Piedmontese and Ligurian schools in the late 15th century. These were influenced in various ways by Foppa and by the French, Burgundian and Provençal schools of painting. In the Veneto the Paduan school (c) took its style from a mixture of local tradition and the influence of artistic circles in Florence. The Humanist trend of the Venetian school in Emilia (e) dictated a style of expression which is translated in terms of drama. In Tuscany, on the one hand, Humanism triumphed in the Florentine school (f), while on the other clung the remnants of the decorative Gothic-Oriental tradition that came from Siena (h). Having fallen under the spell of Piero della Francesca, the Umbrian school (g) gave rise to a generally lyrical conception — a mystic, tender interpretation of nature. In Rome the variety of converging influences created a derivative school (i) from which a few strong personalities emerged. Southern Italy (j) and Sicily remained for a long time in the thrall of the International Gothic style that originated in southern France.

b

c

d

e

f

g

h

f Alessio Baldovinetti
(Florentine school)
The Annunciation, after 1473
oil on panel $65\frac{3}{4} \times 53\frac{7}{8}$ *in.*
Florence, Uffizi

g Umbrian School
The Miracle of St. Bernardino, 1473
Perugia, Gall. Naz. dell'Umbria

h Sano di Pietro
(Sienese school)
St. Jerome, about 1440
tempera on panel $14\frac{1}{8} \times 10\frac{5}{8}$ *in.*
Siena, Pinacoteca

i Antoniazzo Romano
(Roman school)
The Madonna and Child with
St. Peter and St. Paul
tempera on panel $61 \times 65\frac{5}{8}$ *in.*
Rome, Museo di Palazzo Venezia

j Colantonio
(Neapolitan school)
St. Jerome and the Lion
oil on panel $59 \times 49\frac{1}{2}$ *in.*
Naples, Galleria Nazionale

j

i

401

a

The 15th Century—Links with Northern Painters

Throughout the 15th century the characteristics of the new style in Italian art and those of painting in other European countries showed a profound difference. Even so, there were exchanges between the flourishing art of the North and that of Italy. This is first noticeable in Lombardy, where the Visconti court attracted Transalpine artists. Thus local painting showed the influence of Fouquet (a) and Broederlam (b), and even that trend of which Marmion (d) was the chief exponent. There was, moreover, an increasing acquaintance with van Eyck (c), while echoes of Roger van der Weyden (e), who probably made a journey to Italy in mid-century, are to be found especially in Ferrarese painting. The work of Nicolas Froment (f) was known in Florence, but more interesting to local artists was the *Portinari Altarpiece* which Hugo van der Goes had executed at Bruges in about 1476 for the altar of S. Egidio in Florence (g). Another Fleming who was already known in Italy was Joos van Ghent (j), who since 1469 had been established in Urbino where he had made contact with Piero della Francesca. Shortly afterwards, Pedro Berruguete the Spaniard (i) worked in Urbino. His previous style had been tied to the International tradition, but now he gave it an Italian interpretation.

c

d

b

e

f **g** **h**

j

a Jean Fouquet
The Madonna and Child
about 1450
oil on panel 37⅜ × 33⅞ in.
Antwerp, Musée Royal des Beaux-Arts

b Melchior Broederlam
The Annunciation (detail) 1393-99
oil on panel 65¾ × 49¼ in.
Dijon, Musée

c Jan van Eyck
St. Francis Receiving the Stigmata
oil on panel 11 × 13 in.
Turin, Galleria Sabauda

d Simon Marmion
The Crucifixion
oil on panel 17⅞ × 11⅝ in.
Rome, Palazzo Barberini

e Roger van der Weyden
The Entombment, about 1450
oil on panel 43¼ × 37¾ in.
Florence, Uffizi

f Nicolas Froment
The Raising of Lazarus, 1461
oil on canvas 68⅞ × 52¾ in.
Florence, Uffizi

g Hugo van der Goes
The Portinari Altarpiece:
The Adoration of the Shepherds
(center-panel) about 1476
oil on panel 99¾ × 119⅝ in.
Florence, Uffizi

h Hans Memling
The Passion (detail) about 1470
oil on panel 21⅝ × 35¼ in.
Turin, Galleria Sabauda

i Pedro Berruguete
Federico da Montefeltro, 1476
Urbino, Ducal Palace
Gallery of the Marches

j Joos van Ghent
The Institution of the Eucharist
about 1474
Urbino, Ducal Palace,
Gallery of the Marches

i

a

A Comparison between Italian and Northern Architecture of the 15th Century

The expression of the Italian Renaissance in the early 15th century may also be seen in the changing architectural forms. The famous dome that Filippo Brunelleschi built on to the Gothic structure of Florence Cathedral (see p. 398) reveals the same preoccupation with space he had demonstrated in the Basilica of S. Lorenzo (a). The classical proportions of these buildings form an antithesis to the fanciful trend in North European architecture (b). A monumentality distinguished the work of Leon Battista Alberti (c), when the complex ornamentation of the Flamboyant and Perpendicular Gothic styles was at its height. Luciano Laurana left examples of his serenely rationalistic style in the Palazzo Ducale at Urbino (d), while in Flanders the excessively over-elaborate town halls were being constructed (e). Even in Venice local traditions, still full of Oriental and International motifs, were engulfed by the new trends. Although they had to be adapted to the background of the canals (f), they found their place in a series of Renaissance buildings.

In France, the typical turreted châteaux (g) were still tied to medieval ideas. Elsewhere, as in Spain, the flowery Gothic and exuberant Moorish decoration were still merged into a highly-wrought, extremely ornamental style (i).

At the end of the century Bramante created the architecture of the 1500's by the greater unity and co-ordination of his style (h), which anticipated the controlled energy and centralization of space in later buildings.

b

c

d

e

f

g

h

i

a Filippo Brunelleschi
The Nave, about 1446
Florence, S. Lorenzo

b The Nave, about 1388
Cologne, Cathedral

c Leon Battista Alberti
The Basilica of S. Andrea
from 1470
Mantua

d Luciano Laurana
The Courtyard, about 1475
Urbino, Ducal Palace

e The Town Hall, 15th century
Brussels

f Mauro Coducci
Palazzo Corner Spinelli, about 1480
Venice

g The Royal Apartments, from 1434
Amboise, Château

h Donato Bramante
The Dome and Apse, from 1492
Milan, S. Maria delle Grazie

i Juan Guas
The Church of the Monastery
of S. Cruz, 1482-94
Segovia, Spain

a Rosso Fiorentino
Moses Defending the Daughters of
Jethro, about 1520   *oil on canvas*
63 × 46¼ in.   Florence, Uffizi

b Raphael
Baldassare Castiglione, 1519
oil on canvas   32¼ × 26¾ in.
Paris, Louvre

c Titian
Francis I, King of France,
about 1539   *oil on canvas*
42⅞ × 35 in.   Paris, Louvre

d Sodoma (Giovanni Antonio Bazzi)
The Marriage of Alexander and
Roxana, 1512   *fresco*
Rome, Villa Farnesina

e Giorgione
Fête Champêtre
oil on canvas   43¼ × 54¼ in.
Paris, Louvre

f Jacopo Bassano
A Pastoral Scene, after 1550
oil on canvas   54¾ × 50 in.
Lugano, Thyssen Collection

The 16th Century — Themes and Iconography

The Renaissance in Italy witnessed not only an aesthetic revolution in the fine arts but also an important revision of ethical ideas. This began to be apparent as early as the 1400's and reached its climax in the following century. As a result a change came about in the traditions of iconography, and although the religious themes did not in themselves warrant radical changes, certain entirely new ideas brought artists into contact with nature and the countryside, and were decisive factors in the approach to portraiture. The chief effect of the Humanist culture was that painters of the time began to choose mythological and historical subjects (d). This led to even Biblical themes being treated on Humanist lines (a) and is most apparent in the contemporary portrait painted in honor of emperors, princes, and men of letters (b, c). Nature eventually became a direct source of inspiration, particularly in the case of painters in the Veneto who showed their preference for the romantic ideal (e). In this way they moved toward the naturalistic conceptions (f) which characterize one aspect of 17th-century painting.

a

c

d

b

e

f

The Diffusion of Renaissance Thought in European Painting

The links which existed between Italian Humanists and artists from all over Europe caused Renaissance thought to spread into Germany, Flanders, the Netherlands, France, and Spain. Dürer attempted to formulate a systematic and rational theory of aesthetics (a) and the journeys he had previously made to Italy were certainly relevant to it. The Mannerist themes found a specially sympathetic reception in Northern countries (b), as they coincided with intellectual tendencies which were the fruits of International Gothic. Thus the phenomenon of "Romanism" (inspired by Raphael and Michelangelo) was particularly evident in Belgium and Holland. The same Mannerism also found firm roots in France during the reigns of Francis I and Henry II (c, d). Artists from Italy—Andrea del Sarto, Rosso Fiorentino, Francesco Primaticcio, Niccolò dell'Abbate, and Benvenuto Cellini among them—made the Château at Fontainebleau into a center for their special brand of art. The Spanish court was also subject to Italian influence, brought by such artists as Luca Cambiaso, Pellegrino Tibaldi, and Federico Zuccari, who went to Castille, or by Spanish painters who visited Rome, Urbino, and Bologna. Luis Morales, called " the Divine," went back to Leonardo for his inspiration (e), while El Greco left his native Crete for Venice to develop his own unique style before going on to Spain where he was to display the full extent of his genius(f).

a

b

c   d

e   f

a Albrecht Dürer
The Adoration of the Magi, 1504
oil on panel 39⅜ × 56¾ in.
Florence, Uffizi

b Lucas Cranach the Elder
Adam and Eve, 1528
oil on panel
Adam 67¾ × 24¾ in. Eve 65¾ × 24 in.
Florence, Uffizi

c School of Fontainebleau
The Toilet of Venus
oil on canvas 38¼ × 49⅝ in.
Paris, Louvre

d Jean Cousin the Elder
Eva Prima Pandora
oil on canvas
Paris, Louvre

e Luis de Morales
The Madonna and Child
oil on panel 33⅛ × 25¼ in.
Madrid, Prado

f El Greco
The Burial of Count Orgaz, 1586-88
oil on canvas 191⅞ × 141¾ in.
Toledo, S. Tomè

a

Architecture of the 16th Century

The fusion of Humanist and Renaissance ideals was reached in Italian architecture in the 16th century. The monumental character of Roman buildings in the Imperial age constituted a starting point. This classicism did not, however, preclude an early indication of the dynamic concepts of the 17th century. The dome of St. Peter's in Rome (a) was a symbol of this new vision, contradicting the strictly rational outlook of the 1400's by its imaginative power. This tendency was sometimes emphasized by elements drawn from former regional traditions—as occurred in the Veneto with the work of Sansovino and Palladio (c, g)—while the Mannerists, among them Peruzzi and Vasari (i), were at the outset content with merely linear innovations. These gave way later to a more scenic concept that indicated, as in the work of Vignola (e), the imminence of Baroque architecture.

In the meantime, the rest of Europe adopted the Renaissance style in a rather superficial manner, in most cases striking a compromise with local custom. Only the outward forms of Italian architecture were developed, that is certain geometrical rules and the introduction of elements borrowed from ancient buildings. These motifs were usually grafted on to already established styles. In France the vertical elevation and power of the Gothic edifices were overlaid with pilasters and columns (b); in Flanders rusticated façades appeared (d); in Spain, alongside the last remains of late Gothic and Moorish styles, a particularly austere and rigorous manner was adopted, as for instance, in the Escorial (j); in England the Elizabethan style (h) represented a clash between the Perpendicular Gothic and a classicism derived from the Mannerists; in Germany the ornamental Renaissance type motifs acquired a new decorative importance (f) that set the tone for the Baroque age.

b

c

d

408

e

f

g

h

i

j

a Michelangelo and others
The Apse and Dome, 1547-90
Rome, St. Peter's

b The West front, from 1499
Dijon, S. Michel

c Jacopo Sansovino
The Library, begun 1537
Venice, Piazza di S. Marco

d Cornelis Floris
The Town Hall, 1561-66
Antwerp

e Jacopo Vignola
The Villa Farnese, about 1552
Caprarola

f The Woolmarket (after an
engraving by James Redway, 1840)
Brunswick, Germany

g Andrea Palladio
The Basilica, from 1545
Vicenza

h Robert Smythson
Wollaton Hall, 1580
Nottinghamshire, England

i Giorgio Vasari
The Uffizi Gallery, begun 1560
Florence

j Juan Battista di Toledo
and Juan Hevere
The Escorial, 1563-84
Madrid

409

The 17th Century—New Themes in Italian Painting

Italian painting of the 17th century presents a broad and complex scene. The severe morality of the Counter-Reformation determined certain attitudes toward the subject matter of religious paintings. Devout sentiments were of prime importance, with a search for outward effects of pathos, favorite subjects being the martyrdom of saints (b)—a fact that reveals a renewed spiritual torment. Symbols of dogma and faith were also highly important. Therefore a propagandist type of painting prevailed with a sense of decoration and ritualistic worship (a), while here and there the more savage aspects of scriptural subjects were highlighted.

At the same time classicism was revived in forms which strike a contrast with the cold, academic style of the 16th-century Mannerists. Idealism was its guiding principle, and a more direct contact with nature was established by way of landscape painting, which often assumed an Arcadian tone (c). Mythology too became a source of inspiration, in which the intellectual culture of the age merged with its imaginative spirit (d).

The emphasis on nature also implies that the artists turned more often to the realities of daily life. Still-life painting became a means of expression in its own right, and there was a more vital and sensual Italian counterpart of the Dutch analytical precision (e). Genre subjects, arising from a more detailed, anecdotal version of Caravaggio's powerful realism, began to be painted. At times they still retained vaguely allegorical undertones (f), but—also through direct contact with Northern painters—were eventually confined to the narration of everyday incidents.

a

b

c

d

e

f

Italian Influences on European Painting

The repercussions of Caravaggio's revolution were felt throughout Europe; many artists—Dutch, French, Flemish, German, and Spanish—drew their inspiration directly from his work. Great painters with strong personalities used it to produce their own interpretations; thus a Caravaggesque period may be discerned in Rubens' early work (a). Velázquez experienced a similar phase (b), while Georges de La Tour found an ingenious approach to Caravaggio's studies of light (c). Rembrandt's fiery glow may be traced back to the same source, though treated in an entirely different way (d). By the same process the ultimate refinement of color-form-light relationship was reached in the work of Vermeer (e). Among the lesser masters who coupled Caravaggio's influence with the naturalism of the Veneto, should be mentioned the German, Adam Elsheimer. In spite of this, the Venetian school of Titian, Veronese, and Tintoretto continued to thrive; Titian's pathos and Veronese's subtle use of color were united by Anthony van Dyck.

The 16th-century classicism—which originated in Bologna and was taken to Rome by Annibale Carracci, Domenichino, Reni, and Albani—gave rise through landscape painting to fresh discoveries by a group of French painters who settled in Rome, Poussin, Claude Lorraine, and Dughet (f, g). These artists brought to fruition a classical ideal imbued with naturalistic doctrines, and opened up new avenues of exploration which led to the very threshold of modern painting.

a Rubens
The Adoration of the Shepherds
(detail) about 1606
oil on canvas   118¾ × 75⅜ in.
Fermo, S. Filippo Neri

b Velázquez
The Water Carrier, about 1620
Florence, collection Count Contini-Bonacossi

c Georges de La Tour
St. Joseph the Carpenter
oil on canvas   54½ × 40⅜ in.
Paris, Louvre

d Rembrandt
An Old Man Asleep, about 1629
oil on panel   20½ × 16⅛ in.
Turin, Galleria Sabauda

e Jan Vermeer
Girl at a Window
oil on canvas   16 × 18 in.
New York, Metropolitan Museum

f Nicolas Poussin
Landscape with Serpent
and Nymphs
oil on canvas   46½ × 70½ in.
Chantilly, Musée Condé

g Claude Lorraine
View of Delphi with a
Procession, 1650
oil on canvas   59 × 78¾ in.
Rome, Doria Gallery

a   b   c   d

e   f   g

Baroque Architecture

Baroque architecture had its true origins in Italy. The Renaissance contention between reason and imagination was settled entirely in favor of the latter by the adoption of certain methods which broke up the previously established balance of structure and space. The monumental concept of architecture was developed still further, acquiring added significance from outside sources including the introduction of religious propaganda, promoted by the Jesuits. There was a striving after theatrical effect, the illogical superimposition of the architectural orders and increasingly complicated ornamental devices, with broken lines and curves piled on one another. This process came about gradually: Maderno and Bernini were still building up a synthesis of the Classic and the Baroque in the façade and colonnade of St. Peter's (a) while Borromini and Guarini were allowing unbridled fantasy to run riot in their extravagant creations (b, c). At Venice Longhena adapted local tradition to the forms of the Baroque (d), and although Milanese architecture (f) retained the imprint of Counter-Reformation and Mannerist austerity, in Southern Italy, particularly at Lecce (g), there was an outburst of decoration with affinities to the Spanish style. In the Spanish peninsula itself, following a phase in which the Roman Baroque was assimilated but while the preceding "plateresque" style was still influential, are to be found examples of a spectacular decoration called Churrigueresque after the artist who began it (h). French Baroque style followed more solemn and classical lines (e), but it was subject all the same to theatrical contrivances. Finally, in England, there was a marked return to Neo-Renaissance classicism (i), mainly inspired by Palladio.

a

b

c

d

e

f

g

h

i

e Jules Hardouin Mansart
The Garden Façade, from 1678
Versailles, France, Palace

f Francesco Maria Ricchini
The Courtyard and Gallery
from 1615
Milan, Brera

g Gabriele Riccardi and Cesare Penna
The Façade, from about 1582-1644
Lecce, Italy, S. Croce

h Juan Gomez de Mora
The Façade, after 1617
*Salamanca, Spain,
Church of the Clerecía*

i Inigo Jones
The Banqueting House,
Whitehall, 1619-22
London

413

Architecture and the Development of Town Planning

The 18th century should not be considered merely as the triumph of the Rococo —that is, a more frivolous version of the Baroque, elegant decoration refined by a process of subtle rationalization. Precisely because of the rationalistic tendencies of the Age of Enlightenment this was an epoch in which everything connected with previous traditions was subjected to a methodical and critical reappraisal.

In architecture this meant the restraint of the confusion of movement in Baroque buildings, and it led eventually to the art of fitting every building into the right place in the scheme of its town or country setting to fulfil its practical purpose. The well-ordered geometrical lay-out of Turin is a typical example of this; the town was conceived as a network of broad, straight streets intersecting at right angles, with squares and gardens to avoid monotony. The greatest Italian architect of the early 18th century was Filippo Juvarra, who worked at the court of Savoy. He achieved a marvelous harmony between nature and architecture in the royal hunting lodge at Stupinigi near Turin (c). Plans of this type were the common heritage of the century, as is proved by the fact that Francesco de Sanctis's Spanish Steps in Rome (a) were taken as a model for solving a similar problem of perspective in Portugal (b). The buildings are embellished with carefully proportioned ceremonial staircases, and the parks and gardens blend successfully with the surrounding countryside, as in Vanvitelli's designs for the Royal Palace of Caserta (f). Even in Sicily the new ideas of town planning were quickly put into effect, especially in Catania (g).

The rational tendencies found superb expression in England (d) and France while in Germany and Austria Rococo took the form of ostentatiously resplendent interior and exterior decoration (e). The feeling behind such ideas, which were already well on the way to Neoclassicism (h), was eventually taken by Italian architects as far afield as Tsarist Russia (i).

a

c

d

b

e

f

g   h

The Growth of the Minor Arts

All over Europe there was a tremendous upsurge in the minor arts in the 18th century. This originated in the regard for superficial magnificence which was the hallmark of the Baroque and Rococo eras, and which was also revealed in the lavishly rich costume. It became still more evident with the emergence of more highly organized craftsmanship which was later to suffer a fatal blow from the growth of industry in the 19th century. This increase was one of quality as well as quantity, for craftsmanship often reached the level of genuine artistry.

During this period cabinetmaking rose to its height, and furniture was inspired by the emphasis on movement and the fanciful ornamentation of Baroque architecture. The shapes became more and more intricate by virtue of the depth of molding. France with the reigns of the Roi Soleil and Louis XV (c), and England, in the work of Chippendale (a), led the field, but the 18th-century Venetian style in Italy was dignified by a rare finesse, and often enhanced by oriental lacquered motifs (f), while Piedmontese and Ligurian late Baroque vied with it in refinement and delicacy. Towards the end of the century, with the advent of Neoclassicism, Maggiolini's workshop flourished in Lombardy where models were produced on clear-cut lines with the decoration supplied by inlay (b).

In ceramics, biscuit-ware, and porcelain (d, e), Italy competed with the tremendous German, French, and English output in a variety of regional styles, one being that produced by the Capodimonte factory in Naples.

a

a Thomas Chippendale
The "Violin" Cabinet
*Wilton House, England,
collection the Earl of Pembroke*

415

b

d

e

c

f

g

h

THE VOLUMES